15

an

AMERICAN

CONSTITUTIONAL LAW

reader

A collection of materials on American
constitutional law, including excerpts
from Supreme Court opinions, commentary by students of the constitutional
process, and supplemental observations
of the editor.

Selected and Edited by
ROBERT B. McKAY
Professor of Law
New York University School of Law

DOCKET SERIES
Volume 12

CONTENTS

Part IV
CONSTITUTIONAL LIMITATIONS ON THE POWER OF GOVERNMENT

INTRODUCTION

Seldom in American constitutional history has so much interest been centered upon Supreme Court interpretation of the Constitution of the United States as during the decade of the 1950's. The period of acute interest, indeed active controversy, dates essentially from the 1954 decision in the *School Segregation Cases* that "in the field of public education the doctrine of 'separate but equal' has no place." The abandonment of the nearly sixty-year-old doctrine of "separate but equal" was succeeded the next year by the Court's ordering an end of segregated public schools "with all deliberate speed." This in turn was succeeded by other decisions which put renewed vigor in the first and fifth amendments as a restraint upon congressional investigations and federal prosecutions; and due process concepts in the fifth and fourteenth amendments were given new dimension. These matters, along with now-accepted interpretations of other portions of the Constitution, are discussed in the pages that follow. Frequently explanation of constitutional doctrine is in the words of the Court itself; there are opinions ranging from those of the first Chief Justice, John Marshall, to the present Chief Justice, Earl Warren. In addition, there is commentary by a number of constitutional law scholars; and connecting text has been furnished by the editor. It is hoped that this volume, while of course not a comprehensive treatise on all the subtleties of American constitutional law, will provide the essential materials for comprehension of the document upon which the American system of government depends, the Constitution of the United States.

As an aid to the reader footnotes in judicial opinions have been almost entirely dispensed with, and they have been much reduced in the materials extracted from books and articles. Where footnotes have been retained, they appear immediately following the text to which they relate. The editor wishes to express his appreciation to the following authors, publishers, and periodicals for granting permission to reprint material originally copyrighted by them:

The Harvard University Press for portions of chapter I of *The Supreme Court in the American System of Government,* by the late Mr. Justice Robert H. Jackson; *The American Bar Association Journal* for "The Scope of the Phrase 'Interstate Commerce': Should It Be Redefined?," by Robert L. Stern, and for "The Self-Incrimination Clause," by Beecher N. Claflin; the New York University Press for portions of chapter II of *The Presidency Today,* by Edward S. Corwin and Louis W. Koenig; the Harvard Law Review Association for "Federalism and State Procedure," by Justice Walter V. Schaefer; the Princeton University Press for portions of *The Constitution and What It Means Today,* by Edward S. Corwin.

ROBERT B. MCKAY
New York City
January 1958

PART I

Judicial Review:
Balance Wheel of the Federal System

INTRODUCTION

It may be fairly open to question whether the men who signed the United States Constitution as drafted in the Convention of 1787 would recognize today the government which operates pursuant to that document. Probably even John Marshall, who gave the scant 7,000-word instrument of government its first important interpretations, would find some surprises in the details of its present-day significance. But we can surmise that he would be neither astonished nor disappointed in the overall development of constitutional doctrine. After all, Marshall had said, "we must never forget, that it is a *constitution* we are expounding," and had noted that the Constitution was "intended to endure for ages to come, and, consequently, to be adapted to the various crises of human affairs." *McCulloch* v. *Maryland,* 17 U.S. (4 Wheat.) 316, 407, 415 (1819).

The essential features of the Constitution, though variously "adapted" to changing economic, social, and political situations, are basically the same now as they were when John Marshall was Chief Justice. The most important characteristic of the governmental structure provided by the United States Constitution is the so-called federal system. The essence of that scheme of government consists in the fact that there are two complete structures of government, one for the nation and one for each state. Each of these dual sovereignties is supreme in its own sphere of activity, and thus each complements the other. But there is also an area of overlap of authority which creates, under the most favorable conditions, a certain stiffness at the joints and, in less harmonious circumstances, may result in avowed hostility between competing sovereigns. The rationalizing principle which permits the nation and the states to exist together, nearly all the time without conflict, is the constitutional concept that the national government is a government of enumerated powers delegated to it by the body politic, "We the People of the United States." The corollary to the doctrine of enumerated powers is provided in the tenth amendment, which explicitly provides that "The powers not delegated to the United States by the Constitution, nor prohibited by it to the States, are reserved to the States respectively, or to the people."

A second basic tenet of the Constitution is the doctrine of the separation of powers. While this is nowhere specifically stated in the Constitution, the intention so to provide is clear from the structural organization of the Constitution, from the resulting interaction among the branches of government, and from the proceedings of the Convention. The separation depends upon the creation of three departments of government—legislative, executive, and judiciary—each essentially independent from the other two, although each is at the same time subject to some restraints, known as "checks and balances," which may be exerted by each of the other two coordinate arms of government. Thus, members of the judiciary, sometimes said to be the weakest branch, are subject to presidential nomination and Senate confirmation; and of course the judiciary depends upon Congress for appropriations and for definition of the principal parts of its jurisdiction. On the other hand, federal judges, once appointed, may not be removed except by impeachment and trial upon proof of failure to live up to the constitutional requirement of "good behavior"; and their compensation may not be reduced by Congress during such service. Moreover, and most important of all, the federal courts, and particularly the United States Supreme Court, are empowered to test the validity of federal legislative or executive actions against the standard of the Court's interpretation of the Constitution, and to test the validity of state legislative, executive, *and* judicial action against the standard of the Court's interpretation, not only of the Constitution, but also of federal treaties and laws. By virtue of the possession of this powerful weapon of judicial review, the Supreme Court is sometimes said not to be the weakest branch, but in fact the most powerful.

Fortunately, no absolutist answer to this query is necessary or even possible. History reminds that the power of the Supreme Court may not be much stronger than the base of support for its important decisions, and for the Court as an institution meriting respect. Indeed, the Supreme Court has weathered many a constitutional crisis, taking renewed strength from each victory. When Andrew Jackson as President is alleged to have said, "John Marshall has made his decision; now let him enforce it," the institution may have seemed imperiled. That crisis passed, however, as did the period of disrepute into which the Court declined after the *Dred Scott* decision which refused to free a slave, describing him as property, and may thus have contributed its bit to the Civil War. *Scott v. Sandford*, 60 U.S. (19 How.) 393 (1857). Similarly, when President Franklin D. Roosevelt proposed what has come to be known as the "Court-packing" plan, great though the provocation may have been, the scheme was destined to failure. It may be anticipated that present demands for impeachment of members of the Supreme Court, as well as drastic proposals to limit the judicial power, will similarly not succeed.

In short, the doctrine of judicial review is firmly rooted. But it was not always so. As Alexander Hamilton pointed out in *The Federalist*, No. 81, "there is not a syllable in the [Constitution] which *directly* empowers the national courts to construe the laws according to the spirit of the Constitution. . . ." However, he went on there, and more particularly in *The Federalist*, No. 78, to demonstrate that judicial review was deducible from the general theory of a "limited Constitution." He continued:

> "There is no position which depends on clearer principles, than that every act of a delegated authority, contrary to the tenor of the commission under which it is exercised, is void. No legislative act, therefore, contrary to the Constitution, can be valid. . . .
>
> "Nor does this conclusion by any means support a superiority of the judicial to the legislative power. It only supposes that the power of the people is superior to both; and that where the will of the legislature, declared in its statutes, stands in opposition to that of the people, declared in the Constitution, the judges ought to be governed by the latter rather than the former. . . ."

As the extracts from Supreme Court opinions which are reproduced below indicate, judicial review in the United States is premised upon the concept of national supremacy of the Constitution, federal treaties, and federal laws over conflicting action on the part of states or their agents. To enforce this supremacy the Supreme Court passes judgment on laws enacted by Congress and by state legislatures, executive acts of federal, state, and local officials, and the decisions of state and lower federal courts. At the apex of the two great judicial systems, state and federal, the Supreme Court exercises its twin functions as final arbiter and single unifier of inconsistent interpretations. Estimates of the importance of the Court's role in supervising state legislative acts as compared with its authority over acts of Congress have varied. Mr. Justice Holmes, for example, said: "I do not think the United States would come to an end if we lost our power to declare an act of Congress void. I do think the Union would be imperilled if we could not make that declaration as to the laws of the several states." *Collected Legal Papers* 295 (1921). Whatever may have been the thinking of other members of the Court, it is true that the power to invalidate acts of Congress has been used sparingly, while the invalidation of legislative acts of the several states has proceeded at a much more rapid pace. After the decision in *Marbury* v. *Madison, infra,* no congressional act was held unconstitutional until 1857 when portions of the Missouri Compromise were invalidated in *Scott* v. *Sandford, supra.* All told, there have been only seventy-five acts of Congress invalidated in whole or in part, only four of which were based on decisions after May 1936, and two of those were of minor importance.

This does not mean, however, that there has been agreement, on the Court or off, as to how wisely the power of judicial review has been used. The harshest criticism of the Court may have come from its own members who have often spoken sharply in dissent. For example:

> "The [state] legislature must be free to choose unless government is to be rendered impotent. The Fourteenth Amendment has no more embedded in the Constitution our preference for some particular set of ecomonic beliefs than it has adopted, in the name of liberty, the system of theology which we may happen to approve." Mr. Justice Stone: *Morehead* v. *New York* ex rel. *Tipaldo,* 298 U.S. 587, 636 (1936).

or

> "The judicial function is that of interpretation; it does not include the power of amendment under the guise of interpreta-

tion. To miss the point of difference between the two is to miss all that the phrase 'supreme law of the land' stands for and to convert what was intended as inescapable and enduring mandates into mere moral reflections." Mr. Justice Sutherland: *West Coast Hotel Co.* v. *Parrish*, 300 U.S. 379, 404 (1937).

In view of such dissension displayed from time to time within the Court itself, the student of constitutional law should be neither shocked nor distressed by the statement of Chief Justice Hughes (when governor of New York): "We are under a Constitution, but the Constitution is what the judges say it is." While this statement is candid to the point of bluntness, is it not simply a modern recognition of what Chief Justice Marshall first declared, that "it is a *constitution* we are expounding"? Through nearly all its history, the Supreme Court has taken note of the changing "crises of human affairs," and has frankly recognized the possibility of past error of interpretation, in showing that it does not consider itself irrevocably tied to precedent by the doctrine of *stare decisis*. Thus, the Court's reversal of its own decisions has a long-standing history of respectability, most recently evidenced in the companion cases of *Reid* v. *Covert* and *Kinsella* v. *Krueger*, 354 U.S. 1 (1957), reversing decisions of the previous term [351 U.S. 487 (1955)], and holding that court-martial jurisdiction could not constitutionally be applied to the trial outside the United States of persons accompanying United States armed forces. In other instances the elapsed period between original decision and reversal has sometimes been almost a century, as in *Erie R.R.* v. *Tompkins*, 304 U.S. 64 (1938). A number of illustrations are well discussed by Mr. Justice Douglas in *Stare Decisis*, 49 *Columbia Law Review* 735 (1949). Throughout, however, this has been but another example of the necessary accommodation made by the Court to fulfill as wisely and as well as may be its important responsibility in the field of judicial review.

MARBURY V. MADISON

5 U.S. (1 Cr.) 137 (1803)

[Pursuant to an act of the outgoing Federalist Congress, John Adams, as one of his last presidential acts, appointed a number of new justices of the peace for the District of Columbia. The commissions were prepared in the office of John Marshall who was simultaneously Secretary of State and Chief Justice, but the commissions of Marbury and at least three others had not been delivered when Thomas Jefferson took office as President. When the new Secretary of State, James Madison, refused to deliver these commissions, Marbury sought to compel Madison to deliver his commission by seeking a writ of mandamus in the Supreme Court in the exercise of its original jurisdiction pursuant to section 13 of the Judiciary Act of 1789. The resulting case established the supremely important doctrine of judicial review of acts of Congress.]

MARSHALL, C. J.: At the last term on the affidavits then read and filed with the clerk, a rule was granted in this case, requiring the Secretary of State to show cause why a mandamus should not issue, directing him to deliver to William Marbury his commission as a justice of the peace for the county of Washington, in the district of Columbia. . . .

In the order in which the court has viewed this subject, the following questions have been considered and decided:

1st. Has the applicant a right to the commission he demands?

2d. If he has a right, and that right has been violated, do the laws of this country afford him a remedy?

3d. If they do afford him a remedy, is it a mandamus issuing from this court? . . .

[The first and second questions were answered in the affirmative, the discussion being here omitted. On these questions the Court concluded:]

1st. That by signing the commission of Mr. Marbury, the President of the United States appointed him a justice of peace for the county of Washington, in the District of Columbia; and that the seal of the United States, affixed thereto by the Secretary of State, is conclusive testimony of the verity of the signature, and of the completion of the appointment, and that the appointment conferred on him a legal right to the office for the space of five years.

2d. That, having this legal title to the office, he has a consequent right to the commission; a refusal to deliver which is a plain violation of that right, for which the laws of his country afford him a remedy.
. . .

This, then, is a plain case for a mandamus, either to deliver the commission, or a copy of it from the record; and it only remains to be enquired,

Whether it can issue from this court.

The act to establish the judicial courts of the United States authorizes the Supreme Court "to issue writs of mandamus in cases warranted by the principles and usages of law, to any courts appointed, or persons holding office, under the authority of the United States."

The Secretary of State, being a person holding an office under the authority of the United States, is precisely within the letter of the description, and if this court is not authorized to issue a writ of mandamus to such an officer, it must be because the law is unconstitutional, and therefore absolutely incapable of conferring the authority, and assigning the duties which its words purport to confer and assign.

The constitution vests the whole judicial power of the United States in one Supreme Court, and such inferior courts as congress shall, from time to time, ordain and establish. This power is expressly extended to all cases arising under the laws of the United States; and, consequently, in some form, may be exercised over the present case; because the right claimed is given by a law of the United States.

In the distribution of this power it is declared that "the Supreme Court shall have original jurisdiction in all cases affecting ambassadors, other public ministers and consuls, and those in which a state shall be a party. In all other cases, the Supreme Court shall have appellate jurisdiction."

It has been insisted, at the bar, that as the original grant of jurisdiction, to the supreme and inferior courts, is general, and the clause, assigning original jurisdiction to the Supreme Court, contains no negative or restrictive words, the power remains to the legislature, to assign original jurisdiction to that court in other cases than those specified in the article which has been recited; provided those cases belong to the judicial power of the United States.

If it had been intended to leave it in the discretion of the legislature to apportion the judicial power between the supreme and inferior courts according to the will of that body, it would certainly have been useless to have proceeded further than to have defined the judicial power, and the tribunals in which it should be vested. The subsequent part of the section is mere surplusage, is entirely without meaning, if such is to be the construction. If congress remains at liberty to give this court appellate jurisdiction, where the constitution has declared their jurisdiction shall be original; and original jurisdiction where the constitution has declared it shall be appellate; the distribution of jurisdiction, made in the constitution, is form without substance.

Affirmative words are often, in their operation, negative of other objects than those affirmed; and in this case, a negative or exclusive sense must be given to them, or they have no operation at all.

It cannot be presumed that any clause in the constitution is intended to be without effect; and, therefore, such a construction is inadmissible, unless the words require it.

If the solicitude of the convention, respecting our

peace with foreign powers, induced a provision that the Supreme Court should take original jurisdiction in cases which might be supposed to affect them; yet the clause would have proceeded no further than to provide for such cases, if no further restriction on the powers of congress had been intended. That they should have appellate jurisdiction in all other cases, with such exceptions as congress might make, is no restriction; unless the words be deemed exclusive of original jurisdiction.

When an instrument organizing fundamentally a judicial system, divides it into one supreme, and so many inferior courts as the legislature may ordain and establish; then enumerates its powers, and proceeds so far to distribute them, as to define the jurisdiction of the Supreme Court by declaring the cases in which it shall take original jurisdiction, and that in others it shall take appellate jurisdiction; the plain import of the words seems to be, that in one class of cases its jurisdiction is original, and not appellate; in the other it is appellate, and not original. If any other construction would render the clause inoperative, that is an additional reason for rejecting such other construction and for adhering to their obvious meaning.

To enable this court, then, to issue a mandamus, it must be shown to be an exercise of appellate jurisdiction, or to be necessary to enable them to exercise appellate jurisdiction.

It has been stated at the bar that the appellate jurisdiction may be exercised in a variety of forms, and that if it be the will of the legislature that a mandamus should be used for that purpose that will must be obeyed. This is true, yet the jurisdiction must be appellate, not original.

It is the essential criterion of appellate jurisdiction, that it revises and corrects the proceedings in a cause already instituted, and does not create that cause. Although, therefore, a mandamus may be directed to courts, yet to issue such a writ to an officer for the delivery of a paper, is in effect the same as to sustain an original action for that paper, and, therefore, seems not to belong to appellate, but to original jurisdiction. Neither is it necessary in such a case as this, to enable the court to exercise its appellate jurisdiction.

The authority, therefore, given to the Supreme Court by the act establishing the judicial courts of the United States, to issue writs of mandamus to public officers, appears not to be warranted by the constitution; and it becomes necessary to inquire whether a jurisdiction so conferred can be exercised.

The question, whether an act, repugnant to the constitution, can become the law of the land, is a question deeply interesting to the United States; but, happily, not of an intricacy proportioned to its interest. It seems only necessary to recognize certain principles, supposed to have been long and well established, to decide it.

That the people have an original right to establish, for their future government, such principles, as, in their opinion, shall most conduce to their own happiness is the basis on which the whole American fabric has been erected. The exercise of this original right is a very great exertion; nor can it, nor ought it, to be frequently repeated. The principles, therefore, so established, are deemed fundamental. And as the authority from which they proceed is supreme, and can seldom act, they are designed to be permanent.

This original and supreme will organizes the government, and assigns to different departments their respective powers. It may either stop here, or establish certain limits not to be transcended by those departments.

The government of the United States is of the latter description. The powers of the legislature are defined and limited; and that those limits may not be mistaken, or forgotten, the constitution is written. To what purpose are powers limited, and to what purpose is that limitation committed to writing, if these limits may, at any time, be passed by those intended to be restrained? The distinction between a government with limited and unlimited powers is abolished, if those limits do not confine the persons on whom they are imposed, and if acts prohibited and acts allowed are of equal obligation. It is a proposition too plain to be contested, that the constitution controls any legislative act repugnant to it; or, that the legislature may alter the constitution by an ordinary act.

Between these alternatives there is no middle ground. The constitution is either a superior paramount law, unchangeable by ordinary means, or it is on the level with ordinary legislative acts, and like other acts, is alterable when the legislature shall please to alter it.

If the former part of the alternative be true, then a legislative act contrary to the constitution is not law: if the latter part be true, then written constitutions are absurd attempts, on the part of the people, to limit a power in its own nature illimitable.

Certainly all those who have framed written constitutions contemplate them as forming the fundamental and paramount law of the nation, and consequently, the theory of every such government must be, that an act of the legislature, repugnant to the constitution, is void.

This theory is essentially attached to a written constitution, and is, consequently, to be considered, by this court, as one of the fundamental principles of our society. It is not therefore to be lost sight of in the further consideration of this subject.

If an act of the legislature, repugnant to the Constitution, is void, does it, notwithstanding its invalidity, bind the courts, and oblige them to give it effect? Or, in other words, though it be not law, does it constitute a rule as operative as if it was a law? This would be to overthrow in fact what was established in theory; and would seem, at first view, an absurdity too gross to be insisted on. It shall, however, receive a more attentive consideration.

It is emphatically the province and duty of the judicial department to say what the law is. Those who apply the rule to particular cases, must of necessity expound and interpret that rule. If two laws conflict with each other, the courts must decide on the operation of each.

So if a law be in opposition to the constitution; if both the law and the constitution apply to a particular case, so that the court must either decide that case conformable to the law, disregarding the constitution; or conformable to the constitution, disregarding the law; the court must determine which of these conflicting rules governs the case. This is of the very essence of judicial duty.

If, then, the courts are to regard the constitution, and the constitution is superior to any ordinary act of the legislature, the constitution, and not such ordinary act, must govern the case to which they both apply.

Those, then, who controvert the principle that the constitution is to be considered, in court, as a paramount law, are reduced to the necessity of maintaining that courts must close their eyes on the constitution, and see only the law.

This doctrine would subvert the very foundation of all written constitutions. It would declare that an act which, according to the principles and theory of our government, is entirely void, is yet, in practice, completely obligatory. It would declare that if the legislature shall do what is expressly forbidden, such act, notwithstanding the express prohibition, is in reality effectual. It would be giving to the legislature a practical and real omnipotence, with the same breath which professes to restrict their powers within narrow limits. It is prescribing limits, and declaring that those limits may be passed at pleasure.

That it thus reduces to nothing what we have deemed the greatest improvement on political institutions—a written constitution—would of itself be sufficient, in America, where written constitutions have been viewed with so much reverence, for rejecting the construction. But the peculiar expressions of the constitution of the United States furnish additional arguments in favour of its rejection.

The judicial power of the United States is extended to all cases arising under the constitution.

Could it be the intention of those who gave this power, to say that in using it the constitution should not be looked into? That a case arising under the constitution should be decided without examining the instrument under which it rises?

This is too extravagant to be maintained.

In some cases, then, the constitution must be looked into by the judges. And if they can open it at all, what part of it are they forbidden to read or to obey? . . .

It is also not entirely unworthy of observation, that in declaring what shall be the supreme law of the land, the constitution itself is first mentioned; and not the laws of the United States generally, but those only which shall be made in pursuance of the constitution, have that rank.

Thus, the particular phraseology of the constitution of the United States confirms and strengthens the principle, supposed to be essential to all written constitutions, that a law repugnant to the constitution is void; and that courts, as well as other departments, are bound by that instrument.

The rule must be discharged.

MARTIN v. HUNTER'S LESSEE

14 U.S. (1 Wheat.) 304 (1816)

[In 1810 Chief Justice Marshall, in a case involving a gigantic land fraud in which the Georgia Legislature was involved, held that the Supreme Court had the right of judicial review over the acts of state legislatures. *Fletcher* v. *Peck*, 10 U.S. (6 Cr.) 87 (1810). However, since that case had come up through the federal courts, the review and possible reversal of state court *decisions* was not at issue in that case. Nevertheless, provision for that very situation had been made in section 25 of the Judiciary

Act of 1789, which provided explicitly for Supreme Court review of state court decisions involving cases arising under the Constitution, treaties, or laws of the United States. The validity of this provision was at issue in *Martin* v. *Hunter's Lessee* since the Virginia Court of Appeals had expressed itself as "unanimously of opinion that the appellate power of the Supreme Court of the United States does not extend to this court. . . ." The case involved a Revolutionary wartime act of the Virginia Legislature claimed to have been invalidated by a clause in the treaty of peace or a clause in the 1794 treaty with England. Marshall, who did not participate in the decision, benefited from the reversal of the Virginia court to invalidate the state act.]

STORY, J.: . . .

The questions involved in this judgment are of great importance and delicacy. Perhaps it is not too much to affirm, that, upon their right decision, rest some of the most solid principles which have hitherto been supposed to sustain and protect the Constitution itself. . . .

The Constitution unavoidably deals in general language. It did not suit the purposes of the people, in framing this great charter of our liberties, to provide for minute specifications of its powers or to declare the means by which those powers should be carried into execution. It was foreseen that this would be a perilous and difficult, if not an impracticable, task. The instrument was not intended to provide merely for the exigencies of a few years, but was to endure through a long lapse of ages, the events of which were locked up in the inscrutable purposes of Providence. It could not be foreseen what new changes and modifications of power might be indispensable to effectuate the general objects of the charter; and restrictions and specifications, which, at the present, might seem salutary, might, in the end, prove the overthrow of the system itself. Hence its powers are expressed in general terms, leaving to the legislature, from time to time, to adopt its own means to effectuate legitimate objects, and to mould and model the exercise of its powers, as its own wisdom, and the public interest, should require.

With these principles in view, principles in respect to which no difference of opinion ought to be indulged, let us now proceed to the interpretation of the Constitution, so far as regards the great points in controversy.

The third article of the Constitution is that which must principally attract our attention. . . . The language of the article throughout is manifestly designed to be mandatory upon the legislature. Its obligatory force is so imperative, that Congress could not, without a violation of its duty, have refused to carry it into operation. The judicial power of the United States *shall be vested* (not may be vested) in one supreme court, and such inferior courts as Congress may, from time to time, ordain and establish. . . .

If, then, it is a duty of Congress to vest the judicial power of the United States, it is a duty to vest the *whole judicial power*. The language, if imperative as to one part, is imperative as to all. If it were otherwise, this anomaly would exist, that Congress might successively refuse to vest the jurisdiction in any one class of cases enumerated in the constitution, and thereby defeat the jurisdiction as to all; for the constitution has not singled out any class on which congress are bound to act in preference to others.

The next consideration is as to the courts in which the judicial power shall be vested. It is manifested that a supreme court must be established; but whether it be equally obligatory to establish inferior courts, is a question of some difficulty. If congress may lawfully omit to establish inferior courts, it might follow, that in some of the enumerated cases the judicial power could nowhere exist. The supreme court can have original jurisdiction in two classes of cases only, viz., in cases affecting ambassadors, other public ministers and consuls, and in cases in which a state is a party. Congress cannot vest any portion of the judicial power of the United States, except in courts ordained and established by itself; and if in any of the cases enumerated in the constitution, the state courts did not then possess jurisdiction, the appellate jurisdiction of the supreme court (admitting that it could act on state courts) could not reach those cases, and, consequently, the injunction of the constitution, that the judicial power *"shall be vested,"* would be disobeyed. It would seem, therefore, to follow, that congress are bound to create some inferior courts, in which to vest all that jurisdiction which, under the constitution, is *exclusively* vested in the United States, and of which the supreme court cannot take original cognizance. They might establish one or more inferior courts; they might parcel out the jurisdiction among such courts, from time to time, at their own pleasure. But the whole judicial power of the United States should be, at all times, vested either in an original or appellate form, in some courts created under its authority. . . .

It being, then, established that the language of this clause is imperative, the next question is as to the cases to which it shall apply. The answer is found in the constitution itself. The judicial power shall extend to all the cases enumerated in the constitution. As the mode is not limited, it may extend to all such cases, in any form, in which judicial power may be exercised. It may, therefore, extend to them in the shape of original or appellate jurisdiction, or both; for there is nothing in the nature of the cases which binds to the exercise of the one in preference to the other. . . .

But, even admitting that the language of the constitution is not mandatory, and that congress may constitutionally omit to vest the judicial power in courts of the United States, it cannot be denied that when it is vested, it may be exercised to the utmost constitutional extent.

This leads us to the consideration of the great question as to the nature and extent of the appellate jurisdiction of the United States. We have already seen that appellate jurisdiction is given by the constitution to the supreme court in all cases where it has not original jurisdiction; subject, however, to such exceptions and regulations as congress may prescribe. It is, therefore, capable of embracing every case enumerated in the constitution, which is not exclusively to be decided by way of original jurisdiction. But the exercise of appellate jurisdiction is far from being limited by the terms of the constitution to the supreme court. There can be no doubt that congress may create a succession of inferior tribunals, in each of which it may vest appellate as well as original jurisdiction. The judicial power is delegated by the constitution in the most general terms, and may, therefore, be exercised by congress under every variety of form, of appellate or original jurisdiction. And as there is nothing in the constitution which restrains or limits this power, it must, therefore, in all other cases, subsist in the utmost latitude of which, in its own nature, it is susceptible.

As, then, by the terms of the constitution, the appellate jurisdiction is not limited as to the supreme court, and as to this court it may be exercised in all other cases than those of which it has original cognizance, what is there to restrain its exercise over state tribunals in the enumerated cases? The appellate power is not limited by the terms of the third article to any particular courts. The words are, "the judicial power (which includes appellate power) shall extend to *all cases*," &c., and "in all other cases before mentioned the supreme court shall have appellate jurisdiction." It is the *case*, then, and not *the court*, that gives the jurisdiction. If the judicial power extends to the case, it will be in vain to search in the letter of the constitution for any qualification as to the tribunal where it depends. It is incumbent, then, upon those who assert such a qualification to show its existence by necessary implication. If the text be clear and distinct, no restriction upon its plain and obvious import ought to be admitted, unless the inference be irresistible.

If the constitution meant to limit the appellate

jurisdiction to cases pending in the courts of the United States, it would necessarily follow that the jurisdiction of these courts would, in all the cases enumerated in the constitution, be exclusive of state tribunals. How otherwise could the jurisdiction extend to *all* cases arising under the constitution, laws, and treaties of the United States, or *to all cases* of admiralty and maritime jurisdiction? If some of these cases might be entertained by state tribunals, and no appellate jurisdiction as to them should exist, then the appellate power would not extend to *all*, but to *some*, cases. If state tribunals might exercise concurrent jurisdiction over all or some of the other classes of cases in the constitution without control then the appellate jurisdiction of the United States might, as to such cases, have no real existence, contrary to the manifest intent of the constitution. Under such circumstances, to give effect to the judicial power, it must be construed to be exclusive; and this not only when the casus faederis should arise directly, but when it should arise, incidentally, in cases pending in state courts. This construction would abridge the jurisdiction of such court far more than has been ever contemplated in any act of congress.

On the other hand, if, as has been contended, a discretion be vested in congress to establish, or not to establish, inferior courts at their own pleasure, and congress should not establish such courts, the appellate jurisdiction of the supreme court would have nothing to act upon, unless it could act upon cases pending in the state courts. Under such circumstances it must be held that the appellate power would extend to state courts; for the constitution is peremptory that it shall extend to certain enumerated cases, which cases could exist in no other courts. Any other construction, upon this supposition, would involve this strange contradiction, that a discretionary power vested in congress, and which they might rightfully omit to exercise, would defeat the absolute injunctions of the constitution in relation to the whole appellate power.

But it is plain that the framers of the constitution did contemplate that cases within the judicial cognizance of the United States not only might but would arise in the state courts, in the exercise of their ordinary jurisdiction. With this view the sixth article declares, that "this constitution, and the laws of the United States which shall be made in pursuance thereof, and all treaties made, or which shall be made, under the authority of the United States, shall be the supreme law of the land, and the judges in every state shall be bound thereby, any thing in the constitution or laws of any state to the contrary notwithstanding." It is obvious that this obligation is imperative upon the state judges in their official, and not merely in their private, capacities. From the very nature of their judicial duties they would be called upon to pronounce the law applicable to the case in judgment. They were not to decide merely according to the laws or constitution of the state, but according to the constitution, laws and treaties of the United States—"the supreme law of the land." . . .

It must, therefore, be conceded that the constitution not only contemplated, but meant to provide for cases within the scope of the judicial power of the United States, which might yet depend before state tribunals. It was foreseen that in the exercise of their ordinary jurisdiction, state courts would incidentally take cognizance of cases arising under the constitution, the laws and treaties of the United States. Yet to all these cases the judicial power, by the very terms of the constitution, is to extend. It cannot extend by original jurisdiction if that was already rightfully and exclusively attached in the state courts, which (as has been already shown) may occur; it must, therefore, extend by appellate jurisdiction, or not at all. It would seem to follow that the appellate power of the United States must, in such cases, extend to state tribunals; and if in such cases, there is no reason why it should not equally attach upon all others within the purview of the constitution.

It has been argued that such an appellate jurisdiction over state courts is inconsistent with the genius of our governments, and the spirit of the constitution. That the latter was never designed to act upon state sovereignties, but only upon the people, and that if the power exists, it will materially impair the sovereignty of the states, and the independence of their courts. We cannot yield to the force of this reasoning; it assumes principles which we cannot admit, and draws conclusions to which we do not yield our assent.

It is a mistake that the constitution was not designed to operate upon states, in their corporate capacities. It is crowded with provisions which restrain or annul the sovereignty of the states in some of the highest branches of their prerogatives. The tenth section of the first article contains a long list of disabilities and prohibitions imposed upon the states. Surely, when such essential portions of state sovereignty are taken away, or prohibited to be exercised, it cannot be correctly asserted that the constitution does not act upon the states. The language of the constitution is also imperative upon the states as to the performance of many duties. It is imperative upon the state legislatures to make laws prescribing the time, places, and manner of holding elections for senators and representatives, and for elections for senators and representatives, and for electors of president and vice-president. And in these, as well as some other cases, congress have a right to revise, amend, or supersede the laws which may be passed by state legislatures. When, therefore, the states are stripped of some of the highest attributes of sovereignty, and the same are given to the United States; when the legislatures of the states are, in some respects, under the control of congress, and in every case are under the constitution, bound by the paramount authority of the United States; it is certainly difficult to support the argument that the appellate power over the decisions of state courts is contrary to the genius of our institutions. The courts of the United States can, without question, revise the proceedings of the executive and legislative authorities of the states, and if they are found to be contrary to the constitution, may declare them to be of no legal validity. Surely the exercise of the same right over judicial tribunals is not a higher or more dangerous act of sovereign power. . . .

It is further argued, that no great public mischief can result from a construction which shall limit the appellate power of the United States to cases in their own courts: first, because state judges are bound by oath to support the constitution of the United States, and must be presumed to be men of learning and integrity; and, secondly, because congress must have an unquestionable right to remove all cases within the scope of the judicial power from the state courts to the courts of the United States, at any time before final judgment, though not after final judgment. As to the first reason—admitting that the judges of the state courts are, and always will be, of as much learning, integrity, and wisdom, as those of the courts of the United States, (which we very cheerfully admit), it does not aid the argument. It is manifest that the constitution has proceeded upon a theory of its own, and given or withheld powers according to the judgment of the American people, by whom it was adopted. . . .

This is not all. A motive of another kind, perfectly compatible with the most sincere respect for state tribunals, might induce the grant of appellate power over their decisions. That motive is the importance, and even necessity of *uniformity* of decisions throughout the whole United States, upon all subjects within the purview of the constitution. Judges of equal learning and integrity, in different states, might differently interpret a statute, or a treaty of the United States, or even the constitution itself; if there were no revising authority to control these jarring and discordant judgments, and harmonize them into uniformity, the laws, the treaties, and the constitution of the United States would be different in different states, and might, perhaps, never have precisely the same construction, obligation, or efficacy, in any two states. The public mischiefs that would attend such a state of things would be truly deplorable; and it cannot be believed that they could have escaped the enlightened convention which formed the constitution. What, indeed, might then have been only phophecy, has now become fact; and the appellate jurisdiction must continue to be the only adequate remedy for such evils. . . .

On the whole, the court are of opinion, that the appellate power of the United States does extend to cases pending in the state courts; and that the 25th section of the judiciary act, which authorizes the exercise of this jurisdiction in the specified cases, by a writ of error, is supported by the letter and spirit of the constitution. We find no clause in that instrument which limits this power; and we dare not interpose a limitation where the people have not been disposed to create one.

Strong as this conclusion stands upon the general language of the constitution, it may still derive support from other sources. It is an historical fact, that this exposition of the constitution, extending its appellate power to state courts, was, previous to its adoption, uniformly and publicly avowed by its friends, and admitted by its enemies, as the basis of their respective reasonings, both in and out of the state conventions. It is an historical fact, that at the time when the judiciary act was submitted to the deliberations of the first congress, composed, as it was, not only of men of great learning and ability, but of men who had acted a principal part in framing, supporting, or opposing that constitution, the same exposition was explicitly declared and admitted by the friends and by the opponents of that system. It is an historical fact, that the supreme court of the United States have, from time to time, sustained this appellate jurisdiction in a great variety of cases, brought from the tribunals of many of the most important states in the union, and that no state tribunal has ever breathed a judicial doubt on the subject, or declined to obey the mandate of the supreme court, until the present occasion. This weight of contemporaneous exposition by all parties, this acquiescence of enlightened state courts, and these judicial decisions of the supreme court through so long a period, do, as we think, place the doctrine upon a foundation of authority which cannot be shaken, without delivering over the subject to perpetual and irremediable doubts. . . .

THE FEDERAL COURT SYSTEM AND JUDICIAL REVIEW IN OPERATION

At the apex of the federal judicial system the nine-member United States Supreme Court exercises original jurisdiction over a small number of matters which come to it in the first instance and exercises its appellate function of judicial review in connection with a large number of cases coming to it from the state courts and from the lower federal courts. In the October 1956 Term (extending into July 1957), for example, the total number of cases on the Supreme Court dockets was 2,052, divided as follows: Original Docket, 14; Appellate Docket, 1,160; and Miscellaneous Docket, 878. By the end of the Term all except 351 had been disposed of, including 111 opinions handed down by the Court.

The trial court of general jurisdiction in the federal court structure is the United States District Court, of which there are some eighty-seven. Because of multiple judgeships in many districts there are nearly 250 federal district judges. The district courts have jurisdiction over some cases without regard to the amount of money involved; but in most cases there must be in dispute $3,000.00 or more, and the case must involve a federal question or parties of diverse citizenship. The so-called "federal question" jurisdiction, to oversimplify, requires that the decision of the case must depend upon a construction of the United States Constitution or a federal treaty or law. "Diversity" jurisdiction is present whenever the opposing litigants are from different states. As can be readily seen, many of these cases could alternatively be brought in state courts. But where the plaintiff chooses the state forum, the defendant is ordinarily allowed to remove the case, that is, to have it transferred to the appropriate federal court.

In the typical case there is an automatic right of appeal from an adverse decision in the district court to the appropriate United States Court of Appeals, of which there are eleven—one for the District of Columbia and ten numbered circuits into which the remainder of the United States has been divided. The number of judges authorized for each court of appeals varies from three to nine, depending on the congressional estimate of the workload for the court. The total stands at sixty-eight.

Review of determinations of the courts of appeals is sometimes available in the Supreme Court on appeal as a matter of right; but more often review must be on petition for writ of certiorari, the grant or denial of which is discretionary with the Supreme Court. The conditions under which Supreme Court review may be sought are prescribed by Congress in Title 28 of the United States Code, as authorized by article III of the Constitution.

In addition to the restrictions imposed by Congress upon the original jurisdiction of all federal courts and the appellate jurisdiction of the United States Supreme Court, the Court has devised other limitations upon the exercise of judicial review. Thus, before the merits of a case will be heard in the federal courts, it must be established that there is a "case or controversy," that is, a genuine dispute between parties whose interests are substantial and adverse to each other. On this basis the federal courts will neither render advisory opinions nor pass on moot questions. From the beginning it has been the accepted rule that political questions will not be decided, including such problems as voting apportionment within the states and determination of whether a "Republican Form of Government" has been preserved within a particular state, as guaranteed by section 4 of article IV of the Constitution.

Beyond these limitations the Court has developed additional restrictions, even as to cases admittedly within its jurisdiction, which permit it to avoid a large portion of the constitutional issues pressed upon it for decision. These were stated by Mr. Justice Brandeis, concurring, in *Ashwander* v. *Tennessee Valley Authority*, 297 U.S. 288, 346-48 (1936), as follows:

> "1. The Court will not pass upon the constitutionality of legislation in a friendly, non-adversary, proceeding, declining because to decide such questions 'is legitimate only in the last resort, and as a necessity in the determination of real, earnest and vital controversy between individuals. It never was the thought that, by means of a friendly suit, a party beaten in the legislature could transfer to the courts an inquiry as to the constitutionality of the legislative act.' *Chicago & Grand Trunk Ry.* v. *Wellman*, 143 U.S. 339, 345. Compare *Lord* v. *Veazie*, 8 How. 251; *Atherton Mills* v. *Johnston*, 259 U.S. 13, 15.

> "2. The court will not 'anticipate a question of constitutional law in advance of the necessity of deciding it.' *Liverpool, N.Y. & P.S.S. Co.* v. *Emigration Commissioners*, 113 U.S. 33, 39; *Abrams* v. *Van Schaick*, 293 U.S. 188; *Wilshire Oil Co.* v. *United States*, 295 U.S. 100. 'It is not the habit of the Court to decide questions of a constitutional nature unless absolutely necessary to a decision of the case.' *Burton* v. *United States*, 196 U.S. 283, 295.

> "3. The Court will not 'formulate a rule of constitutional law broader than is required by the precise facts to which it is to be applied.' *Liverpool, N.Y. & P.S.S. Co.* v.

Emigration Commissioners, supra. Compare *Hammond* v. *Schappi Bus Line,* 275 U.S. 164, 169-172.

"4. The Court will not pass upon a constitutional question although properly presented by the record, if there is also present some other ground upon which the case may be disposed of. This rule has found most varied application. Thus, if a case can be decided on either of two grounds, one involving a constitutional question, the other a question of statutory construction or general law, the Court will decide only the latter. *Siler* v. *Louisville & Nashville R. Co.,* 213 U.S. 175, 191; *Light* v. *United States,* 220 U.S. 523, 538. Appeals from the highest court of a state challenging its decision of a question under the Federal Constitution are frequently dismissed because the judgment can be sustained on an independent state ground. *Berea College* v. *Kentucky,* 211 U.S. 45, 53.

"5. The Court will not pass upon the validity of a statute upon complaint of one who fails to show that he is injured by its operation. *Tyler* v. *The Judges,* 179 U.S. 405; *Hendrick* v. *Maryland,* 234 U.S. 610, 621. Among the many applications of this rule, none is more striking than the denial of the right of challenge to one who lacks a personal or property right. Thus, the challenge by a public official interested only in the performance of his official duty will not be entertained. *Columbus & Greenville Ry.* v. *Miller,* 283 U.S. 96, 99-100. In *Fairchild* v. *Hughes,* 258 U.S. 126, the Court affirmed the dismissal of a suit brought by a citizen who sought to have the Nineteenth Amendment declared unconstitutional. In *Massachusetts* v. *Mellon,* 262 U.S. 447, the challenge of the federal Maternity Act was not entertained although made by the Commonwealth on behalf of all its citizens.

"6. The Court will not pass upon constitutionality of a statute at the instance of one who has availed himself of its benefits. *Great Falls Mfg. Co.* v. *Attorney General,* 124 U.S. 581; *Wall* v. *Parrot Silver & Copper Co.,* 244 U.S. 407, 411-412; *St. Louis Malleable Casting Co.* v. *Prendergast Construction Co.,* 260 U.S. 469.

"7. 'When the validity of an act of the Congress is drawn in question, and even if a serious doubt of constitutionality is raised, it is a cardinal principle that this Court will first ascertain whether a construction of the statute is fairly possible by which the question may be avoided.' *Crowell* v. *Benson,* 285 U.S. 22, 62."

For an insight into the decision-making process as it operates in the Supreme Court, instruction is offered by the late Justice Robert H. Jackson, in words composed shortly before his death, and posthumously published in 1955 by the Harvard University Press. The extracts below are taken from pages 9-27 of that book.

The Supreme Court in the American System of Government

By Robert H. Jackson

The Supreme Court of the United States was created in a different manner from most high courts. In Europe, most judiciaries evolved as subordinates to the King, who delegated to them some of his functions. For example, while the English judges have developed a remarkably independent status, they still retain the formal status of Crown servants. But here, the Supreme Court and the other branches of the Federal Government came into existence at the same time and by the same act of creation. "We the People of the United States" deemed an independent Court equally as essential as a Congress or an Executive, especially, I suppose, to "establish Justice, insure domestic Tranquility," and to "secure the Blessings of Liberty to ourselves and to our Posterity." The status of the Court as a unit of the Government, not as an institution subordinate to it, no doubt has given it prestige, for the people do not regard the Justices as employees of the Government of the day or as civil servants, as in continental Europe. Also, federal judges enjoy two bulwarks of independence—life tenure (except for impeachable misbehavior) and irreducible salaries (except by taxation and inflation).

Nonetheless, the Constitution-makers left the Court in vital respects a dependent body. The political branches nominate and confirm the Justices, a control of the Court's composition which results in a somewhat lagging political influence over its trend of decision, and any party that prevails in the Federal Government through several presidential terms will gradually tend to impress its political philosophy on the Court. The political branches also from time to time may alter the number of Justices, and that power was used to influence the course of decision several times before it was again proposed by President Roosevelt.

The Court also is dependent on the political branches for its powers in other vital respects. Its only irrevocable jurisdiction is original, and that reaches only cases affecting Ambassadors, public Ministers, or Consuls, or cases in which a state is a party. In all other cases it has appellate jurisdiction, but "with such exceptions and under such regulations as Congress shall make." One Congress, fearing a decision unfavorable to its post-Civil War enactments, ousted the court of jurisdiction in a case that had already been argued, and the Court submitted. The Court also is dependent upon the political branches for the execution of its mandates, for it has no physical force at its command. The story is traditional that

President Jackson once withheld enforcement, saying, "John Marshall has made his decision:—*now let him enforce it!*" Also, the Court, of course, depends upon Congress for the appropriation of funds with which to operate. These all add up to a fairly formidable political power over the Supreme Court, if there were a disposition to exert it.

But perhaps the most significant and least comprehended limitation upon the judicial power is that this power extends only to cases and controversies. We know that this restriction was deliberate, for it was proposed in the Convention that the Supreme Court be made part of a Council of Revision with a kind of veto power, and this was rejected.

The result of the limitation is that the Court's only power is to decide lawsuits between adversary litigants with real interests at stake, and its only method of proceeding is by the conventional judicial, as distinguished from legislative or administrative, process. This precludes the rendering of advisory opinions even at the request of the nation's President and every form of pronouncement on abstract, contingent, or hypothetical issues. It prevents acceptance for judicial settlement of issues in which the interests and questions involved are political in character. It also precludes imposition on federal constitutional courts of nonjudicial duties. Recent trends to empower judges to grant or deny wire-tapping rights to a prosecutor or to approve a waiver of prosecution in order to force a witness to give self-incriminating testimony raise interesting and dubious questions. A federal court can perform but one function—that of deciding litigations—and can proceed in no manner except by the judicial process.

In his pioneering studies, Judge Cardozo demonstrated that this is not the rigid and inflexible process some of our ancestors thought it to be. But its inherent methods make it unfit for solving some kinds of problems which elements of our society have from time to time expected the Supreme Court to settle.

While the President or the Congress can take up

any subject at any time, a court in our Anglo-American system is a substantially passive instrument, to be moved only by the initiative of litigants. The Supreme Court cannot take most cases until at least one and generally two courts below have heard and decided them, which, with the present congestion of calendars, may be very long indeed. Also, as an appellate court, it properly can act only on the state of facts revealed by the record made in the court below, supplemented sometimes by general information of which it may take judicial notice. Hence a claim of right may be prejudiced by the incompetence, carelessness, or collusion of attorneys, as where they fail to make an adequate record to support the question sought to be raised. The decision of a case also may depend on its peculiarities of fact, for it is still true that hard cases make bad law. And when it is all over, the judicial decree, however broadly worded, actually binds, in most instances, only the parties to the case. As to others, it is merely a weather vane showing which way the judicial wind is blowing—a precedent that the Court in a similar case is likely to follow. Its real weight in subsequent cases, however, will depend on many factors, such as the quality of the prevailing opinion, the strength of any dissent, the acceptance or criticism by the profession, and the experience in application of the rule. Thus, the process of the courts is adapted to the intensive examination of particular legal grievances.

No conclusion as to what can be expected of the Court is valid which overlooks the measure of its incapacity to entertain and decide cases under its traditional working methods. With few exceptions, Congress has found it necessary to make review in the Supreme Court not the right of a litigant but a discretionary matter with the Court itself, in order to keep the volume of its business within its capacity. Last term, review was sought by appeal and certiorari in 1,452 cases, only 119 of which were allowed. It is not necessary to detail the considerations which move the Court to grant review beyond saying that the grant is not intended merely to give a litigant another chance, nor does it depend on the dollars involved or the private interests affected, but upon the importance of the case to a uniform and just system of federal law.

The routine during the Court term has been to hear arguments the first five days of each two weeks, followed by two weeks of recess for the writing of opinions and the study of the appeals and certiorari petitions, which must be disposed of periodically. The time allowed for each side to argue its case is normally one hour, and, in cases where the question seems not complex, it is half of that. In the early days of the Supreme Court, the volume of work permitted argument to extend over several days, as it still does in the House of Lords. Many cases argued before us today in two hours have taken days, weeks, and even months in the trial court or administrative body.

What really matters to the lawyer and the law is what happens between the argument and the decision. On each Saturday following argument or preceding a decision Monday, the Court holds its only regularly scheduled conference.* It begins at 11 a.m. and rarely ends before 5:30 p.m. With a half-hour for lunch, this gives about 360 minutes in which to complete final consideration of forthcoming opinions, the noting of probable jurisdiction of appeals, the disposition of petitions for certiorari, petitions for rehearing and miscellaneous matters, and the decision of argued cases. The largest conference list during the October 1953 term contained 145 items, the shortest 24, the average 70. A little computation will show that the average list would permit, at the average conference, an average of five minutes of deliberation per item, or about 33 seconds of discussion per item by each of the nine Justices, assuming, of course, that each is an average Justice who does the average amount of talking.

---

* The practice has been changed so that conferences are now held on Fridays. [Editor.]

All that saves the Court from being hopelessly bogged down is that many of these items are so frivolous on mere inspection that no one finds them worthy of discussion, and they are disposed of by unanimous consent. Even eliminating these, the time devoted at conference to argued cases is inadequate for detailed deliberation and results, more or less, in a canvass of impressions with the understanding that a vote on any case is tentative and on later consideration may be changed. And not infrequently the detailed study required to write an opinion, or the persuasiveness of an opinion or dissent, will lead to a change of a vote or even to a change of result. If there is further conferring, it is unofficial, usually between two or more Justices of like mind in the particular case.

The pressure of time may induce an attitude that discussion in conference is futile and thereby contributes to the multiplicity of individual opinions. It is often easier to write out one's own view than for nine men in such short time to explore their doubts and difficulties together, or to reach a reconciliation of viewpoints. The fact is that the Court functions less as one deliberative body than as nine, each Justice working largely in isolation except as he chooses to seek consultation with others. These working methods tend to cultivate a highly individualistic rather than a group viewpoint.

The individual study which any case receives before or after argument is the affair of each Justice. All receive the printed briefs and record, in some cases short, in others running to a great many volumes. Some records take five feet of shelf space. It is easily demonstrated that no Justice possibly could read more than a fraction of the printed matter filed with the Court each year. Nor is it necessary that he should. But as to his individual labors, with this mountain of papers, each Justice is the keeper of his own conscience.

In argued cases, conferences are followed by the preparation and circulation of opinions by Justices designated by the Chief Justice when he is with the prevailing view and, if not, by the senior Associate who is. But any Justice is free to write as he will, and there may be one or more opinions concurring in the result but reaching it by different reasons, and there may be a dissenting opinion or opinions. This occasions complaint by laymen and the bar that they are required to piece all these contributions together in order to make out where the Supreme Court really stands as an institution.

All of this is at odds with the practice of most courts of continental Europe, which make it a rule to announce the decision in one statement only and to issue no dissents or concurrences. Moreover, their work is institutionalized and depersonalized. The court's opinion bears the name of no author. Like our *per curiam* opinion, it may be the work of any member or of several in collaboration. This anonymity diminishes any temptation to exploit differences within the court, but it may also diminish the incentive for hard work on opinions. In any event, I am sure that not only Anglo-American tradition but judicial and professional opinion favors the identification of writers and the full disclosure of important differences within the Court. Mr. Jefferson would have required each Justice to write his reasons in every case, as proof that he gave it consideration and did not merely follow a leader.

The dissenting opinion strives to undermine the Court's reasoning and discredit its result. At its best, the dissent, as Mr. Hughes said, is "an appeal to the brooding spirit of the law, to the intelligence of a future day. . . ." But Judge Cardozo has written:

". . . Comparatively speaking at least, the dissenter is irresponsible. The spokesman of the court is cautious, timid, fearful of the vivid word, the heightened phrase. He dreams of an unworthy brood of scions, the spawn of careless *dicta* disowned by the *ratio decidendi,* to which all legitimate offspring must be able to trace their lineage. The result is to cramp and paralyze. One fears to say anything when the peril of misunderstanding puts a warning finger to the lips. Not so, however, the dissenter. . . . For the moment, he is the gladiator making a last stand against the lions. The poor man must be forgiven a freedom of expression, tinged at rare moments with a touch of bitterness, which magnanimity as well as caution would reject for one triumphant."

Dissent has a popular appeal, for it is an underdog judge pleading for an underdog litigant. Of course, one party or the other must always be underdog in a lawsuit, the purpose of which really is to determine which one it shall be. But the tradition of great dissents built around such names as Holmes, Brandeis, Cardozo, and Stone is not due to the frequency or multiplicity of their dissents, but to their quality and the importance of the few cases in which they carried their disagreement beyond the conference table. Also, quite contrary to the popular notion, relatively few of all the dissents recorded in the Supreme Court have later become law, although some of these are of great importance.

There has been much undiscriminating eulogy of dissenting opinions. It is said they clarify the issues. Often they do the exact opposite. The technique of the dissenter often is to exaggerate the holding of the Court beyond the meaning of the majority and then to blast away at the excess. So the poor lawyer with a similar case does not know whether the majority opinion meant what it seemed to say or what the minority said it meant. Then, too, dissenters frequently force the majority to take positions more extreme than was originally intended. The classic example is the *Dred Scott Case*, in which Chief Justice Taney's extreme statements were absent in his original draft and were inserted only after Mr. Justice McLean, then a more than passive candidate for the presidency, raised the issue in dissent.

The *right of dissent* is a valuable one. Wisely used on well-chosen occasions, it has been of great service to the profession and to the law. But there is nothing good, for either the Court or the dissenter, in dissenting per se. Each dissenting opinion is a confession of failure to convince the writer's colleagues, and the true test of a judge is his influence in leading, not in opposing, his court.

If the Supreme Court were any kind of institution except a court, it would be easy to suggest methods by which it could dispose of an increased volume of work. The objection to most such proposals is that they are incompatible with the personal and individual responsibility inherent in judicial office.

It has been suggested that a small committee of the Court could pass on certiorari applications. Some lawyers believe that this is done. That is not true. The Supreme Court does not function on any case by committee. Every qualified Justice acts on every petition expressly or by acquiescence.

It is often suggested that the Court could create a staff of assistants like those of administrative tribunals to take much of the drudgery of judicial work from the Justices. In fact, a suspicion has grown at the bar that the law clerks already constitute a kind of junior court which decides the fate of certiorari petitions. This idea of the law clerks' influence gave rise to a lawyer's waggish statement that the Senate no longer need bother about confirmation of Justices but ought to confirm the appointment of law clerks. Twice during the last term I was asked by prominent lawyers, once by letter and once orally, how they could get their petitions for certiorari past law clerks and to the consideration of the Justices themselves. The answer is that every petition is on the conference list, and its fate is decided by the vote or agreement without formal vote of every Justice who does not disqualify himself. . . .

From what I have said it might almost be assumed that the Supreme Court could be ignored in the power equation of the American Government. But in living history this institution has profoundly influenced, for better or for worse, the course of the nation. Not only has it been the center of bitter debate itself, but its decisions have played some part in nearly every great political issue that has vexed our people.

What authority does the Court possess which generates this influence? The answer is its power to hold unconstitutional and judicially unenforceable an act of the President, of Congress, or of a constituent state of the Federation. That power is not expressly granted or hinted at in the Article defining judicial power, but rests on logical implication. It is an incident of jurisdiction to determine what really is the law governing a particular case or controversy. In the hierarchy of legal values, if the higher law of the Constitution prohibits what the lower law of the legislature attempts, the latter is a nullity; otherwise, the Constitution would exist only at the option of Congress. Thus it comes about that in a private litigation the Court may decide a question of power that will be of great moment to the nation or to a state.

The assertion of this power over the enactments of the states met with strong resistance, and its application to laws of Congress provoked bitter and persistent opposition. It is needless to trace the evolution of the power as now exercised. The Rooseveltian struggle with the Court did not impair the power, which is as positively asserted today as in pre-Roosevelt days. But neither did that struggle end the controversy over the proper use of the power, a controversy which lies just beneath the surface and is likely to break forth from time to time as long as the Republic shall last.

Public opinion, however, seems always to sustain the power of the Court, even against attack by popular executives and even though the public more than once has repudiated particular decisions. It is inescapable in our form of government that authority exist somewhere to interpret an instrument which sets up our whole structure and defines the powers of the Federal Government in about 4,000 words, to which a century and a half have added only about half as many amendatory words. The people have seemed to feel that the Supreme Court, whatever its defects, is still the most detached, dispassionate, and trust-

worthy custodian that our system affords for the
translation of abstract into concrete constitutional
commands.

The Constitution has gone through several cycles
of interpretation, each of which is related to the
political and economic condition of the period. Federal powers were consolidated and invigorated under
Marshall. A reaction marked by conflict over the very
nature and binding force of the compact embittered
the time of Taney. There followed a period when
attention turned to nationalism and to railroad building and industrial growth stimulated by a long period
of almost uninterrupted peace. That came to an end
in 1914, and we entered the period of international
violence which now burdens and vexes us and puts
our internal liberties under new strains.

That the Supreme Court, in some instances, can interpose judicial authority between political forces and
those whose liberty they would override is a great
distinction from those governments abroad which
have been subverted by dictatorship. But I have tried
to point out that while our judiciary is an effective
instrument for applying to the case of an individual
the just laws enacted by representatives of a free-
dom-respecting society, it has grave jurisdictional,
procedural, and political shortcomings. These counsel against leaving the protection of liberty wholly to
the judiciary while heedlessly allowing the elected
branches of the Government to be constituted without regard to their members' attitudes toward liberty.

Let us take the factor of delay. Since the Court
may pronounce a judgment of unconstitutionality
only in deciding a case or controversy, obviously it
cannot take the initiative in checking what the Justices may know to be constitutional violations. It has
no self-starting capacity and must await the action of
some litigant so aggrieved as to have a justiciable
case. Also, its pronouncement must await the decision in the lower courts. Often it is years after a
statute is put on the books and begins to take effect
before a decision on a constitutional question can be

heard by the Supreme Court. The Smith Act of 1940 was held constitutional for the first time in 1951, and the Alien Registration Act, also of 1940, was passed on in 1952. The run of constitutional litigation, like that of all litigations, is slow and costly.

Such delays often mean that the damage is done before the remedy for invasion of civil liberties is available. For example: In 1951 the Court cast serious doubt upon the legality of the Attorney General's list of subversive organizations promulgated in 1947. But the list had long been widely circulated and accepted, and despite the Court's views it has never ceased to be used in the press, in the executive department, by and before congressional committees, and even in courts to prejudice individuals in their liberty, position, and good name.

Then, too, many of the most vital acts of government cannot be challenged at all by the case and controversy route, because the questions are political or involve the spending power, foreign affairs, or the war power. The Supreme Court is a tribunal of limited jurisdiction, narrow processes, and small capacity for handling mass litigation; it has no force to coerce obedience, and is subject to being stripped of jurisdiction or smothered with additional Justices any time such a disposition exists and is supported strongly enough by public opinion. I think the Court can never quite escape consciousness of its own infirmities, a psychology which may explain its apparent yielding to expediency, especially during war time.

If I may borrow a summation from my former self, I will repeat to you the conclusion of a lecture to the lawyers of the Ministry of Justice of France, delivered at their invitation in April 1946, when they were in the throes of writing a new constitution for France. After discussing the judicial vis-à-vis the political power in our system, I said:

"Opinion, of course, will differ as to the advantages and disadvantages of this constitutional and judicial system. The United States on the whole has been a prosperous country, with varied resources, making a favorable background for any experiment in government. Its inhabitants have not faced the strains that beset some less-favored nations. Even so, our history has not been free of sanguinary internal conflicts. It would not be realistic to contend that judicial power always has been used wisely. The Court has been sharply attacked by Presidents Jefferson, Jackson, Lincoln, and both Roosevelts. Yet no substantial sentiment exists for any curtailment of the Court's powers. Even President Roosevelt in the bitterest conflict with judicial power in our history suggested only change in the Court's composition, none in its constitutional prerogatives. The real strength of the position of the Court is probably in its indispensability to government under a written Constitution. It is difficult to see how the provisions of a 150-year-old written document can have much vitality if there is not some permanent institution to translate them into current commands and to see to their contemporary application. Courts will differ from time to time in the emphasis they will place on one or another of the Constitution's provisions, in part no doubt responsive to the atmosphere of the changes in public opinion. Interpretations will change from one generation to another, precedents will sometimes be overruled, innovations will be made that will not always be predictable. This always has been the history of the Court.

"The legal profession in all countries knows that there are only two real choices of government open to a people. It may be governed by law or it may be governed by the will of one or of a group of men. Law, as the expression of the ultimate will and wisdom of a people, has so far proven the safest guardian of liberty yet devised. I think our constitutional and judicial system has made a valuable and enduring contribution to the science of government under law. We commend it to your notice, not because we think it is perfect, but because it is an earnest effort to fulfill those aspirations for freedom and the general welfare which are a common heritage of your people and of mine."

PART II

Congress and the Legislative Power

THE ENUMERATED POWERS

"All legislative Powers herein granted shall be vested in a Congress of the United States, which shall consist of a Senate and House of Representatives."

Thus reads section 1 of article I of the Constitution, from which is derived the doctrine that the national government is one of "enumerated powers," as described by Chief Justice Marshall in *McCulloch* v. *Maryland*, 17 U.S. (4 Wheat.) 316 (1819), *infra*. Two consequences would seem to follow from this central proposition: First, no branch of the national government except Congress may make law; and second, Congress may legislate only in connection with the matters enumerated in the legislative article of the Constitution. Both propositions, while true in a general way, require interpretation if not modification.

As to the first proposition, that only Congress may legislate, it should be remembered that treaties, negotiated by the President and ratified by the Senate, also have the force of law. Even executive agreements, entered into by the President alone in the exercise of his diplomatic powers, may have the same effect. Moreover, presidential executive orders and proclamations and regulations validly promulgated by administrative agencies also have the force of law. Finally, it can be argued that the Supreme Court, in interpreting terms of such uncertain content as "commerce among the several States" or "due process of law," is constantly engaged in a kind of law-making process.

The second proposition, that Congress can act only in relation to the subjects enumerated in article I, requires an expanded interpretation rather than one of limitation. Section 8 of article I specifies seventeen fairly specific matters as to which legislative power is conferred on Congress. The most important of these are the power to regulate commerce, discussed in section B, *infra*, and the taxing power, discussed in section C, *infra*.

A. The "Necessary and Proper" Clause

In addition to the specifically enumerated powers in section 8 of article I, the eighteenth clause gives to Congress the following power:

> "To make all Laws which shall be necessary and proper for carrying into Execution the foregoing Powers, and all other Powers vested by this Constitution in the Government of the United States, or in any Department or Officer thereof."

The vastly important issue as to whether this clause was a limitation upon the exercise of the previously enumerated powers or was by implication the source of significant additional powers, was decided in a powerful opinion by Chief Justice Marshall.

McCulloch v. Maryland

17 U.S. (4 Wheat.) 316 (1819)

[The Bank of the United States was first established in 1791, but its charter was allowed to expire in 1811. In the period of financial difficulty following the War of 1812 the charter was renewed in 1816. The management was never very efficient, and its unfortunate handling of credit created difficulties for many state banks. The resulting unpopularity of the national bank, particularly in the South and West, induced many special taxes designed to drive the bank out of existence. The State of Maryland enacted a tax upon notes issued by the national bank, which could be commuted by the payment of $15,000 a year. McCulloch, an official of the bank, was held liable for the nonpayment of the tax; and the Court was confronted with two questions: First, has Congress the power to incorporate a bank? Second, if so, may a state tax the activities of such a bank?]

MR. CHIEF JUSTICE MARSHALL delivered the opinion of the Court: . . .

The first question made in the cause is, has congress power to incorporate a bank?

It has been truly said that this can scarcely be considered as an open question, entirely unprejudiced by the former proceedings of the nation respecting it. The principle now contested was introduced at a very early period of our history, has been recognized by many successive legislatures, and has been acted upon by the judicial department, in cases of peculiar delicacy, as a law of undoubted obligation.

It will not be denied, that a bold and daring usurpation might be resisted, after an acquiescence still longer and more complete than this. But it is conceived that a doubtful question, one on which human reason may pause, and the human judgment be suspended, in the decision of which the great principles of liberty are not concerned, but the respective powers of those who are equally the representatives of the people, are to be adjusted; if not put at rest by the practice of the government, ought to receive a considerable impression from that practice. An exposition of the constitution, deliberately established by legislative acts, on the faith of which an immense property has been advanced, ought not to be lightly disregarded.

The power now contested was exercised by the
first Congress elected under the present constitution.
The bill for incorporating the bank of the United
States did not steal upon an unsuspecting legislature,
and pass unobserved. Its principle was completely
understood, and was opposed with equal zeal and
ability. After being resisted, first in the fair and open
field of debate, and afterwards in the executive cabinet, with as much persevering talent as any measure
has ever experienced, and being supported by arguments which convinced minds as pure and as intel-
ligent as this country can boast, it became a law. The
original act was permitted to expire; but a short experience of the embarrassments to which the refusal
to revive it exposed the government, convinced those
who were most prejudiced against the measure of its
necessity and induced the passage of the present law.
It would require no ordinary share of intrepidity to
assert that a measure adopted under these circumstances was a bold and plain usurpation, to which
the constitution gave no countenance.

These observations belong to the cause; but they
are not made under the impression that, were the
question entirely new, the law would be found irre-
concilable with the constitution.

In discussing this question, the counsel for the
State of Maryland have deemed it of some importance, in the construction of the constitution, to consider that instrument not as emanating from the
people, but as the act of sovereign and independent
States. The powers of the general government, it has
been said, are delegated by the States, who alone are
truly sovereign; and must be exercised in subordina-
tion to the States, who alone possess supreme
dominion.

It would be difficult to sustain this proposition.
The Convention which framed the constitution was
indeed elected by the state legislatures. But the instrument, when it came from their hands, was a mere
proposal, without obligation, or pretensions to it. It
was reported to the then existing Congress of the

United States, with a request that it might "be submitted to a convention of delegates, chosen in each State by the people thereof, under the recommendation of its legislature, for their assent and ratification." This mode of proceeding was adopted; and by the convention, by Congress, and by the state legislatures, the instrument was submitted to the people. They acted upon it in the only manner in which they can act safely, effectively, and wisely, on such a subject, by assembling in convention. It is true they assembled in their several States—and where else should they have assembled? No political dreamer was ever wild enough to think of breaking down the lines which separate the States, and of compounding the American people into one common mass. Of consequence, when they act, they act in their States. But the measures they adopt do not, on that account, cease to be the measures of the people themselves, or become the measures of the state governments.

From these conventions the constitution derives its whole authority. The government proceeds directly from the people; is "ordained and established" in the name of the people; and is declared to be ordained, "in order to form a more perfect union, establish justice, insure domestic tranquillity, and secure the blessings of liberty, to themselves and to their posterity." The assent of the States, in their sovereign capacity, is implied in calling a convention, and thus submitting that instrument to the people. But the people were at perfect liberty to accept or reject it; and their act was final. It required not the affirmance, and could not be negatived, by the state governments. The constitution, when thus adopted, was of complete obligation, and bound the state sovereignties. . . .

The government of the Union, then, (whatever may be the influence of this fact on the case), is, emphatically, and truly, a government of the people. In form and in substance it emanates from them. Its powers are granted by them, and are to be exercised directly on them, and for their benefit.

This government is acknowledged by all to be one of enumerated powers. The principle, that it can exercise only the powers granted to it, would seem too apparent to have required to be enforced by all those arguments which its enlightened friends, while it was depending before the people, found it necessary to urge. That principle is now universally admitted. But the question respecting the extent of the powers actually granted, is perpetually arising, and will probably continue to arise, as long as our system shall exist.

In discussing these questions, the conflicting powers of the general and state governments must be brought into view, and the supremacy of their respective laws, when they are in opposition, must be settled.

If any one proposition could command the universal assent of mankind, we might expect it would be this—that the government of the Union, though limited in its powers, is supreme within its sphere of action. This would seem to result necessarily from its nature. It is the government of all; its powers are delegated by all; it represents all, and acts for all. Though any one State may be willing to control its operations, no State is willing to allow others to control them. The nation, on those subjects on which it can act, must necessarily bind its component parts. But this question is not left to mere reason: the people have, in express terms, decided it, by saying, "this constitution, and the laws of the United States, which shall be made in pursuance thereof," "shall be the supreme law of the land," and by requiring that the members of the state legislatures, and the officers of the executive and judicial departments of the states shall take the oath of fidelity to it.

The government of the United States, then, though limited in its powers, is supreme; and its laws, when made in pursuance of the constitution, form the supreme law of the land, "anything in the constitution or laws of any state to the contrary notwithstanding."

Among the enumerated powers, we do not find that of establishing a bank or creating a corporation. But there is no phrase in the instrument which, like the articles of confederation, excludes incidental or implied powers; and which requires that everything granted shall be expressly and minutely described. Even the 10th amendment, which was framed for the purpose of quieting the excessive jealousies which have been excited, omits the word "expressly," and declares only that the powers "not delegated to the United States, nor prohibited to the States, are reserved to the States or to the people"; thus leaving the question, whether the particular power which may become the subject of contest has been delegated to the one government, or prohibited to the other, to depend on a fair construction of the whole instrument. The men who drew and adopted this amendment had experienced the embarrassments resulting from the insertion of this word in the articles of confederation, and probably omitted it to avoid those embarrassments. A constitution, to contain an accurate detail of all the subdivisions of which its great powers will admit, and of all the means by which they may be carried into execution, would partake of a prolixity of a legal code, and could scarcely be embraced by the human mind. It would probably never be understood by the public. Its nature, therefore, requires, that only its great outlines should be marked, its important objects designated, and the minor ingredients which compose those objects be deduced from the nature of the objects themselves. That this idea was entertained by the framers of the American constitution, is not only to be inferred from the nature of the instrument, but from the language. Why else were some of the limitations, found in the ninth section of the 1st article, introduced? It is also, in some degree, warranted by their having omitted to use any restrictive term which might prevent its receiving a fair and just interpretation. In considering this question, then, we must never forget that it is a *constitution* we are expounding.

Although, among the enumerated powers of government, we do not find the word "bank" or "incorporation," we find the great powers to lay and collect taxes; to borrow money; to regulate commerce; to declare and conduct a war; and to raise and support armies and navies. The sword and the purse, all the external relations, and no inconsiderable portion of the industry of the nation, are entrusted to its government. It can never be pretended that these vast powers draw after them others of inferior importance, merely because they are inferior. Such an idea can never be advanced. But it may with great reason be contended, that a government, entrusted with such ample powers, on the due execution of which the happiness and prosperity of the nation so vitally depends, must also be entrusted with ample means for their execution. . . . But it is denied that the government has its choice of means; or, that it may employ the most convenient means, if, to employ them, it be necessary to erect a corporation.

On what foundation does this argument rest? On this alone: The power of creating a corporation, is one appertaining to sovereignty, and is not expressly conferred on Congress. This is true. But all legislative powers appertain to sovereignty. The original power of giving the law on any subject whatever, is a sovereign power; and if the government of the Union is restrained from creating a corporation, as a means for performing its functions, on the single reason that the creation of a corporation is an act of sovereignty; if the sufficiency of this reason be acknowledged, there would be some difficulty in sustaining the authority of Congress to pass other laws for the accomplishment of the same objects.

The government which has a right to do an act, and has imposed on it the duty of performing that act, must, according to the dictates of reason, be allowed to select the means; and those who contend that it may not select any appropriate means, that one particular mode of effecting the object is excepted, take upon themselves the burden of establishing that exception. . . . The power of creating a corporation, though appertaining to sovereignty, is not, like the power of making war, or levying taxes, or of regulating commerce, a great substantive and independent power, which cannot be implied as incidental to other powers, or used as a means of executing them. It is never the end for which other powers are exercised, but a means by which other objects are accomplished. . . . The power of creating a corporation is never used for its own sake, but for the purpose of effecting something else. No sufficient reason is, therefore, perceived, why it may not pass as incidental to those powers which are expressly given, if it be a direct mode of executing them.

But the constitution of the United States has not left the right of Congress to employ the necessary means, for the execution of the powers conferred on the government, to general reasoning. To its enumeration of powers is added that of making "all laws which shall be necessary and proper, for carrying into execution the foregoing powers, and all other powers vested by this constitution, in the government of the United States, or in any department thereof."

The counsel for the State of Maryland have urged various arguments, to prove that this clause, though in terms a grant of power, is not so in effect; but is really restrictive of the general right, which might otherwise be implied, of selecting means for executing the enumerated powers.

In support of this proposition, they have found it necessary to contend, that this clause was inserted for the purpose of conferring on Congress the power of making laws. . . . That a legislature, endowed with legislative powers, can legislate, is a proposition too self-evident to have been questioned.

But the argument on which most reliance is placed, is drawn from the peculiar language of this clause. Congress is not empowered by it to make all laws, which may have relation to the powers conferred on the government, but such only as may be *necessary and proper* for carrying them into execution. The word *"necessary"* is considered as controlling the whole sentence, and as limiting the right to pass laws for the execution of the granted powers, to such as are indispensable, and without which the power would be nugatory. That it excludes the choice of means, and leaves to Congress, in each case, that only which is most direct and simple.

Is it true, that this is the sense in which the word "necessary" is always used? Does it always import an absolute physical necessity, so strong, that one thing, to which another may be termed necessary, cannot exist without that other? We think it does not. If reference be had to its use, in the common affairs of the world, or in approved authors, we find that it frequently imports no more than that one thing is convenient, or useful, or essential to another. To employ the means necessary to an end, is generally understood as employing any means calculated to produce the end, and not as being confined to those single means, without which the end would be entirely unattainable. Such is the character of human language, that no word conveys to the mind, in all situations, one single definite idea; and nothing is more common than to use words in a figurative sense. Almost all compositions contain words, which, taken in their rigorous sense, would convey a meaning different from that which is obviously intended. It is essential to just construction, that many words which import something excessive should be understood in a more mitigated sense—in that sense which common usage justifies. The word "necessary" is of this description. It has not a fixed character peculiar to itself. It admits of all degrees of comparison; and is often connected with other words, which increase or diminish the impression the mind receives of the urgency it imports. A thing may be necessary, very necessary, absolutely or indispensably necessary. To no mind would the same idea be conveyed by these several phrases. This comment on the word is well illustrated by the passage cited at the bar, from the 10th section of the 1st article of the constitution. It is, we think, impossible to compare the sentence which prohibits a State from laying "imposts or duties on imports or exports, except what may be *absolutely* necessary for executing its inspection laws," with that which authorizes Congress "to make all laws which shall be necessary and proper for carrying into execution" the powers of the general government, without feeling a conviction that the convention understood itself to change materially the meaning of the word "necessary," by prefixing the word "absolutely." This word, then, like others, is used in various senses; and, in its construction, the subject, the context, the intention of the person using them, are all to be taken into view.

Let this be done in the case under consideration. The subject is the execution of those great powers on which the welfare of a nation essentially depends. It must have been the intention of those who gave these powers, to insure, as far as human prudence could insure, their beneficial execution. This could not be done by confining the choice of means to such narrow limits as not to leave it in the power of Congress to adopt any which might be appropriate, and which were conducive to the end. This provision is made in a constitution intended to endure for ages to come, and, consequently, to be adapted to the various *crises* of human affairs. . . .

But the argument which most conclusively demonstrates the error of the construction contended for by the counsel for the State of Maryland, is founded on the contention of the convention, as manifested in the whole clause. To waste time and argument in proving that, without it, Congress might carry its powers into execution, would be not much less idle than to hold a lighted taper to the sun. As little can it be required to prove, that in the absence of this clause, Congress would have some choice of means. That it might employ those which, in its judgment, would most advantageously effect the object to be accomplished. That any means adapted to the end, any means which tended directly to the execution of the constitutional powers of the government, were in themselves constitutional. This clause, as construed by the State of Maryland, would abridge, and almost annihilate this useful and necessary right of the legislature to select the means. That this could not be intended, is, we should think, had it not been already controverted, too apparent for controversy. We think so for the following reasons:

1st. The clause is placed among the powers of Congress, not among the limitations on those powers.

2d. Its terms purport to enlarge, not to diminish the powers vested in the government. It purports to be an additional power, not a restriction on those already granted. . . . Had the intention been to make this clause restrictive, it would unquestionably have been so in form as well as in effect.

The result of the most careful and attentive consideration bestowed upon this clause is, that if it does not enlarge, it cannot be construed to restrain the powers of Congress, or to impair the right of the legislature to exercise its best judgment in the selection of measures to carry into execution the constitutional powers of the government. If no other motive for its insertion can be suggested, a sufficient one is found in the desire to remove all doubts respecting the right to legislate on that vast mass of incidental powers which must be involved in the constitution, if that instrument be not a splendid bauble.

We admit, as all must admit, that the powers of the government are limited, and that its limits are not to be transcended. But we think the sound construction of the constitution must allow to the national legislature that discretion, with respect to the means by which the powers it confers are to be carried into execution, which will enable that body to perform the high duties assigned to it, in the manner most beneficial to the people. Let the end be legitimate, let it be within the scope of the constitution, and all means which are appropriate, which are plainly adapted to that end, which are not prohibited, but consistent with the letter and spirit of the constitution, are constitutional.

That a corporation must be considered as a means not less usual, not of higher dignity, not more requiring a particular specification than other means, has been sufficiently proved. If we look to the origin of corporations, to the manner in which they have been framed in that government from which we have derived most of our legal principles and ideas, or to the uses to which they have been applied, we find no reason to suppose that a constitution, omitting, and wisely omitting, to enumerate all the means for carrying into execution the great powers vested in government, ought to have specified this. Had it been intended to grant this power as one which should be distinct and independent, to be exercised in any case whatever, it would have found a place among the enumerated powers of the government. But being considered merely as a means, to be employed only for the purpose of carrying into execution the given powers, there could be no motive for particularly mentioning it. . . .

If a corporation may be employed indiscriminately with other means to carry into execution the powers of the government, no particular reason can be assigned for excluding the use of a bank, if required for its fiscal operations. To use one, must be within the discretion of Congress, if it be an appropriate mode of executing the powers of government. That it is a convenient, a useful, and essential instrument in the prosecution of its fiscal operations, is not now a subject of controversy. All those who have been concerned in the administration of our finances, have concurred in representing its importance and necessity; and so strongly have they been felt, that statesmen of the first class, whose previous opinions against it had been confirmed by every circumstance which can fix the human judgment, have yielded those opinions to the exigencies of the nation. . . .

After the most deliberate consideration, it is the unanimous and decided opinion of this Court, that the act to incorporate the Bank of the United States is a law made in pursuance of the constitution, and is a part of the supreme law of the land. . . .

It being the opinion of the Court, that the act incorporating the bank is constitutional; and that the power of establishing a branch in the State of Maryland might be properly exercised by the bank itself, we proceed to inquire—

2. Whether the State of Maryland may, without violating the constitution, tax that branch? . . .

That the power to tax involves the power to destroy; that the power to destroy may defeat and render useless the power to create; that there is a plain repugnance, in conferring on one government a power to control the constitutional measures of another, which other, with respect to those very measures, is declared to be supreme over that which exerts the control, are propositions not to be denied. But all inconsistencies are to be reconciled by the magic of the word CONFIDENCE. Taxation, it is said, does not necessarily and unavoidably destroy. To carry it to the excess of destruction would be an abuse, to presume which, would banish that confidence which is essential to all government. . . .

But is this a case of confidence? Would the people of any one State trust those of another with a power to control the most insignificant operations of their state government? We know they would not. Why, then, should we suppose that the people of any one State should be willing to trust those of another with a power to control the operations of a government to which they have confided the most important and most valuable interests? In the legislature of the Union alone, are all represented. The legislature of the Union alone, therefore, can be trusted by the people with the power of controlling measures which concern all, in the confidence that it will not be abused. This, then, is not a case of confidence, and we must consider it as it really is. . . .

If the States may tax one instrument, employed by the government in the execution of its powers, they may tax any and every other instrument. They may tax the mail; they may tax the mint; they may tax patent rights; they may tax the papers of the custom-house; they may tax judicial process; they may tax all the means employed by the government, to an excess which would defeat all the ends of government. . . . This is not all. If the controlling power of the States be established; if their supremacy as to taxation be acknowledged; what is to restrain their exercising this control in any shape they may please to give it? Their sovereignty is not confined to taxation. That is not the only mode in which it might be displayed. The question is, in truth, a question of supremacy; and if the right of the States to tax the means employed by the general government be conceded, the declaration that the constitution, and the laws made in pursuance thereof, shall be the supreme law of the land, is empty and unmeaning declamation. . . .

We are unanimously of opinion, that the law passed by the legislature of Maryland, imposing a tax on the Bank of the United States, is unconstitutional and void. . . .

B. *The Commerce Clause*

The principal source of affirmative power in the national government is found in the following few words:

> "To regulate Commerce with foreign Nations, and among the several States, and with the Indian Tribes;"

The leading case is again an early opinion of Chief Justice Marshall.

GIBBONS V. OGDEN

22 U.S. (9 Wheat.) 1 (1824)

[Robert R. Livingston and Robert Fulton had been granted by the New York Legislature a monopoly of steamboat navigation in the waters of New York. Ogden, who had previously operated steamboats across the Hudson in partnership with Gibbons, accepted a license from the monopoly; but his partner Gibbons refused to do so. Thereupon Ogden brought an action to restrain Gibbons from continuing his trade between New York and New Jersey.]

Mr. Chief Justice Marshall delivered the opinion of the Court, and after stating the case, proceeded as follows:

The appellant contends that this decree is erroneous, because the laws which purport to give the exclusive privilege it sustains, are repugnant to the constitution and laws of the United States.

They are said to be repugnant—

1st. To that clause in the constitution which authorizes Congress to regulate commerce. . . .

The subject to be regulated is commerce; and our constitution being, as was aptly said at the bar, one of enumeration, and not of definition, to ascertain the extent of the power it becomes necessary to settle the meaning of the word. The counsel for the appellee would limit it to traffic, to buying and selling, or the interchange of commodities, and do not admit that it comprehends navigation. This would restrict a general term, applicable to many objects, to one of its significations. Commerce, undoubtedly, is traffic, but it is something more: it is intercourse. It describes the commercial intercourse between nations, and parts of nations, in all its branches, and is regulated by prescribing rules for carrying on that intercourse. The mind can scarcely conceive a system for regulating commerce between nations, which shall exclude all laws concerning navigation, which shall be silent on the admission of the vessels of the one nation into the ports of the other, and be confined to prescribing rules for the conduct of individuals, in the actual employment of buying and selling, or of barter.

If commerce does not include navigation, the government of the Union has no direct power over that subject, and can make no law prescribing what shall constitute American vessels, or requiring that they shall be navigated by American seamen. Yet this power has been exercised from the commencement of the government, has been exercised with the consent of all, and has been understood by all to be a commercial regulation. All America understands, and has uniformly understood, the word "commerce" to comprehend navigation. It was so understood, and must have been so understood, when the constitution was framed. The power over commerce, including navigation, was one of the primary objects for which the people of America adopted their government, and must have been contemplated in forming it. The convention must have used the word in that sense; because all have understood it in that sense, and the attempt to restrict it comes too late.

If the opinion that "commerce," as the word is used in the constitution, comprehends navigation also, requires any additional confirmation, that additional confirmation is, we think, furnished by the words of the instrument itself.

It is a rule of construction, acknowledged by all, that the exceptions from a power mark its extent; for it would be absurd, as well as useless, to except from a granted power, that which was not granted—that which the words of the grant could not comprehend. If, then, there are in the constitution plain exceptions from the power over navigation, plain inhibitions to the exercise of that power in a particular way, it is a proof that those who made these exceptions, and prescribed these inhibitions, understood the power to which they applied as being granted.

The 9th section of the 1st article declares that "no preference shall be given, by any regulation of commerce or revenue, to the ports of one State over those of another." This clause cannot be understood as applicable to those laws only which are passed for the purposes of revenue, because it is expressly applied to commercial regulations; and the most obvious preference which can be given to one port over another, in regulating commerce, relates to navigation. But the subsequent part of the sentence is still more explicit. It is, "nor shall vessels bound to or from one State, be obliged to enter, clear, or pay duties, in another." These words have a direct reference to navigation. . . .

The word used in the constitution, then, comprehends, and has been always understood to comprehend, navigation within its meaning; and a power to regulate navigation is as expressly granted as if that term had been added to the word "commerce."

To what commerce does this power extend? The constitution informs us, to commerce "with foreign nations, and among the several States, and with the Indian tribes."

It has, we believe, been universally admitted that these words comprehend every species of commercial intercourse between the United States and foreign nations. No sort of trade can be carried on between this country and any other, to which this power does not extend. It has been truly said, that commerce, as the word is used in the constitution, is a unit, every part of which is indicated by the term.

If this be the admitted meaning of the word, in its application to foreign nations, it must carry the same meaning throughout the sentence, and remain a unit, unless there be some plain intelligible cause which alters it.

The subject to which the power is next applied, is to commerce "among the several States." The word "among" means intermingled with. A thing which is among others, is intermingled with them. Commerce among the States cannot stop at the external boundary line of each State, but may be introduced into the interior.

It is not intended to say that these words comprehend that commerce which is completely internal, which is carried on between man and man in a State, or between different parts of the same State, and which does not extend to or affect other States. Such a power would be inconvenient, and is certainly unnecessary.

Comprehensive as the word "among" is, it may very properly be restricted to that commerce which concerns more States than one. The phrase is not one which would probably have been selected to indicate the completely interior traffic of a State, because it is not an apt phrase for that purpose; and the enumeration of the particular classes of commerce to which the power was to be extended, would not have been made had the intention been to extend the power to every description. The enumeration presupposes something not enumerated; and that something, if we regard the language or the subject of the sentence, must be the exclusively internal commerce of a State. The genius and character of the whole government seem to be, that its action is to be applied to all the external concerns of the nation, and to those internal concerns which affect the States generally; but not to those which are completely within a particular State, which do not affect other States, and with which it is not necessary to interfere, for the purpose of executing some of the general powers of the government. The completely internal commerce of a State, then, may be considered as reserved for the State itself.

But, in regulating commerce with foreign nations, the power of Congress does not stop at the jurisdictional lines of the several States. It would be a very useless power if it could not pass those lines. The commerce of the United States with foreign nations is that of the whole United States. Every district has a right to participate in it. The deep streams which penetrate our country in every direction, pass through the interior of almost every State in the Union, and furnish the means of exercising this right. If Congress has the power to regulate it, that power must be exercised whenever the subject exists. If it exists within the States, if a foreign voyage may commence or terminate at a port within a State, then the power of Congress may be exercised within a State. . . .

We are now arrived at the inquiry—What is this power?

It is the power to regulate; that is, to prescribe the rule by which commerce is to be governed. This power, like all others vested in Congress, is complete in itself, may be exercised to its utmost extent, and acknowledges no limitations, other than are prescribed in the constitution. These are expressed in plain terms, and do not affect the questions which arise in this case, or which have been discussed at the bar. If, as has always been understood, the sovereignty of Congress, though limited to specified objects, is plenary as to those objects, the power over commerce with foreign nations, and among the several States, is vested in Congress as absolutely as it would be in a single government, having in its constitution the same restrictions on the exercise of the power as are found in the constitution of the United States. The wisdom and the discretion of Congress, their identity with the people, and the influence which their constituents possess at elections, are, in this, as in many other instances, as that, for example, of declaring war, the sole restraints on which they have relied to secure them from its abuse. They are the restraints on which the people must often rely solely, in all representative governments. . . .

But it has been urged with great earnestness, that although the power of Congress to regulate commerce with foreign nations, and among the several States, be co-extensive with the subject itself, and have no other limits than are prescribed in the constitution, yet the States may severally exercise the same power within their respective jurisdictions. In support of this argument, it is said that they possessed it as an inseparable attribute of sovereignty, before the formation of the constitution, and still retain it, except so far as they have surrendered it by that instrument; that this principle results from the nature of the government, and is secured by the tenth amendment; that an affirmative grant of power is not exclusive, unless in its own nature it be such that the continued exercise of it by the former possessor is inconsistent with the grant, and that this is not of that description.

. . .

In our complex system, presenting the rare and difficult scheme of one general government, whose action extends over the whole, but which possesses only certain enumerated powers, and of numerous State governments, which retain and exercise all powers not delegated to the Union, contests respecting power must arise. Were it even otherwise, the measures taken by the respective governments to execute their acknowledged powers, would often be of the same description, and might sometimes, interfere. This, however does not prove that the one is exercising, or has a right to exercise, the powers of the other.

The acts of Congress, passed in 1796 and 1799 [2 U.S.L. p. 545; 3 U.S.L. p. 126], empowering and directing the officers of the general government to conform to, and assist in the execution of the quarantine and health laws of a State, proceed, it is said, upon the idea that these laws are constitutional. It is undoubtedly true that they do proceed upon that idea; and the constitutionality of such laws has never, so far as we are informed, been denied. But they do not imply an acknowledgment that a state may rightfully regulate commerce with foreign nations, or among the States; for they do not imply that such laws are an exercise of that power, or enacted with a view to it. On the contrary, they are treated as quarantine and health laws, are so denominated in the acts of Congress, and are considered as flowing from the acknowledged power of a State, to provide for the health of its citizens. . . . But in making these provisions, the opinion is unequivocally manifested, that Congress may control the State laws, so far as it may be necessary to control them, for the regulation of commerce. . . .

It has been said that the act of August 7, 1789 [declaring that pilots shall continue to be regulated "by such laws as the States may respectively hereafter enact for that purpose"], acknowledges a concurrent power in the States to regulate the conduct of pilots, and hence is inferred an admission of their concurrent right with Congress to regulate commerce with foreign nations, and amongst the States. But this inference is not, we think, justified by the fact.

Although Congress cannot enable a State to legislate, Congress may adopt the provisions of a State on any subject. When the government of the Union was brought into existence, it found a system for the regulation of its pilots in full force in every State. The act which has been mentioned adopts this system, and gives it the same validity as if its provisions had been specially made by Congress. But the act, it may be said, is prospective also, and the adoption of laws to be made in the future, presupposes the right in the maker to legislate on the subject.

The act unquestionably manifests an intention to leave this subject entirely to the States, until Congress should think proper to interpose; but the very enactment of such a law indicates an opinion that it was necessary; that the existing system would not be applicable to the new state of things, unless expressly applied to it by Congress. . . .

It has been contended by the counsel for the appellant, that, as the word "to regulate" implies in its nature, full power over the thing to be regulated, it excludes, necessarily, the action of all others that would perform the same operation on the same thing. That regulation is designed for the entire result, applying to those parts which remain as they were, as well as to those which are altered. It produces a uniform whole, which is as much disturbed and deranged by changing what the regulating power designs to leave untouched, as that on which it has operated.

There is great force in this argument, and the Court is not satisfied that it has been refuted.

Since, however, in exercising the power of regulating their own purely internal affairs, whether of trading or police, the States may sometimes enact laws, the validity of which depends on their interfering with and being contrary to, an act of Congress passed in pursuance of the constitution, the court will enter upon the inquiry, whether the laws of New

York, as expounded by the highest tribunal of that State, have, in their application to this case, come into collision with an act of Congress, and deprived a citizen of a right to which that act entitles him. Should this collision exist, it will be immaterial whether those laws were passed in virtue of a concurrent power "to regulate commerce with foreign nations and among the several States," or in virtue of a power to regulate their domestic trade and police. In one case and the other, the acts of New York must yield to the law of Congress; and the decision sustaining the privilege they confer, against a right given by a law of the Union, must be erroneous.

[The laws of New York were found to be in conflict with the Act of Congress. The decree below was reversed, and the bill of Ogden was dismissed.]

Despite the sweeping character of the commerce power which the Court recognized in *Gibbons* v. *Ogden*, Congress took no significant action in furtherance of that authority until the enactment of the Interstate Commerce Act in 1887 and the Sherman Antitrust Act in 1890. However, these acts, and other legislation enacted as late as the mid-thirties of the twentieth century, received a more restrictive interpretation than the Marshall opinion seemed to require. It was not until 1937 that the return to the full scope of the power suggested by Marshall was again voiced by the Court.

NLRB v. Jones & Laughlin Steel Corp.

301 U.S. 1 (1937)

Mr. Chief Justice Hughes delivered the opinion of the Court.

In a proceeding under the National Labor Relations Act of 1935, the National Labor Relations Board found that the respondent, Jones & Laughlin Steel

Corporation, had violated the Act by engaging in unfair labor practices affecting commerce. The proceeding was instituted by the Beaver Valley Lodge No. 200, affiliated with the Amalgamated Association of Iron, Steel and Tin Workers of America, a labor organization. The unfair labor practices charged were that the corporation was discriminating against members of the union with regard to hire and tenure of employment, and was coercing and intimidating its employees in order to interfere with their self-organization. The discriminatory and coercive action alleged was the discharge of certain employees.

The National Labor Relations Board, sustaining the charge, ordered the corporation to cease and desist from such discrimination and coercion, to offer reinstatement to ten of the employees named, to make good their losses in pay, and to post for thirty days notices that the corporation would not discharge or discriminate against members, or those desiring to become members, of the labor union. As the corporation failed to comply, the Board petitioned the Circuit Court of Appeals to enforce the order. The court denied the petition, holding that the order lay beyond the range of federal power. 83 F.2d 998. We granted certiorari. . . .

The procedure in the instant case followed the statute. The labor union filed with the Board its verified charge. The Board thereupon issued its complaint against the respondent alleging that its action in discharging the employees in question constituted unfair labor practices affecting commerce within the meaning of § 8, subdivisions (1) and (3), and § 2, subdivisions (6) and (7) of the Act. Respondent, appearing specially for the purpose of objecting to the jurisdiction of the Board, filed its answer. Respondent admitted the discharges, but alleged that they were made because of inefficiency or violation of rules or for other good reasons and were not ascribable to union membership or activities. As an affirmative defense respondent challenged the constitutional validity of the statute and its applicability in the instant case. Notice of hearing was given and respondent appeared by counsel. The Board first took up the issue of jurisdiction and evidence was presented by both the Board and the respondent. Respondent then moved to dismiss the complaint for lack of jurisdiction and, on denial of that motion, respondent in accordance with its special appearance withdrew from further participation in the hearing. The Board received evidence upon the merits and at its close made its findings and order.

Contesting the ruling of the Board, the respondent argues (1) that the Act is in reality a regulation of labor relations and not of interstate commerce; (2) that the Act can have no application to the respondent's relations with its production employees because they are not subject to regulation by the federal government; and (3) that the provisions of the Act violate § 2 of Article III and the Fifth and Seventh Amendments of the Constitution of the United States.

The facts as to the nature and scope of the business of the Jones & Laughlin Steel Corporation have been found by the Labor Board and, so far as they are essential to the determination of this controversy, they are not in dispute. The Labor Board has found: The corporation is organized under the laws of Pennsylvania and has its principal office at Pittsburgh. It is engaged in the business of manufacturing iron and steel in plants situated in Pittsburgh and nearby Aliquippa, Pennsylvania. It manufactures and distributes a widely diversified line of steel and pig iron, being the fourth largest producer of steel in the United States. With its subsidiaries—nineteen in number—it is a completely integrated enterprise, owning and operating ore, coal and limestone properties, lake and river transportation facilities and terminal railroads located at its manufacturing plants. It owns or controls mines in Michigan and Minnesota. It operates four ore steamships on the Great Lakes, used in the transportation of ore to its factories. It owns coal mines in Pennsylvania. It operates towboats and steam barges used in carrying coal to its factories. It owns limestone properties in various places in Pennsylvania and West Virginia. It owns the Monongahela connecting railroad which connects the plants of the Pittsburgh works and forms an interconnection with the Pennsylvania, New York Central and Baltimore and Ohio Railroad systems. It owns the Aliquippa and Southern Railroad Company which connects the Aliquippa works with the Pittsburgh and Lake Erie, part of the New York Central system. Much of its product is shipped to its warehouses in Chicago, Detroit, Cincinnati and Memphis,—to the last two places by means of its own barges and transportation equipment. In Long Island City, New York, and in New Orleans it operates structural steel fabricating shops in connection with the warehousing of semi-finished materials sent from its works. Through one of its wholly-owned subsidiaries it owns, leases and operates stores, warehouses and yards for the distribution of equipment and supplies for drilling and operating oil and gas mills and for pipe lines, refineries and pumping stations. It has sales offices in twenty cities in the United States and a wholly-owned subsidiary which is devoted exclusively to distributing its product in Canada. Approximately 75 per cent. of its product is shipped out of Pennsylvania.

Summarizing these operations, the Labor Board concluded that the works in Pittsburgh and Aliquippa "might be likened to the heart of a self-contained, highly integrated body. They draw in the raw materials from Michigan, Minnesota, West Virginia, Pennsylvania in part through arteries and by means controlled by the respondent; they transform the materials and then pump them out to all parts of the nation through the vast mechanism which the respondent has elaborated." . . .

While respondent criticises the evidence and the attitude of the Board, which is described as being hostile toward employers and particularly toward those who insisted upon their constitutional rights, respondent did not take advantage of its opportunity to present evidence to refute that which was offered to show discrimination and coercion. In this situation, the record presents no ground for setting aside the order of the Board so far as the facts pertaining to the circumstances and purpose of the discharge of the employees are concerned. Upon that point it is sufficient to say that the evidence supports the findings of the Board that respondent discharged these men "because of their union activity and for the purpose of discouraging membership in the union." We turn to the questions of law which respondent urges in contesting the validity and application of the Act.

First. The scope of the Act.—The Act is challenged in its entirety as an attempt to regulate all industry, thus invading the reserved powers of the States over their local concerns. It is asserted that the references in the Act to interstate and foreign commerce are colorable at best; that the Act is not a true regulation of such commerce or of matters which directly affect it but on the contrary has the fundamental object of placing under the compulsory supervision of the federal government all industrial labor relations within the nation. The argument seeks support in the broad words of the preamble (section one) and in the sweep of the provisions of the Act, and it is further insisted that its legislative history shows an essential universal purpose in the light of which its scope cannot be limited by either construction or by the application of the separability clause.

If this conception of terms, intent and consequent inseparability were sound, the Act would necessarily fall by reason of the limitation upon the federal power which inheres in the constitutional grant, as well as because of the explicit reservation of the Tenth Amendment. *Schechter Corp.* v. *United States,* 295 U.S. 495, 549, 550, 554. The authority of the federal government may not be pushed to such an extreme as to destroy the distinction, which the commerce clause itself establishes, between commerce "among the several States" and the internal concerns of a State. That distinction between what is national and

what is local in the activities of commerce is vital to
the maintenance of our federal system. Id.

But we are not at liberty to deny effect to specific
provisions, which Congress has constitutional power
to enact, by superimposing upon them inferences
from general legislative declarations of an ambiguous
character, even if found in the same statute. The
cardinal principle of statutory construction is to save
and not to destroy. We have repeatedly held that as
between two possible interpretations of a statute, by
one of which it would be unconstitutional and by the
other valid, our plain duty is to adopt that which will
save the act. Even to avoid a serious doubt the rule
is the same. . . .

We think it clear that the National Labor Relations
Act may be construed so as to operate within the
sphere of constitutional authority. The jurisdiction
conferred upon the Board, and invoked in this instance, is found in § 10(a), which provides:

"Sec. 10(a). The Board is empowered, as herein-
after provided, to prevent any person from engaging
in any unfair labor practice (listed in section 8) affecting commerce."

The critical words of this provision, prescribing the
limits of the Board's authority in dealing with the
labor practices, are "affecting commerce." The Act
specifically defines the "commerce" to which it refers
(§ 2(6)):

"The term 'commerce' means trade, traffic, commerce, transportation, or communication among the
several States, or between the District of Columbia
or any Territory of the United States and any State
or other Territory, or between any foreign country
and any State or other Territory, or the District of
Columbia, or within the District of Columbia or any
Territory, or between points in the same State but
through any other State or any Territory or the District of Columbia or any foreign country."

There can be no question that the commerce thus
contemplated by the Act (aside from that within a
Territory or the District of Columbia) is interstate

and foreign commerce in the constitutional sense. The Act also defines the term "affecting commerce" (§ 2(7)):

"The term 'affecting commerce' means in commerce, or burdening or obstructing commerce or the free flow of commerce, or having led or tending to lead to a labor dispute burdening or obstructing commerce or the free flow of commerce."

This definition is one of exclusion as well as inclusion. The grant of authority to the Board does not purport to extend to the relationship between all industrial employees and employers. Its terms do not impose collective bargaining upon all industry regardless of effects upon interstate or foreign commerce. It purports to reach only what may be deemed to burden or obstruct that commerce and, thus qualified, it must be construed as contemplating the exercise of control within constitutional bounds. It is a familiar principle that acts which directly burden or obstruct interstate or foreign commerce, or its free flow, are within the reach of the congressional power. Acts having that effect are not rendered immune because they grow out of labor disputes. See *Texas & N. O. R. Co.* v. *Railway Clerks*, 281 U.S. 548, 570; *Schechter Corp.* v. *United States, supra,* pp. 544, 545; *Virginian Railway* v. *System Federation, No. 40,* 300 U.S. 515. It is the effect upon commerce, not the source of the injury, which is the criterion. Second Employers' Liability Cases, 223 U. S. 1, 51. Whether or not particular action does affect commerce in such a close and intimate fashion as to be subject to federal control, and hence to lie within the authority conferred upon the Board, is left by the statute to be determined as individual cases arise. We are thus to inquire whether in the instant case the constitutional boundary has been passed.

Second. The unfair labor practices in question.— The unfair labor practices found by the Board are those defined in § 8, subdivisions (1) and (3). These provide:

"Sec. 8. It shall be an unfair labor practice for an employer—

"(1) To interfere with, restrain, or coerce employees in the exercise of the rights guaranteed in section 7."

"(3) By discrimination in regard to hire or tenure of employment or any term or condition of employment to encourage or discourage membership in any labor organization. . . ."

Section 8, subdivision (1), refers to § 7, which is as follows:

"§ 7. Employees shall have the right to self-organization, to form, join, or assist labor organizations, to bargain collectively through representatives of their own choosing, and to engage in concerted activities, for the purpose of collective bargaining or other mutual aid or protection."

Thus, in its present application, the statute goes no further than to safeguard the right of employees to self-organization and to select representatives of their own choosing for collective bargaining or other mutual protection without restraint or coercion by their employer.

That is a fundamental right. Employees have as clear a right to organize and select their representatives for lawful purposes as the respondent has to organize its business and select its own officers and agents. Discrimination and coercion to prevent the free exercise of the right of employees to self-organization and representation is a proper subject for condemnation by competent legislative authority. Long ago we stated the reason for labor organizations. We said that they were organized out of the necessities of the situation; that a single employee was helpless in dealing with an employer; that he was dependent ordinarily on his daily wage for the maintenance of himself and family; that if the employer refused to pay him the wages that he thought fair, he was nevertheless unable to leave the employ and resist arbitrary and unfair treatment; that union was essential to give laborers opportunity to deal on an equality with their employer. *American Steel Foundries* v. *Tri-City Central Trades Council*, 257 U.S. 184, 209; . . .

Third. The application of the Act to employees engaged in production.—The principle involved.—Respondent says that whatever may be said of employees engaged in interstate commerce, the industrial relations and activities in the manufacturing department of respondent's enterprise are not subject to federal regulation. The argument rests upon the proposition that manufacturing in itself is not commerce. *Kidd* v. *Pearson*, 128 U.S. 1, 20, 21; *United Mine Workers* v. *Coronado Coal Co.*, 259 U.S. 344, 407, 408; *Oliver Iron Co.* v. *Lord*, 262 U.S. 172, 178; *United Leather Workers* v. *Herkert & Meisel Trunk Co.*, 265 U.S. 457, 465; *Industrial Association* v. *United States*, 268 U.S. 64, 82; *Coronado Coal Co.* v. *United Mine Workers*, 268 U.S. 295, 310; *Schechter Corp.* v. *United States, supra,* p. 547; *Carter* v. *Carter Coal Co.*, 298 U.S. 238, 304, 317, 327.

The Government distinguishes these cases. The various parts of respondent's enterprise are described as interdependent and as thus involving "a great movement of iron ore, coal and limestone along well-defined paths to the steel mills, thence through them, and thence in the form of steel products into the consuming centers of the country—a definite and well-understood course of business." It is urged that these activities constitute a "stream" or "flow" of commerce, of which the Aliquippa manufacturing plant is the focal point, and that industrial strife at that point would cripple the entire movement. Reference is made to our decisions sustaining the Packers and Stockyards Act [42 Stat. 159.] *Stafford* v. *Wallace*, 258 U.S. 495. . . .

We do not find it necessary to determine whether these features of defendant's business dispose of the asserted analogy to the "stream of commerce" cases. The instances in which that metaphor has been used are but particular, and not exclusive, illustrations of the protective power which the Government invokes in support of the present Act. The congressional authority to protect interstate commerce from burdens and obstructions is not limited to transactions which can be deemed to be an essential part of a "flow" of interstate or foreign commerce. Burdens and obstructions may be due to injurious action springing from other sources. The fundamental principle is that the power to regulate commerce is the power to enact "all appropriate legislation" for "its protection and advancement" (The Daniel Ball, 10 Wall. 557, 564); to adopt measures "to promote its growth and insure its safety" (*Mobile County* v. *Kimball,* 102 U.S. 691, 696); "to foster, protect, control and restrain." Second Employers' Liability Cases, *supra,* p. 47. See *Texas & N. O. R.* v. *Railway Clerks, supra.* That power is plenary and may be exerted to protect interstate commerce "no matter what the source of the dangers which threaten it." Second Employers' Liability Cases, [223 U.S.] p. 51; *Schechter Corporation* v. *United States, supra.* Although activities may be intrastate in character when separately considered, if they have such a close and substantial relation to interstate commerce that their control is essential or appropriate to protect that commerce from burdens and obstructions, Congress cannot be denied the power to exercise that control. *Schechter Corporation* v. *United States, supra.* Undoubtedly the scope of this power must be considered in the light of our dual system of government and may not be extended so as to embrace effects upon interstate commerce so indirect and remote that to embrace them, in view of our complex society, would effectually obliterate the distinction between what is national and what is local and create a completely centralized government. . . .

That intrastate activities, by reason of close and intimate relation to interstate commerce, may fall within federal control is demonstrated in the case of carriers who are engaged in both interstate and intrastate transportation. . . . It is said that this exercise of federal power has relation to the maintenance of adequate instrumentalities of interstate commerce.

But the agency is not superior to the commerce which uses it. The protective power extends to the former because it exists as to the latter. . . .

Fourth. Effects of the unfair labor practice in respondent's enterprise.—Giving full weight to respondent's contention with respect to a break in the complete continuity of the "stream of commerce" by reason of respondent's manufacturing operations, the fact remains that the stoppage of those operations by industrial strife would have a most serious effect upon interstate commerce. In view of respondent's far-flung activities, it is idle to say that the effect would be indirect or remote. It is obvious that it would be immediate and might be catastrophic. . . . When industries organize themselves on a national scale, making their relation to interstate commerce the dominant factor in their activities, how can it be maintained that their industrial labor relations constitute a forbidden field into which Congress may not enter when it is necessary to protect interstate commerce from the paralyzing consequences of industrial war? We have often said that interstate commerce itself is a practical conception. It is equally true that interferences with that commerce must be appraised by a judgment that does not ignore actual experience. . . .

Our conclusion is that the order of the Board was within its competency and that the Act is valid as here applied. The judgment of the Circuit Court of Appeals is reversed and the cause is remanded for further proceedings in conformity with this opinion.

Reversed.

[JUSTICE McREYNOLDS delivered a dissenting opinion, concurred in by JUSTICES VAN DEVANTER, SUTHERLAND, and BUTLER, covering the principal case and two others decided the same day.]

THE SCOPE OF THE PHRASE "INTERSTATE COMMERCE": SHOULD IT BE REDEFINED?

(41 American Bar Association Journal 823, 1955)

By Robert L. Stern

Whether "interstate commerce" should be redefined depends upon the content of the present definition and upon whether a change in that meaning will better serve the interests of the people of the United States. Neither the broad question nor its parts can be answered, however, unless they are placed in proper focus. The principal importance of an inquiry into the meaning of "interstate commerce" lies in its relation to the extent of the power of Congress under the commerce clause of the Constitution. And yet the words "interstate commerce" are not found in that clause, which authorizes Congress to regulate "commerce . . . among the several states", nor anywhere else in the Constitution. Nor is the definition of "interstate commerce" coextensive with the bounds of the federal regulatory power.

Nevertheless, it is true that for years "interstate commerce" has been used (as it will be in this paper) as a shorter synonym for the language of the Constitution without substantial criticism until very recently. In that capacity the phrase has also served as the starting point from which the scope of the power of Congress has been derived. Indeed the phrase is often loosely used as the equivalent or symbol of the line between the state and the federal authority. For these reasons, exploration into the meaning of "interstate commerce" still has constitutional significance.

1. *The meaning of interstate commerce.*

The phrase "interstate commerce" is now commonly understood to describe all trading and movements across state lines, whether of tangible commodities or of intangibles such as documentary material, radio waves or information.[1] It has been held to include, despite occasional criticism,[2] such non-commercial interstate movements as those of kidnappers,[3] polygamists' brides[4] and fleeing witnesses.[5] It includes those parts of an interstate journey which take place solely within one state,[6] and it extends from the moment the journey has begun[7] until the final destination where the goods become an inseparable part of the mass of products within a state.[8] It embraces the sale of goods for interstate shipment and the terms of such sales, as well as the transportation itself.[9] It also encompasses "activities so closely related to interstate transportation as to be in practice and legal relation a part thereof".[10]

The only notable exception to the general definition of interstate commerce had been the line of cases holding that "contracts of insurance" and the "business of insurance", apparently because they dealt in intangibles, "are not commerce at all, neither state nor interstate", and that the activities of the interstate insurance companies were therefore not in interstate commerce.[11] In 1944 these cases were repudiated as out of line with doctrines which the Court had long applied in other cases.[12] This year the "baseball" offshoot of the insurance cases[13] was also abandoned, except that, as a matter of *stare decisis*, the Court still adheres to the bare holding that organized baseball is exempt from the Sherman Act.[14]

With the elimination of the insurance exception, the decisions applying the general definition of interstate commerce have turned upon a close analysis of facts, not upon controversial differences in legal theory. Accordingly a discussion of the scope of interstate commerce from the viewpoint of precisely where the boundaries should be drawn would not appear to be particularly fruitful. This paper will be devoted to the fundamental principles and theories.

. . . In the first great commerce clause decision, *Gibbons* v. *Ogden*,[20] Chief Justice Marshall appeared to recognize that the word "among" which he defined as "intermingled with", was broader than "between". "Comprehensive as the word 'among' is", he declared, "it may very properly be restricted to that commerce which concerns more States than one. . . ." The opinion continues, "The genius and character of the whole government seems to be that its action is to be applied to all the external concerns of the nation, and to those internal concerns which affect the States generally; but not to those which are completely within a particular State, which do not affect other States, and with which it is not necessary to interfere, for the purpose of executing some of the general powers of the government".

This passage has been referred to approvingly in a number of subsequent cases,[21] although there have also been many cases which have been inconsistent with it.[22] Thus in the *Minnesota Rate Cases*,[23] Mr. Justice Hughes stated in 1913 "The words 'among the several States' distinguish between the commerce which concerns more States than one and that commerce which is confined within one State and does not affect other States." In *United States* v. *South-Eastern Underwriters Association*,[24] the Court, speaking through Mr. Justice Black, declared in 1944, with literal correctness, that "No decision of this Court has ever questioned this as too comprehensive a description of the subject matter of the Commerce Clause." A unanimous Court in 1946 applied the same test to the constitutionality of the Public Utility Holding Company Act.[25]

2. *The Scope of the Commerce Power.*

If the Court had consistently adhered to and applied Marshall's famous pronouncement, the history of the commerce clause would have run a different and less interesting course. There would have been no occasion to differentiate between the meaning of the constitutional phrase and the scope of the congressional power derived from it. For if "among" the states had continued to be construed as covering all commercial transactions affecting more than one state and not merely as transactions "between" states, there would have been no need for the various "affectation"[26] doctrines of recent years under which the commerce power has been expanded to reach intrastate activities.

Nevertheless, despite occasional obeisance to *Gibbons* v. *Ogden*, the Court has generally interpreted the clause as if "among" read "between". The result was that acts not themselves closely connected with the interstate movement were not "interstate", for purpose of the commerce clause, and could not be regulated unless the commerce power authorized Congress in certain circumstances to reach intrastate transactions. Such authority could find its constitutional bases in the "necessary and proper" clause and the doctrine of implied powers, both of which were held in *McCulloch* v. *Maryland*[28] to permit Congress to select appropriate means for carrying out the enumerated powers.

Gibbons v. *Ogden* itself first intimated that the power extended to incidental intrastate activities.[29] This dictum was given effect the next year by the highest court of New York in holding that the power of Congress to license shipping in "coastal waters" included vessels operating between points in New York as well as between New York and New Jersey.[30]

For many years thereafter, during which the affirmative power of Congress over commerce was not exercised in any important respect, the Court's pronouncements on the commerce clause were made in cases which, like *Gibbons* v. *Ogden* itself, were connected with the effect of the commerce clause on state legislative action. In a number of those cases the Court held that manufacturing, production and mining were subject to state regulation and taxation because such activities were purely local and not interstate commerce.[31] In the first major case under the Sherman Act of 1890, the *Sugar Trust* case, these generalizations led to the conclusion that a monopoly of sugar refiners throughout the United States could not be prohibited under the commerce clause, since manufacturing was not commerce.[32] The Court subsequently followed this reasoning in some, but by no means all, labor antitrust cases involving strikes in mines and factories,[33] and in *Hammer* v. *Dagenhart*[34] went so far as to hold that Congress could not bar from interstate commerce goods produced by child labor. The Court also invalidated laws which sought to control aspects of railroad labor activities as not closely enough related to interstate commerce.[35]

Nevertheless, after 1900 a much larger body of cases had established the power of Congress over intrastate transactions. The modern doctrine is regarded as stemming from the opinions of Mr. Justice Hughes in the *Minnesota Rate Cases*[36] and the *Shreveport Case*,[37] although these were not the first decisions in which the power had been so extended.[38] These cases held that the federal power extended to intrastate acts which were inseparably commingled, either economically through the forces of competition,[39] or physically,[40] with interstate transactions so that the latter could not be controlled unless the intrastate were too. Other cases held that intrastate acts which directly or necessarily or intentionally affected interstate prices or supplies or movements[41] could be reached under the commerce power.

The constitutional boundary between state and federal power was customarily phrased, in the years prior to 1941, in terms of "direct" or "indirect" effects. In drawing this line the Court was sometimes decisively influenced by its view as to whether the subject regulated was "local" in nature; if so, the effect was "indirect", the Tenth Amendment[42] applied, and the subject was only regulable by the states, no matter how great the effect upon interstate commerce actually was.[43] In 1936 this limitation caused a majority of the Court to hold in *Carter* v. *Carter Coal Co.*[44] that labor relations in the coal industry only "indirectly" affected interstate commerce, although labor disputes might obstruct not only commerce in coal but the railroads and many interstate manufacturing industries as well. "Directness", according to Mr. Justice Sutherland's opinion, connoted lack of an intermediate intervening cause; the "magnitude" of the effect was irrelevant.[45]

Within a year, however, the coal case was discarded, in the cases holding the National Labor Relations Act validly applicable to factories shipping goods in interstate commerce.[46] These and subsequent cases continued to apply the "directly affecting" test, but without any artificial limitations; the question was whether the acts sought to be regulated would actually affect interstate commerce in a substantial way. In the *Santa Cruz Fruit Packing* case, decided in the following year,[47] Chief Justice Hughes sought to redefine "direct" and "indirect" in terms of substantiality rather than proximate cause, although he recognized that the criterion was still a matter of degree, not of mathematical certitude.

It was Mr. Justice Stone who first shifted the emphasis from the directness or substantiality of an effect on commerce, to "whether the regulation was 'an appropriate means to the attainment of a legitimate end, the exercise of the granted power of Congress to regulate interstate commerce.'" His opinion in the *Darby* case upholding the application of the Fair Labor Standards Act to a lumber manufacturer shipping in commerce[48] used language reminiscent of *McCulloch* v. *Maryland*,[49] the classic authority on the implied powers of Congress and the "necessary and proper" clause. The *Darby* opinion also re-established for the future that the Tenth Amendment, as its words proclaimed, only reserved to the states what had not been granted to Congress, and was therefore not a limitation on the enumerated powers.[50]

Mr. Justice Jackson, shortly thereafter, referred specifically to the "necessary and proper" clause as a basis for the power over intrastate transactions,[51] and in 1947 Mr. Justice Rutledge declared that "the 'affectation' approach was actually a revival of Marshall's 'necessary and proper' doctrine."[52] In the same cases the Court also spoke in terms of the need for a "substantial economic effect" or a "practical impeding effect" upon interstate commerce, and other cases of the same period also used the adjective "substantial."[53] It has already been pointed out that during this same period, the Court also had described the commerce clause in the original language of *Gibbons* v. *Ogden,* as extending to "that commerce which concerns more States than one".

It is thus apparent that the same group of Justices have in the same group of cases stated in three different ways the principles governing application of the commerce power to intrastate activities:

(1) Whether control of the intrastate act was an appropriate means to the end of regulating "interstate commerce," the test historically applied under the "necessary and proper" clause;

(2) Whether there was in fact a relationship to interstate commerce which could be termed substantial;

(3) Whether the problem affected commerce in more than one state. Obviously these formulations of doctrine by the same Justices were not thought to be inconsistent with each other. The tests are complementary, not incompatible. Some will be important in some situations, some in others. Together they indicate the factors which the Court will weigh in coming to a conclusion.

How have these tests been applied? The Court has held that Congress may regulate processes of production and distribution in industries the products of which cross state lines. The labor relations and wages and hours of establishments which produce goods for commerce have been held subject to the commerce power,[54] as have those of industries which receive materials from outside the state.[55] The amount of wheat a farmer can produce, even for use on his own farm, has been held to be an integral part of the supply of an interstate commodity which Congress can regulate in order to maintain the interstate price.[56] A retail druggist has been prohibited from selling a product locally without the label required for the interstate movement, since the object of the federal interstate labeling regulation was the protection of the ultimate consumer.[57]

Many of these cases seem to involve relatively small

transactions, which in themselves could have little effect on commerce. But the Court has pointed out that even though the effect of a single person's conduct "may be trivial by itself", Congress is entitled to consider the total impact of "his contribution, taken together with that of many others similarly situated".[58]

This brief review of what may be regarded as the more extreme cases demonstrates that almost every aspect of a business or industry which has interstate ramifications may be subjected to the federal commerce power. This results (1) from the fact that, in part because of the commerce clause itself,[59] American business can and does ignore state boundaries, and (2) from the economic interrelationship between all aspects of an industry or business enterprise. The Court is now unwilling to sever for legal purposes what Congress has determined to be economically united. Thus Congress now has the authority, which it may exercise or not as it deems the public interest to require, to determine what features of interstate industry should be federally regulated.

This application of the clause to all business activities which concern more states than one, and not merely to direct trade and transportation between states, would seem to be precisely what was meant by Marshall's prophetic declaration. Thus, although the Court has generally continued to define interstate commerce narrowly, as commerce *between* the states, the theories which the Court has employed to sustain federal regulation of non-interstate acts have brought the substance of the commerce power back to where Marshall originally placed it when he defined the phrase more broadly.

3. *Should interstate commerce be redefined?* (a) *The affirmative power of Congress.* The foregoing discussion shows that under the current doctrines, which only occasionally make direct use of Marshall's test, the phrase "interstate commerce" is considerably narrower in scope than the regulatory power of Congress. The breadth of the constitutional power is

obviously more important than the meaning of the phrase. The latter has not in itself been the cause of much dissatisfaction or dispute. . . . In its modern context its principal significance is that it provides the foundation upon which the constitutional power rests. It is accordingly necessary to appraise the present doctrines as to the scope of the power as a prerequisite to determining whether there is justifiable reason for redefining the phrase. . . .

The Constitutional Convention itself furnishes the criterion by which the question may be answered. For almost two months after it first convened, the Convention devoted itself to consideration of the principles which should be followed in the new Constitution, prior to submission to the Committee on Detail for drafting. With respect to the powers to be granted the National Government, the Convention twice approved resolutions based on Randolph's Virginia Plan, which

> Resolved, that the national legislature ought to possess the legislative rights vested in Congress by the confederation; and moreover, to legislate in all cases for the general interests of the Union, and also in those to which the states are separately incompetent, or in which the harmony of the United States may be interrupted by the exercise of individual legislation.[60]

Twice, more restrictive proposals were defeated.[61] When the Committee on Detail reported a draft enumerating the powers of Congress, including the Commerce Clause, substantially in their present form, there was no objection—and no discussion of the commerce power as such.[62] It was obvious that the Convention believed that the enumeration conformed to the principles set forth for the guidance of the Committee in the resolution previously adopted.[63]

It is reasonable to interpret the provisions of a document drafted to achieve these expressed purposes in a manner which will best accomplish the stated objectives, even though it be recognized that developments during the ensuing one hundred and sixty-eight years have greatly enlarged the area which, under these principles, would fall within the federal sphere. Furthermore, these principles for determining the scope of the federal power would seem to be as sensible today as in 1787. What better reasons can there be for the exercise of the national authority than that the regulation is needed for the general interests of the Union, or that the states are separately incompetent, or that uniformity is needed rather than individual legislation?

Which of the suggested ways of defining the scope of the commerce power best conforms with the standards approved by the Convention?

The narrowest test seriously proposed in recent years, that applied by the Supreme Court in cases such as *Carter* v. *Carter Coal Co.*,[64] would allow federal regulation of intrastate transactions "directly affecting" interstate commerce, but not when the activities were in fields, such as production or manufacture, which the Court thought were too "local" in nature. Experience has demonstrated, however, that production problems are national in character. Strikes do interrupt interstate commerce and thereby harm other states than those in which they occur. The amount of a commodity produced has a direct impact on the amount shipped as well as on interstate prices, and cannot be controlled except on a nationwide basis. The forces of competition prevent individual states from fixing minimum wages for employees working in factories which compete with factories in other states. Because the market is interstate, the states are "separately incompetent". The test which the Court has abandoned would have left such problems to the states which could not possibly have coped with them. Such a result is certainly not in harmony with the resolutions approved by the framers. Nor can the creation of an economic hiatus in which the National Government cannot act for "legal" reasons and the states for economic ones possibly be desirable. It is not in the public interest that government, that is the people acting as an entity, be impotent. Those who believe that no government should intermeddle in economic affairs are entitled to present their views to Congress, but not to assert that they find support for freezing them into our basic charter of government in the constitutional provision which affirmatively authorizes the regulation of commerce. . . .

Under the Court's current doctrine, the commerce power is "commensurate with the national needs".[68] The Court considers the substantiality of the relationship to interstate commerce in a practical sense, whether the problem concerns or has an impact on more than one state, whether it is necessary and proper for a regulation to reach intrastate acts in order to make the regulation of commerce effective. As is revealed in the opinions discussed above, the Court has reached this result in large part by returning to the principles first enunciated by Chief Justice Marshall in *Gibbons* v. *Ogden*.

Since he lived through the period in which the Constitution was adopted and had himself been a member of the Virginia ratifying convention, it is not surprising that his classical pronouncements are in harmony with the principles of the framers. His awareness that it was a Constitution "intended to endure for ages to come" which he was expounding (*McCulloch* v. *Maryland*)[69] makes his views as timely now as when they were originally uttered.

There may, of course, be disagreement as to whether particular decisions in recent years conform to the above standards. This is inevitable no matter what rule is adopted. It is the standard, however, which is important in considering whether there is need to change constitutional concepts.

For the foregoing reasons, it is submitted that the principles now being applied by the Court in determining the scope of the commerce power best comport with the basic purposes of the Constitution, and also with the needs of the nation. There is thus no reason to redefine the underlying concept of interstate commerce in order to work a change in the scope of the federal power.

(b) *"Interstate commerce" in statutes.* The meaning of interstate commerce also has significance apart from its effect upon the basic constitutional power. Many statutes or parts of statutes regulate "interstate commerce," without going to the limits of Congress' constitutional authority. The Fair Labor Standards Act[70] applies to employees engaged in interstate commerce or in production for interstate commerce. Part II of the Federal Power Act applies to the transmission and sale at wholesale of electric energy "in interstate commerce".[71] The Natural Gas Act has a similar provision.[72] Coverage under statutes such as these depends upon the meaning of "interstate commerce" rather than upon the limits of the constitutional commerce power.

Use of the phrase "interstate commerce" in these statutes, however, affords no basis for changing the meaning of the constitutional expression. Since such statutes do not exhaust Congress' constitutional authority, Congress has ample power to expand or contract statutory coverage by amendment, without redefining the constitutional phrase. That was what happened to the Federal Employers' Liability Act, which originally applied only to injuries to employees engaged in interstate commerce.[73] The overrefinements[74] which resulted from judicial interpretation of that phrase[75] led to the replacement of the "in commerce" test by language which covered all railroad employees.[76]

(c) *The negative side of the commerce power.* The meaning of interstate commerce has also been important in determining the negative effects of the commerce clause. In many more cases than have been concerned with the power affirmatively granted to Congress, the Supreme Court has held that the commerce clause of its own force limited the regulatory and taxing authority of the states.

For two reasons, however, the difficult problems as to the validity of state laws do not call for any re-definition of interstate commerce. In the first place, the Court no longer applies what Chief Justice Stone termed the "mechanical test"[77] whereby the validity of a state law depended on whether it regulated in-terstate or intrastate regulations.[78] State laws which regulate even such clearly interstate activities as rail-road operations have been sustained against constitu-tional attack, where there is no substantial interfer-ence with interstate transportation.[79] The current doc-trine, which is substantially the same as that first pro-claimed in *Cooley* v. *Board of Port Wardens*,[80] makes the validity of a state law depend upon a balancing of the local and national interests affected, or upon the extent and nature of the burden, if any, which the law imposes on interstate commerce.[81] A redefini-tion of interstate commerce would not necessarily af-fect the Court's judgment in applying a formula which is not based on any rigid definition.

It is true that in passing upon state taxes on inter-state transactions, the Court sometimes seems to be applying the "mechanical" test rejected in the regu-latory field.[82] But the Court's adherence to such a rule in an area beset with complications and confu-sion[83] is a policy judgment which would not neces-sarily be automatically followed if the definition of interstate commerce were changed.

In the second place, the negative effects of the commerce clause upon state legislation are subject to the control of Congress. Chief Justice Stone declared, in *Southern Pacific Company* v. *Arizona*[84], that "Con-gress has undoubted power to redefine the distribu-tion of power over interstate commerce. It may either permit the states to regulate the commerce in a man-ner which would otherwise not be permissible, or ex-clude state regulation even of matters of peculiarly local concern which nevertheless affect interstate com-merce". This means that Congress may determine the desirable policy irrespective of the definition of interstate commerce. Since the difficulties in this perplexing field have not resulted from the present definition of interstate commerce, and since their solution by the Court or by Congress is not dependent upon how commerce is defined, the problems as to the negative effects of the Commerce Clause do not call for a redefinition of the constitutional phrase.

There is, of course, no reason to amend the Constitution or otherwise change the accepted meaning of a constitutional phrase unless a substantial public benefit can be achieved. The advocate of change must satisfy a heavy burden. In interpreting the commerce clause the Supreme Court seems to be following principles which make satisfactory adjustments between the needs of the states and those of the nation. Accordingly, no redefinition is needed.

---

[1] *United States* v. *South-Eastern Underwriters Association,* 322 U.S. 533, 549-50 (1944), and cases cited therein.

[2] Willoughby, *Constitution of the United States* (2d ed. 1928) 733-734.

[3] *Gooch* v. *United States,* 297 U.S. 124 (1936).

[4] *Cleveland* v. *United States,* 329 U.S. 14 (1946).

[5] *Hemans* v. *United States,* 163 F. 2d 228, 239 (6th Cir. 1947), certiorari denied, 332 U.S. 801 (1947). Earlier cases holding non-commercial interstate activities to be commerce include *Brooks* v. *United States,* 267 U.S. 432 (1925) (stolen automobiles); *United States* v. *Simpson,* 252 U.S. 465 (1920) (whiskey for personal use); *Thornton* v. *United States,* 271 U.S. 414 (1926) (ranging cattle).

[6] *The Daniel Ball,* 10 Wall. 557 (U.S. 1870).

[7] *Coe* v. *Errol,* 116 U.S. 517 (1886).

[8] *Walling* v. *Jacksonville Paper Co.,* 317 U.S. 564 (1943); *Standard Oil Co.* v. *Federal Trade Commission,* 340 U.S. 231, 237-238 (1951).

[9] *Dahnke-Walker Co.* v. *Bondurant,* 257 U.S. 282 (1921); *Lemke* v. *Farmers Grain Co.,* 258 U.S. 50 (1922); *Currin* v. *Wallace,* 306 U.S. 1 (1939); *United States* v. *Rock Royal Co-operative,* 307 U.S. 533, 568-569 (1939); *Mulford* v. *Smith,* 307 U.S. 38 (1939); *Sunshine Anthracite Coal Co.* v. *Adkins,* 310 U.S. 381 (1940).

[10] *McLeod* v. *Threlkeld*, 319 U.S. 491, 495 (1943); *Mitchell* v. *Vollmer* & *Co.*, 349 U.S. 427. Held in commerce: rate clerk for interstate bus line (*Overnight Motor Co.* v. *Missel*, 316 U.S. 572, 575 (1942); railroad track repair man (*Pedersen* v. *Delaware, L.* & *W. R. Co.*, 229 U.S. 146 (1913); *Fitzgerald Co.* v. *Pedersen*, 324 U.S. 720 (1945); *Alstate Construction Co.* v. *Durkin*, 345 U.S. 13 (1953); bridge tender on interstate highway (*Overstreet* v. *North Shore Corp.*, 318 U.S. 125 (1943)). Held not in commerce: mechanic in railroad back shop (*New York, N. H.* & *H. R. Co.* v. *Bezue*, 284 U.S. 415 (1932); builder of new trackage (*Raymond* v. *Chicago, M.* & *St.P. Ry.*, 243 U.S. 43 (1917). But *cf. Mitchell* v. *Vollmer, supra.*

[11] *New York Life Ins. Co.* v. *Deer Lodge County*, 231 U.S. 495, 503-504, 510 (1913); *Hooper* v. *California*, 155 U.S. 648, 654-655 (1895); *Paul* v. *Virginia*, 8 Wall. 168 (1869). Other cases are listed in *United States* v. *South-Eastern Underwriters Association*, 322 U.S. 533, 544 n. (1944).

[12] *United States* v. *South-Eastern Underwriters Association*, 322 U.S. 533, 539-553 (1944); *Polish National Alliance* v. *NLRB*, 322 U.S. 643 (1944).

[13] *Federal Baseball Club* v. *National League*, 259 U.S. 200 (1922).

[14] *United States* v. *International Boxing Club*, 348 U.S. 236 (1955); *United States* v. *Shubert*, 348 U.S. 222 (1955); cf. *Toolson* v. *New York Yankees*, 346 U.S. 356 (1953). Nothing in the original baseball case had suggested that it was based on anything but constitutional grounds, or on considerations pertaining especially to the antitrust laws.

[20] 9 Wheat. 1, 194-195 (1824).

[21] See *Mayor of New York* v. *Miln*, 11 Pet. 102, 146 (U.S. 1837); *The Daniel Ball*, 10 Wall. 557, 564 (U.S. 1870); *Kidd* v. *Pearson*, 128 U.S. 1, 17 (1888); *Champion* v. *Ames*, 188 U.S. 321, 346 (1903) (The Lottery case; *Employers' Liability Cases*, 207 U.S. 463, 493, 507 (1908) (both majority and dissenting opinions).

[22] E.g., *United States* v. *E. C. Knight* & *Co.*, 156 U.S. 1 (1895); *Employers' Liability Cases*, 207 U.S. 463 (1908); *Hammer* v. *Dagenhart*, 247 U.S. 251 (1918); *Railroad Retirement Board* v. *Alton R.R.*, 295 U.S. 330 (1935); *Carter* v. *Carter Coal Co.*, 298 U.S. 238 (1936).

[23] 230 U.S. 352, 398 (1913).

[24] 322 U.S. 533, 551 (1944).

25 *North American Company* v. *SEC*, 327 U.S. 686, 706 (1946).

26 The phrase is Mr. Justice Rutledge's. See *Mandeville Farms* v. *American Crystal Sugar Co.*, 334 U.S. 219, 232 (1948).

28 4 Wheat. 316 (1819).

29 9 Wheat. 1, 204 (1824).

30 *North River Steamboat Company* v. *Livingston*, 3 Cow. 713 (N.Y. 1825).

31 See *Veazie* v. *Moor*, 14 How. 568, 573-574 (U.S. 1852); *Kidd* v. *Pearson*, 128 U.S. 1, 20-22 (1888); *Heisler* v. *Thomas Colliery Co.*, 260 U.S. 245, 259-60 (1922); *Oliver Iron Mining Co.* v. *Lord*, 262 U.S. 172, 178-79 (1923); *Utah Power & Light Co.* v. *Pfost*, 286 U.S. 165 (1932).

32 *United States* v. *E. C. Knight & Co.*, 156 U.S. 1 (1895); *cf. Hopkins* v. *United States*, 171 U.S. 578 (1898); *Anderson* v. *United States*, 171 U.S. 604 (1898).

33 *United Mine Workers* v. *Coronado Coal Co.*, 259 U.S. 344 (1922); *United Leather Workers* v. *Herkert*, 265 U.S. 457 (1924); *Industrial Association* v. *United States*, 268 U.S. 64 (1925); *Levering & Garrigues Co.* v. *Morrin*, 289 U.S. 103 (1933). But compare *Coronado Coal Co.* v. *United Mine Workers*, 268 U.S. 295 (1925); *Loewe* v. *Lawlor*, 208 U.S. 274 (1908); *Duplex Printing Press Co.* v. *Deering*, 254 U.S. 443 (1921); *Bedford Cut Stone* v. *Journeymen Stone Cutters Association*, 274 U.S. 37 (1927). Except for the second *Coronado* case, the latter cases, holding strikes to violate the Sherman Act, involved interstate secondary boycotts.

34 247 U.S. 251 (1918).

35 *Employers' Liability Cases*, 207 U.S. 463 (1908); *Adair* v. *United States*, 208 U.S. 161 (1908); *Railroad Retirement Board* v. *Alton R. Co.*, 295 U.S. 330 (1935).

36 230 U.S. 352 (1913).

37 234 U.S. 342 (1914).

38 Prior decisions included *Swift & Co.* v. *United States*, 196 U.S. 375 (1905) and *Standard Oil Co.* v. *United States*, 221 U.S. 1 (1911), applying the Sherman Act to monopolies of manufacturers, despite the *Sugar Trust* case; *Southern Railway* v. *United States*, 222 U.S. 20 (1911), which subjected intra-state trains to federal safety regulations; *Baltimore & Ohio*

Railroad Co. v. *Interstate Commerce Commission,* 221 U.S. 612 (1911), applying a federal maximum hour law to railroad employees not themselves in interstate commerce.

39 *Minnesota Rate Cases,* 230 U.S. 352, 398 (1913); *Shreveport Case,* 234 U.S. 342 (1914); *Railroad Commission of Wisconsin* v. *Chicago, B. & Q. R. Co.,* 257 U.S. 563 (1922); *United States* v. *Wrightwood Dairy Co.,* 315 U.S. 110 (1942).

40 *Stafford* v. *Wallace,* 258 U.S. 495 (1922); *Currin* v. *Wallace,* 306 U.S. 1 (1939); *United States* v. *Rock Royal Cooperative,* 307 U.S. 533 (1939); *Mulford* v. *Smith,* 307 U.S. 38 (1939).

41 The antitrust cases cited in note 38, *supra,* would seem to fall in this category. See also *Chicago Board of Trade* v. *Olsen,* 262 U.S. 1 (1923); *United States* v. *Patten,* 226 U.S. 525 (1913); *Standard Oil Co. (Ind.)* v. *United States,* 283 U.S. 163, 169 (1931); *Coronado Coal Co.* v. *United Mine Workers,* 268 U.S. 295, 310 (1925); *Local* 167 v. *United States,* 291 U.S. 293 (1934).

42 "The powers not delegated to the United States by the Constitution, nor prohibited by it to the States, are reserved to the States respectively, or to the people."

43 *Carter* v. *Carter Coal Co.,* 298 U.S. 238 (1936); *United States* v. *Butler,* 297 U.S. 1 (1936). See also cases cited in notes 32, 33, 34, 35, *supra.*

44 298 U.S. 238 (1936).

45 298 U.S. at 307-308.

46 *NLRB* v. *Jones & Laughlin Steel Corp.,* 301 U.S. 1 (1937) and companion cases.

47 *Santa Cruz Fruit Packing Co.* v. *NLRB,* 303 U.S. 453 (1938).

48 *United States* v. *Darby,* 312 U.S. 100 (1941); see also *United States* v. *Wrightwood Dairy Co.,* 315 U.S. 110 (1942).

49 4 Wheat. 316 (U.S. 1819).

50 312 U.S. at 123-124.

51 *Wickard* v. *Filburn,* 317 U.S. 111, 119, 121 (1942).

52 *Mandeville Farms* v. *American Sugar Refining Co.,* 334 U.S. 219, 232 (1948).

53 *United States* v. *Wrightwood Dairy Co.,* 315 U.S. 110 (1942); *North American Company* v. *SEC,* 327 U.S. 686 (1946).

54 *NLRB* v. *Jones & Laughlin Steel Corp.,* 301 U.S. 1 (1937); *Santa Cruz Fruit Packing Co.* v. *NLRB,* 303 U.S. 453

(1938); *United States* v. *Darby,* 312 U.S. 100 (1941); *Kirsch-baum* v. *Walling,* 316 U.S. 517 (1942) (building employees); *Martino* v. *Michigan Window Cleaning Co.,* 327 U.S. 173 (1946) (window cleaners in factories); *Walton* v. *Southern Package Corp.,* 320 U.S. 540 (1944) (watchmen); *Warren-Bradshaw Drilling Co.* v. *Hall,* 317 U.S. 88 (1942) (drillers of oil wells); *Mabee* v. *White Plains Pub. Co.,* 327 U.S. 178 (1946) (newspaper with small out-of-state circulation).

[55] *NLRB* v. *Denver Building Trades Council,* 341 U.S. 675 (1951); *Howell Chevrolet Co.* v. *NLRB,* 346 U.S. 482 (1953).

[56] *Wickard* v. *Filburn,* 317 U.S. 111 (1942).

[57] *United States* v. *Sullivan,* 332 U.S. 689 (1948).

[58] *Wickard* v. *Filburn,* 317 U.S. 111, 127-128 (1942), *NLRB* v. *Denver Building Trades Council,* 341 U.S. 675, 683-684 (1942).

[59] Mr. Justice Rutledge, A DECLARATION OF LEGAL FAITH (Univ. of Kans. Press, 1947) pages 26-27.

[60] *Madison's Debates,* as reported in H.R. Doc. No. 398, 69th Cong. 1st Sess. (1927), entitled DOCUMENTS ILLUSTRA-TIVE OF THE FORMATION OF THE UNION OF THE AMERICAN STATES, pages 466, 117, 129-130, 234-235, 389-390.

[61] *Id.,* at 205, 211, 234, 388-389.

[62] *Id.,* at 475, 555.

[63] *Abel, The Commerce Clause in the Constitutional Convention and in Contemporary Comment,* 25 MINN. L. REV. 432, 440 (1941); Stern, *That Commerce Which Concerns More States Than One,* 47 HARV. L. REV. 1335, 1338-1340 (1934).

[64] 298 U.S. 238 (1936), *supra,* note 43.

[68] *North American Co.* v. *SEC,* 327 U.S. 686, 705-6 (1946).

[69] 4 Wheat. 316, 415 (1819).

[70] Sections 6 and 7, 52 Stat. 1062-3, 29 U.S.C., Sections 206, 207.

[71] Section 201 (b), 49 Stat. 847, 16 U.S.C. 824 (1935).

[72] Section 1 (b), 52 Stat. 821, 15 U.S.C. §717 (b) (1938).

[73] Act of April 22, 1908, 35 Stat. 65.

[74] The word is the Supreme Court's. *McLeod* v. *Threlkeld,* 319 U.S. 491, 495 (1943). See also Schoene and Watson, *Workmen's Compensation on Interstate Railways,* 47 HARV. L. REV. 399 (1934).

[75] See cases cited in note 10.

[76] Act of August 11, 1939, 53 Stat. 1404, 45 U.S.C. §51.

77 *Parker* v. *Brown*, 317 U.S. 341, 362 (1943); *Illinois Natural Gas Co.* v. *Central Illinois Public Service Co.*, 314 U.S. 498, 504-506 (1942). See also *South-Eastern Underwriters Association* v. *United States*, 322 U.S. 533, 548 (1944).

78 *Nathan* v. *Louisiana*, 8 How. 73 (U.S. 1850); *Paul* v. *Virginia*, 8 Wall. 168 (U.S. 1868); *Railroad Co.* v. *Husen*, 95 U.S. 465 (1877); *Coe* v. *Errol*, 116 U.S. 517 (1886); *Bowman* v. *Chicago & N. W. Ry.*, 125 U.S. 465 (1888); *Leloup* v. *Port of Mobile*, 127 U.S. 640 (1888); *Kidd* v. *Pearson*, 128 U.S. 1 (1888); *Rhodes* v. *Iowa*, 170 U.S. 412 (1898); *Caldwell* v. *North Carolina*, 187 U.S. 622 (1903). Cf. *Leisy* v. *Hardin*, 135 U.S. 100 (1890).

79 *Terminal R.R. Association* v. *Brotherhood of Railroad Trainmen*, 318 U.S. 1 (1943); *California* v. *Thompson*, 313 U.S. 109, 113-114 (1941); cf. *Southern Pacific Co.* v. *Arizona*, 325 U.S. 761, 767-769, 779 (1945).

80 12 How. 299 (1852).

81 *E.g.*, *Southern Pacific Co.* v. *Arizona*, 325 U.S. 761 (1945); *Morgan* v. *Virginia*, 328 U.S. 373 (1946); *California* v. *Zook*, 336 U.S. 725, 728 (1949); *Cities Service Gas Co.* v. *Peerless Oil & Gas Co.*, 340 U.S. 179, 186-187 (1950).

82 *Freeman* v. *Hewit*, 329 U.S. 249 (1946); *Spector Motor Service* v. *O'Connor*, 340 U.S. 602 (1951); *Railway Express Agency* v. *Virginia*, 347 U.S. 359 (1954); *Michigan-Wisconsin Pipe Line Co.* v. *Calvert*, 347 U.S. 157 (1954). For a period the Court seemed to have been induced by Mr. Justice Stone to balance competing practical considerations, as in the cases involving state regulatory measures. *Western Live Stock* v. *Bureau of Revenue*, 303 U.S. 250 (1938); *McGoldrick* v. *Berwind-White Coal Mining Co.*, 309 U.S. 33 (1940). There has since been an apparent resurgence of emphasis upon the incidence of the tax.

83 The number of cases in this field is paralleled by the amount of explanatory material which is thought to be needed to understand them. Professor Barrett lists twenty-nine articles and one book in an "incomplete" enumeration of "helpful" articles on the subject. Barrett, *State Taxation of Interstate Commerce—"Direct Burdens", "Multiple Burdens", Or What Have You*, 4 VANDERBILT L. REV. 496 (1951). See also Barrett, *"Substance" vs. "Form" in the Application of the Commerce Clause to State Taxation*, 101 UNIV. OF PA. L. REV. 740 (1953).

84 325 U.S. 761, 769 (1945). See also *Prudential Insurance Co.* v. *Benjamin*, 328 U.S. 408 (1946); Dowling, *Interstate Commerce and State Power*, 47 COL. L. REV. 547, 552 (1947).

C. *The Taxing Power*

Second only to the commerce power is the fiscal and regulatory power which the Supreme Court has approved, based upon the first clause of section 8 of article I, which reads as follows:

> "The Congress shall have Power To lay and collect Taxes, Duties, Imposts and Excises, to pay the Debts and provide for the common Defence and general Welfare of the United States; but all Duties, Imposts and Excises shall be uniform throughout the United States."

From this clause comes the complete power of taxation, except that (1) Congress may levy no tax on exports; (2) direct taxes are subject to the requirement of apportionment by population; and (3) indirect taxes must be uniform in their application, that is, without discrimination for or against any section of the country. The principal significance of these limitations is that there is no practical way for Congress to tax real or personal property, thus leaving these areas of revenue raising exclusively to the states and local units of government. Although the Supreme Court held in *Pollock* v. *Farmers' Loan and Trust Co.*, 157 U.S. 429 and 158 U.S. 601 (1895) that a tax on incomes derived in part from property was a forbidden direct tax, this limitation was removed in 1913 with the adoption of the sixteenth amendment.

The raising of revenue may be the primary purpose behind most federal taxes; but it has been repeatedly recognized that Congress may also regulate, even to the point of virtual exclusion, through the exercise of the taxing power. Thus, Congress has been sustained in its imposition of prohibitively high tax rates upon oleomargarine colored to look like butter, dealing in sawed-off shot guns, and the sale of marihuana to an unregistered person. *McCray* v. *United States*, 195 U.S. 27 (1904); *Sonzinsky* v.

United States, 300 U.S. 506 (1937); *United States* v. *Sanchez,* 340 U.S. 42 (1950).

The money which Congress raises by taxation may be expended "to pay the debts and provide for the common defense and general welfare of the United States." It has occasionally been urged that this provision authorizes Congress to act broadly for "the general welfare of the United States." This interpretation, which would confer almost unrestrained legislative power on Congress, has never been adopted by the Court. However, on another point relating to the proper meaning of the "general welfare clause," the Court did not finally announce its view until 1936 in *United States* v. *Butler.*

UNITED STATES v. BUTLER

297 U.S. 1 (1936)

[In a receivership proceeding the United States sought to recover a balance due on processing and floor-stock taxes assessed against the bankrupt under the provisions of the Agricultural Adjustment Act of 1933. Thus, the ultimate issue was whether the processing taxes and regulatory scheme of the AAA were valid. On this question the Court held against the Government because Congress had sought to do indirectly, that is, by conditions attached to the grants of money, what it could not do directly because it amounted to an invasion of the reserved powers of the states. Preliminarily, however, the Court had to determine whether there was standing to challenge the imposition of the tax. Holding that there was standing, the Court then turned to the question whether the taxing and spending power was an independent power possessed by Congress or whether it was merely a limitation upon the other enumerated powers. This portion of the decision by Mr. Justice Roberts is extracted below.]

Second. The Government asserts that even if the

respondents may question the propriety of the appropriation embodied in the statute, their attack must fail because Article I, § 8 of the Constitution, authorizes the contemplated expenditure of the funds raised by the tax. This contention presents the great and the controlling question in the case. . . .

The clause thought to authorize the legislation,—the first,—confers upon the Congress power "to lay and collect Taxes, Duties, Imposts and Excises, to pay the Debts and provide for the common Defence and general Welfare of the United States. . . ." It is not contended that this provision grants power to regulate agricultural production upon the theory that such legislation would promote the general welfare. The Government concedes that the phrase "to provide for the general welfare" qualifies the power "to lay and collect taxes." The view that the clause grants power to provide for the general welfare, independently of the taxing power, has never been authoritatively accepted. Mr. Justice Story points out that, if it were adopted, "it is obvious that under color of the generality of the words, to 'provide for the common defence and general welfare,' the government of the United States is, in reality, a government of general and unlimited powers, notwithstanding the subsequent enumeration of specific powers." The true construction undoubtedly is that the only thing granted is the power to tax for the purpose of providing funds for payment of the nation's debts and making provision for the general welfare.

Nevertheless, the Government asserts that warrant is found in this clause for the adoption of the Agricultural Adjustment Act. The argument is that Congress may appropriate and authorize the spending of moneys for the "general welfare"; that the phrase should be liberally construed to cover anything conducive to national welfare; that decision as to what will promote such welfare rests with Congress alone, and the courts may not review its determination; and, finally, that the appropriation under attack was in fact for the general welfare of the United States.

The Congress is expressly empowered to lay taxes to provide for the general welfare. Funds in the Treasury as a result of taxation may be expended only through appropriation. (Article I, § 9, cl. 7.) They can never accomplish the objects for which they were collected, unless the power to appropriate is as broad as the power to tax. The necessary implication from the terms of the grant is that the public funds may be appropriated "to provide for the general welfare of the United States." These words cannot be meaningless, else they would not have been used. The conclusion must be that they were intended to limit and define the granted power to raise and to expend money. How shall they be construed to effectuate the intent of the instrument?

Since the foundation of the Nation, sharp differences of opinion have persisted as to the true interpretation of the phrase. Madison asserted it amounted to no more than a reference to the other powers enumerated in the subsequent clauses of the same section; that, as the United States is a government of limited and enumerated powers, the grant of power to tax and spend for the general national welfare must be confined to the enumerated legislative fields committed to the Congress. In this view the phrase is mere tautology, for taxation and appropriation are or may be necessary incidents of the exercise of any of the enumerated legislative powers. Hamilton, on the other hand, maintained the clause confers a power separate and distinct from those later enumerated, is not restricted in meaning by the grant of them, and Congress consequently has a substantive power to tax and to appropriate, limited only by the requirement that it shall be exercised to provide for the general welfare of the United States. Each contention has had the support of those whose views are entitled to weight. . . . Study of all these leads us to conclude that the reading advocated by Mr. Justice Story is the correct one. . . .

PART III

The President and the Executive Power

THE PRESIDENCY TODAY
(New York University Press, 1956)
By Edward S. Corwin and Louis W. Koenig

CHAPTER II

Of Presidential Prerogative

"PRESIDENTIAL PREROGATIVE" is a short term for power claimed by the President primarily on the basis of the Constitution itself. At any particular time it is the product of three factors: personality, crisis (i.e., public necessity as judged by the President), and available constitutional doctrine. In the course of the last half century expansion of the presidential role has been substantially continuous, thanks to a succession of strong Presidents, to our involvement in two world wars, to "an economic crisis more serious than war," to "a cold war" more baffling in some respects than "a shooting war," and to a succession of industrial strikes or threats of strikes. In what fashion, through what verbal apparatus, so to speak, has enlargement of the presidential role been articulated from time to time with the Constitutional document?

The Executive-Power Clause

The opening clause of Article II of the Constitution reads: "The Executive power shall be vested in a President of the United States of America." It is clear from the records of the Philadelphia Convention . . . that the primary purpose of this clause was to settle the question whether the executive branch should be plural or single, while a secondary purpose was to give the President a title. The term "executive power" denoted simply the powers conferred upon him in the succeeding provisions of the Article —"The power, by and with the advice and consent of the Senate, to make treaties," the power to "receive Ambassadors and other public ministers," and so on. Yet the first Congress to assemble under the Constitution was compelled to choose between seeing the President stuck indefinitely with subordinates appointed "by and with the advice and consent of the Senate," and attributing to him on the score of his executive power the right to remove such officers at will. It chose the latter alternative, thereby ousting the Senate once and for all time from any share in the removal power.[1]

Likewise, in 1793 Hamilton invoked the executive-power clause in support of President Washington's proclamation of neutrality upon the outbreak of war between France and Great Britain. Three years earlier Jefferson had cited the clause, in an official opinion, for the proposition that "the transaction of business with foreign nations is Executive altogether," doctrine that John Marshall later reiterated on the floor of Congress: "The President is the sole organ of the nation in its external relations, and its sole representative with foreign nations."

Indeed, throughout the first decade under the Constitution aggrandizement of the President's role in the field of foreign relations was unremitting. In his reception of Genêt, Washington laid claims effectively to the power to recognize new governments, and by his subsequent demand on the French government that it recall its representative he established a precedent followed by later Presidents repeatedly, and more than once in the face of impending war. He also blocked the Senate in its effort to downgrade certain nominees to diplomatic posts, thereby establishing the principle that though that body may assent to or reject nominations by the President, it cannot remodel them. Likewise, he initiated what later became an established practice marking a serious inroad on the Senate's participation in the choice of diplomatic representatives, the designation of a personal agent to conduct negotiations abroad. Meantime the Senate itself had by its own headiness surrendered the right to advise in advance concerning the terms of international agreements.[2]

To all these developments the Court in due course lent its sanction, thereby laying the foundations of the doctrine of "political questions," which has many times afforded executive action an escape hatch from the trammels of judicial review, and especially in the field of foreign relations.[3]

Today, not only is the executive-power clause an ever-available recourse to the President in the field of foreign affairs: it is also an indeterminate factor of any and all presidential powers.

The Commander in Chief Clause

The second, and today the most powerful, timber in the constitutional rooftree of presidential prerogative is the clause that makes the President "Commander-in-Chief of the Army and Navy of the United States and of the Militia of the several States when called into the actual service of the United States." Hamilton, expounding this clause in *The Federalist,* asserted that it would be altogether erroneous to compare the power that it confers with the superficially similar prerogative of the British monarch. The President was top admiral and top general, and nobody could issue him a military command; but that was all. And in 1850, in a case growing out of the Mexican War, the Supreme Court, speaking by Chief Justice Taney, substantially repeated Hamilton's language.[4] The Commander in Chief clause remained the forgotten clause of the Constitution until the day when Sumter fell, April 14, 1861. Then came the great break-through.

Lincoln, first calling Congress to assemble on July 4, at the time more than ten weeks away, proceeded forthwith to take certain measures of his own, based on the idea that in the circumstances the war power was his; and on this premise he proclaimed a blockade of the Southern ports, summoned an army of 300,000 volunteers, increased the regular Army and Navy, took over the rail and telegraph lines between Washington and Baltimore and eventually as far as Boston, and suspended the writ of habeas corpus along these lines.

Several of these extraordinary measures Congress presently ratified; all save that touching habeas corpus were grounded on the theory that the Rebellion possessed from the outset the dimensions of public war, a theory that the Supreme Court underwrote in the Prize Cases of 1863.[5] Lincoln's general suspension of the habeas corpus privilege as to persons arrested for alleged disloyal practices in September 1862 and his order that they be tried by military commission stemmed, however, from the notion that the entire country, and not merely the portion of it within the enemy's lines, constituted "a theatre of military operations," a conception that the Court rejected in 1866 in the famous Milligan Case. The war being now safely over, the Court could indulge its long pent-up constitutional scruples.[6]

Between the Civil War and the First World War two profound contrasts appear in retrospect. In the first place, most of the fighting in the latter—all the land fighting—took place three thousand miles from our shores. There was consequently no question at any time of treating the country at large as a "theatre of military operations" in the conventional sense of that term. In the second place, on the other hand, the vast development between the two wars of the technological aspects of warfare had created in this greatest of industrial nations an industrial theater of war of immense proportions. Great industry in the United States had, in brief, become part and parcel of the fighting forces not only of the United States but of its allies as well, and as such it had to be subjected to detailed regimentation by the government of the United States. To meet this requirement Congress was compelled to develop a new technique in legislative practice, one capable of meeting the fluctuating demands of a fluid war situation. This it did by delegating vast unchanneled powers to the President, to be exercised by him through men of his own choosing. John Locke's ban on delegated legislation simply went by the board, nor has it since been revived so far as concerns powers shared by the two departments. As to these "cognate powers," as it terms them, the Court will not attempt today to plot nicely, or indeed at all, the delimiting line.[7] More than that, President Wilson took upon himself, without consulting Congress, both the government of industrial relations and the screening of information regarding the war, the former function being performed by the War Industries Board under Mr. Baruch, the latter by the Committee of Public Information headed by Mr. Creel. Both agencies were created out of hand by the President.

The Second World War was the First World War writ large, and the quasi-legislative powers of Franklin Roosevelt as "Commander-in-Chief in wartime," to use his own favorite formula, burgeoned correspondingly. The precedents were there, to be sure, most of them from the First World War, but they proliferated amazingly. What is more, Roosevelt took his first step toward war some fifteen months before our entrance into "shooting war." This step occurred in September 1940, when he handed over fifty so-called "overage" destroyers to Great Britain. The truth is, they were not overage, but had been recently reconditioned and recommissioned. The late Robert H. Jackson, subsequently a member of the Supreme Court, duly wrote the required opinion of justification. It boiled down in effect to this: Since everybody admits that the President can, as Commander in Chief, *dispose* the forces of the United States, why then may he not *dispose of* them? Actually, what President Roosevelt did was to take over for the nonce Congress's power to dispose of property of the United States (Article IV, Section 3) and to repeal at least two statutes.[8]

Congress's endorsement was not long delayed, however, and it was given in ungrudging terms. The Lend-Lease Act of March 11, 1941 empowered the President, whenever he deemed it to be in the interest of the national defense, to authorize the Secretary of War, the Secretary of the Navy, or any other head of department or agency of the government to manufacture or "otherwise procure," so long as funds were available, "defense articles"—i.e., anything from butter to battleships—and "sell, transfer, exchange, lease, lend or otherwise dispose of the same to any government whose defense the President deemed vital" to that of the United States, and on any terms that he deemed "satisfactory." . . .

The Steel Seizure Case

. . . even prior to the Second World War Presidents had gradually built up a practice of intervening without legal authorization, sometimes indeed to the derogation of applicable law, in labor-management disputes.[10] The war being over, Congress, now in the control of the Republicans, decided that it was time to subject such informal interventions to a prescribed procedure, and with this end in view brought forward what presently became the Taft-Hartley (Labor Management Relations) Act. The measure was sharply opposed by labor spokesmen on account of a provision authorizing the federal courts on the petition of the Attorney General, to enjoin strikes or lockouts that were found to "imperil the national health or safety." "The inherent power of the President," the protestants alleged, citing Attorney General Clark, "to deal with emergencies affecting the health, safety and welfare of the entire nation is very great." On this showing President Truman vetoed the bill, but when it became law over his veto he gave solemn assurance that he would observe it.[11] Nevertheless, when in April 1952 a nation-wide strike of steel workers threatened, the President, without referring to the Taft-Hartley Act, whose procedures he by-passed, or to any other statutory warrant for such action, directed the Secretary of Commerce to seize and operate most of the steel mills of the country. His stated justification was the requirements of the national security at home and of our allies abroad, and he invoked generally "the authority vested in me by the Constitution and laws of the United States." Before the Secretary could execute the order he was stopped by an injunction, which in due course the Supreme Court affirmed.[12]

The pivotal proposition of "the opinion of the Court," so-called, by Justice Black is that, inasmuch as Congress could have ordered the seizure of the mills, the President lacked power to seize them without its authorization. In support of this position, which purported to have the indorsement of four other members of the Court, Justice Black invoked the principle of the Separation of Powers, but otherwise adduced no proof from previous decisions or from governmental practice. In the circumstances of the case this course of reasoning was self-refuting. If the principle of the Separation of Powers prevents the President from doing anything that Congress may do, then by the same token it bars the Supreme Court from doing anything that Congress may do. Yet everybody conceded that Congress could have ended the seizure of the steel mills at any time—precisely what the Supreme Court undertook to do in this case!

For the rest, the opinion bears all the earmarks of hasty improvisation as well as of strong prepossession, being unquestionably contradicted by a long record of presidential pioneering in territory eventually occupied by Congress. Thus Washington, as we have seen, acting on his own in 1793, issued the first neutrality proclamation. The following year Congress, at the President's suggestion, enacted the first neutrality statute. In 1799 the elder Adams extradited the first fugitive from justice under the Jay Treaty and was successfully defended by Marshall in the House of Representatives for his course. Not till 1848 did Congress provide another method. And in 1799 an American naval vessel, acting under presidential orders, seized a Danish craft trading in the West Indies. Although the Court disallowed the seizure as violative of an act of Congress, it took pains, by Chief Justice Marshall, to assert that but for the act the President could in the circumstances have ordered the seizure by virtue of his duty "to take care that the laws be faithfully executed" and of his power as commander of the forces. That the President, in the absence of legislation by Congress, may control the landing of foreign cables in the United States and the passage of foreign troops through American territory has been demonstrated repeatedly. Likewise, until Congress acts he may set up military commissions in territory occupied by the armed forces of the United States. During the Civil War Lincoln's suspensions of the writ of habeas corpus paved the way to authorizing legislation. Similarly, his action in seizing the railroad and telegraph lines between Washington and Baltimore in 1861 was followed in 1862 by an act of Congress generally authorizing such seizures when dictated by military necessity as judged by the President.[13]

On the specific issue of seizures of industrial property, Justice Frankfurter incorporates many pertinent data in an appendix to his concurring opinion in the steel case. Of statutes authorizing such seizures he lists eighteen between 1916 and 1951; and of Presidential seizures without specific authorization he lists eight for the First World War period and eleven for the Second World War period, several of which occurred before the outbreak of hostilities. While in the War Labor Disputes Act of June 25, 1943 such seizures were put on a statutory basis, in the *United States* v. *Pewee Coal Co., Inc.* they were impliedly sustained as having been validly made.[14]

In consequence of the evident belief of at least four of the Justices who concurred in the judgment in the steel case that Congress, by the procedures that it had laid down in the Taft-Hartley Act, had exercised its powers in the premises of the case in opposition to seizure, the lesson of the case is somewhat blurred. But that the President does possess, in the absence of restrictive legislation, a residual or resultant power above or in consequence of his granted powers, to deal with emergencies that he regards as threatening the national security, is explicitly asserted by Justice Clark, and the same view is evidently shared, with certain vague qualifications, by Justices Frankfurter and Jackson; and the dissenting Justices would apparently go further. Speaking by the late Chief Justice Vinson, they quote with evident approval—not to say gusto—a passage extracted from the government's brief in *United States* v. *Midwest Oil Co.*,[15] in which in 1915 the Court sustained the power of the President to order withdrawals from the public domain not only without the sanction of Congress, but even contrary to its legislation, such legislation having been systematically ignored by successive Presidents through a long term of years. . . .

What, then is the lesson of the Steel Case? Unquestionably it tends to supplement presidential emergency power with a power to adopt temporary remedial legislation when Congress has been, in the judgment of the President, unduly remiss in taking cognizance of and acting on a given situation. In other words, the lesson of the case is that, just as nature abhors a vacuum, so does an age of emergency. Let Congress see to it, then, that no such vacuum occurs. The best escape from presidential autocracy in the age we inhabit is not, in short, judicial review, which can supply only a vacuum, but timely legislation.

In brief, the President's duty "to take care that the

laws be faithfully executed" becomes at times the power to make laws. Nor is this the whole story, as we see when we recur to the practice of Congress in recent decades of making broad unbounded delegations of power to the President. The approach of war with Germany in 1917, the war itself, the economic crisis that confronted the country in 1932 and the years immediately following—these produced a considerable crop of statutory provisions delegating powers to the President to be exercised by him "in cases of emergency," of "extreme emergency," of "sufficient emergency," "in time of war or similar emergency," in "a state of public peril," and so on; and this practice was, of course, resumed following our abrupt precipitation into the Second World War. The dimensions that it assumed are revealed by the fact that President Truman, in his proclamation of December 31, 1946 declaring the war to be at an end, announced that it terminated some twenty statutes at once and foreshadowed the demise of thirty-three others, and that as to still others he intended to ask Congress for their renewal in whole or in part.[16]

Presidential Warmaking

We now return to base, i.e. to the Constitutional document and, more specifically, to the "take-care" clause. The starting point is Hamilton's contention, which he advanced in support of Washington's proclamation of neutrality of 1793, that the laws whose faithful execution the President is obliged to forward comprise not only the Constitution and laws and treaties of the United States, but international law as well, and that hence the President's responsibility extends to the discharge of American duties and to the protection of American rights and interests abroad. Hamilton thus adumbrated a presidential function the performance of which has been difficult at times to demark from the war-declaring power of Congress. The framers of the Constitution had, in fact, pointed the way to this very development.

Thus, when it was proposed in the Federal Convention, on August 17, 1787, to authorize Congress to "make war," Madison and Gerry "moved to insert 'declare,' striking out 'make' war, leaving to the Executive the power to repel sudden attacks," and the motion carried.[17] When, nevertheless, early in Jefferson's first administration, the question arose whether the President had the right to employ naval forces to protect American shipping against the Tripolitan pirates, Jefferson was so doubtful on the point that he instructed his commander that if he took any prisoners he should release them; and that while he might disarm captured vessels in self-defense, he must release those too. These scruples excited the derision of Hamilton;[18] he argued that if we were attacked, we were *ipso facto* at war willy-nilly and that Congress's prerogative was exclusive only when it came to putting the country into a state of war *ab initio*. At the time Jefferson's view prevailed, Congress formally voting him war powers against the Bey of Tripoli. Later developments have abundantly established Hamilton's thesis.[19]

Thus, commenting on the action of Lieutenant Hollins in 1854 in ordering the bombardment of Greytown, Nicaragua, in default of reparations from the local authorities for an attack by a mob on the United States consul stationed there, Justice Nelson, on circuit, said: "As respects the interposition of the Executive abroad for the protection of the lives or property of the citizen, the duty must, of necessity, rest in the discretion of the President . . . under our system of government the citizen abroad is as much entitled to protection as the citizen at home,"[20] words endorsed by the Supreme Court in 1890. The President's duty, said Justice Miller, is not limited "to the enforcement of acts of Congress or of treaties of the United States according to their express terms," but includes "the rights, duties, and obligations growing out of the Constitution itself, our international relations, and all the protection implied by the nature of the Government under the Constitution."[21] . . .

Treaties and Executive Agreements; The Senate's Abdication

The foregoing brings us to a subject that of late has been much before the public: the power of the President to enter into international agreements. The Constitution (Article II, section 2, clause 1) reads: "He [the President] shall have power, by and with the advice and consent of the Senate, to make treaties, provided two-thirds of the Senators present concur." It is usual to regard the process of treaty making as falling into two parts, negotiation and ratification, and to assign the former to the President exclusively and the latter to the Senate exclusively. It will be observed, however, that in fact the Constitution makes no such division of the subject. Originally, indeed, Washington endeavored to take counsel with the Senate regarding the drafting of treaties, but the Senate itself created so many difficulties that he speedily abandoned the procedure, with the result that what was intended to be one authority consisting of two closely collaborating organs became split into two, often antagonistic, authorities performing sharply differentiated functions. Today the actual initiation and negotiation of treaties is, by the vast weight of both practice and opinion, the President's alone.[23]

Furthermore the President frequently negotiates, besides treaties proper, agreements with other governments that are not referred to the Senate for its advice and consent. These are of two kinds: those that he is authorized by Congress to make or that he lays before Congress for approval and implementation; and those that he enters into by virtue simply of his diplomatic powers and powers as Commander in Chief. As early as 1792 Congress authorized the Postmaster General to enter into postal conventions; as recently as 1934 it authorized the President to enter into foreign trade agreements and to lower customs rates as much as fifty per cent on imports from the other contracting countries in return for equivalent concessions, an authorization renewed in 1937, 1940, and 1943. The Lend-Lease Act of March 11, 1941, dealt with previously, belongs to the same category.[24]

Instances of treaty making by the President without the aid or consent of either Congress or the Senate are still more numerous. One was the exchange of notes in 1817 between the British Minister Bagot and Secretary of State Rush for the limitation of naval forces on the Great Lakes. A year later is was submitted to the Senate, which promptly ratified it. Of like sort were the protocol of August 12, 1898 between the United States and Spain, by which Spain agreed to relinquish all title to Cuba and to cede Puerto Rico and her other West Indian possessions to the United States; the exchange of notes between the Department of State and various European governments in 1899 and 1900 with reference to the "open door" in China; the "Gentlemen's Agreement," first drawn in 1907, by which Japanese immigration to this country was long regulated; the *modus vivendi* by which after the termination of the Treaty of Washington in 1885 American fishing rights off the coast of Canada and Newfoundland were defined for more than a quarter of a century; the protocol for ending the Boxer Rebellion in 1901; the notorious Lansing-Ishii agreement of November 2, 1917, recognizing that Japan had special rights in China; and the armistice of November 11, 1918—to say nothing of that entire complexus of conventions and understandings by which our relations with our "associates" in the First World War and our "allies" in the Second World War were determined—the last-named group including two, those labeled "Yalta" and "Potsdam," that have achieved a special notoriety.[25]

Obviously the line between such agreements and those that have to be submitted to the Senate is not easily defined. When the Senate refused in 1905 to ratify a treaty that Theodore Roosevelt had entered into with the government of Santo Domingo for putting its customs houses under United States control, the President simply changed the treaty into an agreement and proceeded to carry out its terms, with the result that a year or so later the Senate capitulated and ratified the agreement, thereby converting it once more into a treaty. Furthermore, by recent decisions of the Supreme Court an executive agreement within the power of the President to make is law of the land to which the courts must give effect, any state law or judicial policy to the contrary notwithstanding.[26] That Congress, which can at any time repeal any treaty as "law of the land or authorization," can do the same to executive agreements would appear to be obvious.[27]

Nor is the executive agreement, whether made with or without the sanction of Congress, the only inroad that practice under the Constitution has made on the original role of the Senate in treaty making. Not only is the business of negotiation today within the President's exclusive province, as was pointed out above, but Congress and the President have also come into possession of a quite indefinite power to legislate with respect to external affairs. The annexation of Texas in 1845 by joint resolution is the leading precedent. The example thus set was followed a half century later in connection with Hawaii; and of similar import are the joint resolution of July 2, 1921 by which war with the Central Powers was brought to a close and the joint resolution of June 19, 1934 by which the President was enabled to accept membership for the United States in the International Labor Organization.[28] Such precedents make it difficult to state any limit to the power of the President and Congress, acting jointly, to implement effectively any foreign policy on which they agree, no matter how "the recalcitrant third plus one man" of the Senate may feel about the matter.

Presidential Confidences and Confidants

The last phase of presidential prerogative to receive attention here, one that has been recently much in the public eye, stems also from the "take-care" clause. The reference is to the President's right to protect official confidences between himself and his subordinates from undue judicial and congressional curiosity. The leading case on the subject is still *Marbury* v. *Madison*.[29] In the course of the argument the Attorney General, pointing out that he was acting as Secretary of State at the time of the transaction involved, stated that "he felt himself bound to maintain the rights of the executive" and that he ought not to answer concerning "any facts which came officially to his knowledge while acting as Secretary of State." The Chief Justice, though of the opinion that nothing confidential was in fact involved, conceded none the less that "if he [the Attorney General] thought that anything was communicated to him in confidence he ought not to answer concerning it."

But even earlier, as Attorney General Brownell recently showed,[30] President Washington had taken the position, apropos of a congressional inquiry, that although he ought to communicate to the committee conducting the inquiry, at its request, such papers as the public interest demanded, he ought, on the other hand, to withhold any the disclosure of which might injure the public interest, *and that he was the judge of this matter.* Nearly a century later the Senate Judiciary Committee tangled with President Cleveland on the same issue. The Attorney General of that day having refused to furnish certain documents, the Committee advanced the sweeping contention that it was entitled to know all that officially takes place in any of the departments of government, to which assertion the President replied that, though he had no intention of withholding any official papers, he denied that "papers inherently private or confidential" became official merely by being lodged in the custody of a public department. In a similar controversy in 1909 between the Senate Judiciary Committee and President Theodore Roosevelt, the President assured the chairman of the committee that he, Roosevelt, had the desired papers, but that the only way the Senate could get them was through his impeachment. Some of the facts contained in the papers, he further explained, were given to the government under the seal of secrecy, and "I will see to it that the word of this government to individuals is kept sacred."

In April 1941, to turn to a more modern instance, the chairman of the House Committee on Naval Affairs, in a letter addressed to Attorney General Jackson, asked that the Committee be furnished with all FBI reports since June 1939 and all future reports. The Attorney General answered: "It is the position of this Department, now repeated with the approval of and at the direction of the President, that all investigative reports are confidential documents of the executive department of the Government, to aid the duty laid upon the President by the Constitution to 'take care that the laws be faithfully executed,' and that congressional or public access to them would not be in the public interest." "Disclosure of the reports could not do otherwise," he continued, "than seriously prejudice law enforcement," as by identifying sources, etc. It "would also prejudice the national defense and be of aid and comfort to the very subversive elements against which you wish to protect the country." It would violate pledges of secrecy and "might produce the grossest kind of injustice to innocent individuals." The opinion is bolstered by a wealth of precedents both of executive and of judicial provenance.[31]

A more recent controversy was precipitated by President Eisenhower's letter of May 17, 1954 to Secretary of Defense Wilson banning certain testimony in the McCarthy-Army dispute. It reads in part:

> Because it is essential to efficient and effective administration that employees of the Executive Branch be in a position to be completely candid in advising with each other

on official matters, and because it is not in the public interest that any of their conversations or communications or any documents or reproductions concerning such advice be disclosed, you will instruct employees of your department that in all of their appearances before the subcommittee of the Senate Committee on Government Operations regarding the inquiry now before it, they are not to testify to any such conversations or communications or to produce any such documents or reproductions.

Although the order was assailed by Senator McCarthy, who demanded that it be "trimmed," it seems to be well within the pattern set by the precedents compiled by the Attorney General.

On the other hand, the President's determination announced on June 6, 1954 to prevent—apparently *in toto*—any investigation of the Central Intelligence Agency by Senator McCarthy plainly exceeds this pattern. Indeed, it contradicts the President's own recognition in his letter to Secretary Wilson of the general right of Congressional committees to request "information relating to any matter" within their jurisdiction, "certain historical exceptions" aside. In the words of the *New York Times* in its editorial column of June 8, 1954: "The intelligence work of the CIA under its able director, Allen W. Dulles, is vital to this Government. . . ." Yet "no one outside the agency itself really knows whether it is doing an efficient job, whether it is overstaffed, whether it duplicates work of other agencies, whether it gets into operations where it has no business, whether it wastes money, whether it interferes with the conduct of our foreign policy, and so forth. Because it is almost completely cut off from Congress, it is an object of suspicion by Congress. Obviously, we are not urging publicity for the work of the CIA, and of course an investigation of the type Senator McCarthy would conduct (or for that matter any public inquiry) could well be disastrous."[32] . . .

Summary and Assessment

It was discovered at the very outset of the government under the Constitution that enlarged views of presidential power commanded an open road into the Constitution in the initial words of Article II—the executive-power clause. Later the Commander-in-Chief clause revealed even greater potentialities, and meantime the "take-care" clause had come to be invoked. Long before this, moreover, the Senate, by abdicating its intended participation in the elaboration of treaties in order to seize upon an unlimited power to amend or reject them, smoothed the way for the assumption by the President of an indefinite power to enter into executive agreements which, so far as subject matter is concerned, are often indistinguishable from treaties. It is, however, in the twentieth century that presidential power, building on accumulated precedents, has taken on at times, under the stimulation of emergency conditions, the dimensions of executive prerogative as described by John Locke; of a power to wit, to fill needed gaps in the law, or even to supersede it so far as may be requisite to realize "the fundamental law of nature and government, namely, that as much as may be all the members of society are to be preserved."

Theodore Roosevelt, expounding his so-called Stewardship Theory of the presidency, wrote in 1913 that "it was not only his [the President's] right but his duty to do anything that the needs of the Nation" —as judged by himself, of course—"demanded unless such action was forbidden by the Constitution or by the laws."[34] . . .

The first Roosevelt, however, wrote in the piping times of peace. The second Roosevelt elaborated his conception of the powers of the President as Commander in Chief in wartime in the midst of hostilities. The occasion was his demand on September 7, 1942 that Congress repeal forthwith certain so-called parity provisions of the Price Control Act. This is what he said:

I ask the Congress to take this action by the first of October. Inaction on your part by that date will leave me an inescapable responsibility to the people of this country to see to it that the war effort is no longer imperiled by the threat of economic chaos.

In the event that the Congress should fail to act, and act adequately, I shall accept the responsibility, and I will act.

At the same time that fair prices are stabilized, wages can and will be stabilized also. This I will do.

The President has the powers, under the Constitution and under congressional acts, to take measures necessary to avert a disaster which would interfere with the winning of the war.

I have given the most thoughtful consideration to meeting this issue without further reference to the Congress. I have determined, however, on this vital matter to consult with the Congress.

The American people can be sure that I will use my powers with a full sense of my responsibility to the Constitution and to my country. The American people can also be sure that I shall not hesitate to use every power vested in me to accomplish the defeat of our enemies in any part of the world where our own safety demands such defeat.

When the war is won, the powers under which I act automatically revert to the people—to whom they belong.[37]

What we have here is certainly a rather far-reaching proposition. The President of the United States is claiming the right to repeal an act of Congress, although he does not deny that Congress had the power to pass it. To be sure, other Presidents have occasionally refused to enforce acts of Congress, though very rarely, and always on the ground that the acts in question were unconstitutional. This was

Andrew Johnson's contention in 1867 respecting the Tenure of Office Act; as it was Woodrow Wilson's respecting the Jones Shipping Act of 1920.[38] But nobody would venture to deny that Congress had the right to pass the Emergency Price Control Act or that it was the only organ of the government that did have that right; and yet the President claimed the right to repeal the law. That was a claim of power to suspend the Constitution, and moreover to suspend it as to its most important feature, the division of power between the President and Congress.

Yet any candid person must admit that a situation might arise in which it would be necessary to suspend the Constitution. Abraham Lincoln admitted that he did not know whether or not he had suspended a part of it when he suspended the writ of habeas corpus; but, said he, "Are all the laws to go unenforced in order that one law may be preserved?" When Mr. Roosevelt spoke, however, Congress was in session, and it might seem that if the situation was so desperate as to require suspension of the Constitution, the safe view to take was that Congress was aware of the fact as well as the President and should be joined in the enterprise. And yet, suppose that an atom bomb were to be dropped on Washington, New York, or Los Angeles: whose duty would it be to proclaim martial law and thereby suspend the Constitution?

For the rest, it must be admitted that Roosevelt's attempt to establish a whole series of new offices and his attempt to rule labor for two years without a whit of authorization by Congress prevailed *in fact;* why not, then, *in law?* And if in law, then does this law hold when peace, in the sense of the absence of a shooting war, once more supervenes?

Nor may we assess the President's powers as Commander in Chief in wartime without reference to the scope of the war power itself. The Court's doctrine on this point was stated succinctly by Chief Justice Hughes more than twenty years ago in the following curt terms: "The war power of the Federal Government is a power to wage war successfully."[39] But who is to judge what measures *are* necessary to bring a war to a successful conclusion? Certainly not the Court, as was amply demonstrated when in 1944 it sustained the measures that the Government adopted early in the Second World War respecting Japanese residents on the West Coast. What, in brief, these measures accomplished was the removal of 112,000 Japanese, two thirds of them citizens of the United States by birth, from their homes and properties and their temporary segregation in assembly centers, later styled relocation centers.[40] No such wholesale or dractic invasion of the rights of citizens of the United States by their own government had ever occurred in the history of the country. These measures, moreover, were initially drafted as a presidential order, although before being put into operation they were formally enacted by Congress. The Court's reliance was on the broad scope of the blended powers of the President and Congress in wartime.

If, then, the question be asked: How does presidential prerogative today compare with the constitutional scheme of things? the answer must undoubtedly be: *The power of the President as Commander in Chief in wartime is subject only to such restraints as Congress may effectively impose.* For the rest, he "is accountable only to his country in his political character and to his own conscience."[41]

---

[1] For the Supreme Court's ratification of the "decision of 1789" see *Myers* v. *U.S.*, 272 U.S. 52 (1926). The ratification was somewhat too sweeping and had to be retracted as to the great independent agencies like the I.C.C., the F.T.C., etc., which are now held not to be in the executive department, but arms of the legislative department. *Humphrey* v. *U.S.*, 295 U.S. 602 (1935).

[2] For particulars *see* Corwin, *The President, Office and Powers* (ed. of 1948), Chapter V and pp. 459-83; also Norman J. Small, *Some Presidential Interpretations of the Presidency* (Baltimore, 1932), Chapter II.

3 *Marbury* v. *Madison*, Cr. 137, 166-67 (1803). Corwin, *The Constitution and What It Means Today* (11th ed., Princeton, 1954), 138 and note.

4 *The Federalist* #69; *Fleming* v. *Page*, 9 How. 603, 615, 618.

5 2 Black. 635 (1863). The Emancipation Proclamation rests on the same assumption and hence raises no fresh question respecting the powers of the President as Commander in Chief. *See* James G. Randall, *Constitutional Problems Under Lincoln* (New York, 1926), Chapter XVI.

6 4 Wall. 2.

7 *United States* v. *Curtiss-Wright Export Corp.*, 299 U.S. 304, 320-27 (1936).

8 For particulars *see* the writer's communication to the *New York Times*, October 13, 1940.

10 This practice stemmed in the first instance from the famous Debs Case of 1895, 158 U.S. 564. For a list of major labor disputes in which Presidents intervened in the capacity of policeman-mediator between 1902 and 1947, *see The President, Office and Powers*, pp. 453-54. *See also* B. M. Rich, *The Presidents and Civil Disorders* (Washington, 1941).

11 *See* Corwin, *A Constitution of Powers in a Secular State* (Charlottesville, 1951), 62-63, 75-76.

12 *Youngstown Sheet and Tube Co.* v. *Sawyer*, 343 U.S. 579 (1952).

13 Corwin, *op. cit.* in note 3, pp. 126-27 and notes.

14 341 U.S. 114 (1951).

15 236 U.S. 459.

16 *The President, Office and Powers*, 496.

17 Farrand, *Records . . .* , II, 318.

18 *Works* (Hamilton, ed.), VII, 745-48.

19 For an effort that didn't come off on the part of Woodrow Wilson to apply the Jeffersonian tactic, *see The President, Office and Powers*, 476-77.

20 *Durand* v. *Hollins*, 4 Blatch. 451, 454 (1860).

21 *In re* Neagle, 135 U.S. 1, 64.

23 *The President, Office and Powers*, 253-59; *see also* reference in note 7 *supra*.

24 *The Constitution and What It Means Today*, 112.

25 *Ibid.*, 112-13.

26 *United States* v. *Belmont*, 301 U.S. (1937); *United States* v. *Pink*, 315 U.S. 203 (1942).

27 Head Money Cases, 112 U.S. 580 (1884); *La Abra Mining Co.* v. *U.S.*, 175 U.S. 423, 460 (1899). *See also* R. S. Secs. 1999, 2000 as indicative of the power of Congress to determine

what law shall be enforced in the courts of these United States.

28 42 Stat. 105; 49 Stat. 2741.

29 See note 3 *supra.*

30 *New York Times,* May 18, 1954.

31 40 *Opinions of the Attorney General,* 45-51 (April 30, 1941).

32 *New York Times* (editorial), June 8, 1954.

34 *Autobiography,* 388-89.

37 *President, Office and Powers,* 303-6.

38 *Ibid.,* 231, 471. The story is amusing.

39 *Home Building and Loan Assoc.* v. *Blaisdell,* 290 U.S. 398, 426 (1934). The war power and other powers of foreign relationship were declared by Justice Sutherland for the Court, in the Curtiss-Wright Case, to devolve on the Federal Government simply "as necessary concomitants of nationality" and so were not dependent "on the affirmative grants of the Constitution." 299 U.S. 304, 317-18 (1936). In the more recent case of *Lichter* v. *United States,* 334 U.S. 742 (1948) the Court appears to regard the war power as derived from the Constitution.

40 *The Constitution and What It Means Today,* 66-67.

41 *See* note 3 *supra.* Secretary Seward summed up his estimate of the Presidency in 1863 on the basis of his observation of President Lincoln's acts as Commander in Chief, as follows: "We elect a king for four years, and give him absolute power within certain limits, which after all he can interpret for himself." Ford, *Rise and Growth,* 291. For a period of war, and civil war at that, he was probably not far from wrong.

"In time of peace," wrote Jefferson in 1810, "the people look most to their representatives; but in war, to the Executive solely." *Writings* (P. L. Ford, ed.), IX, 272.

PRESIDENTIAL INABILITY

Few clauses of the Constitution are more uncertain in meaning than that dealing with the question of when a president is incapable of continuing his duties. The sixth clause of section 1 of article II reads as follows:

> "In case of the Removal of the President from Office, or of his Death, Resignation, or Inability to discharge the Powers and Duties of the said Office, the same shall devolve on the Vice President, and the Congress may by Law provide for the Case of Removal, Death, Resignation or Inability, both of the President and Vice President, declaring what Officer shall then act as President, and such Officer shall act accordingly, until the Disability be removed, or a President shall be elected."

One searches these words in vain for answers to the questions: Who may say whether a President is unable to discharge the duties of his office? When the President is disabled does the Vice President succeed to the "powers and duties of the office" or to the office itself? Is the election referred to in the last phrase the next regular election or one to be called by Congress? And finally, may these and other questions be resolved by Congress, or is a constitutional amendment necessary?

Twice the question has been raised with some acuteness, during the lingering disability of President Garfield after he was shot, and during the long incapacity of President Wilson. But no remedial action followed either episode. Some of the minor questions relating to the failure of a newly elected President and Vice President to qualify were resolved by the twentieth amendment, adopted in 1946, and the 1947 presidential succession act. By the latter act the order of succession after the President and Vice President devolves upon the Speaker of the House, the President *pro tempore* of the Senate, and thereafter the members of the Cabinet commencing with the Secretary of State.

In a study of the problems involved in this matter the House Committee on the Judiciary secured answers to a questionnaire from a number of constitutional law scholars. *Presidential Inability*, 84th Cong., 2d Sess. (1956). The reply of Professor Arthur E. Sutherland of the Harvard Law School is reproduced below.

December 31, 1955

Hon. Emanuel Celler,
Chairman, Committee on the Judiciary,
United States House of Representatives,
Washington, D. C.

Dear Congressman Celler: . . .

Your first question asks what the draftsmen of the Constitution meant by "inability" in article II, section 1, clause 6, and whether a statutory definition is now desirable. I do not know of any material which shows us just what the draftsmen had in mind, and it may be that the absence from the Constitution of any machinery for superseding the President in case of inability indicates that comparatively little thought was given to the matter. I should consider an attempt at legislative definition inadvisable and not helpful. The varieties and degrees of disability, physical and mental, temporary or permanent, which might render a President unable to discharge his duties, are so numerous that an inventory would be impracticable, and a definition would end up as a repetition in different words of what we already know —that inability in the constitutional sense is inability so serious that it requires that the President's duties be taken over by someone else.

Your second question asks who should raise the question of disability. The substitution of another officer for the President, whether temporarily or permanently, is of such grave importance that the arrangements for it should, as far as humanly possible, achieve at least two ends: A factually correct decision as to the President's inability; and a decision which will be accepted by all concerned as having been impartial and without partisan bias. If the question of inability were to be raised by the House of Representatives, with open discussion (by analogy to impeachment) these ends might be attained, though in case of a House bitterly opposed to a President, suspicion of politics would inevitably attach. Furthermore the House might not be in session at the time of some such misfortune as the wounding of President Garfield. One of the committees might have this duty delegated to it by previous legislation. The Cabinet, the President's friends and advisers, would be free of the suggestion of hostile partisanship, though they would tend to a slow action out of loyalty, unless the disability were obvious and the need critical. Perhaps this is a good thing. Some special body, for example like that set up under the act of 1877 (19 Stat. 227) could be set up to be always in existence. I incline to favor leaving this matter with the Cabinet. If real need developed, its members would not be deterred, by sympathy for their chief, from doing what the country needed.

Your third question asks who should pass on the question of disability, once brought forward. Of course the Supreme Court has detachment, and profound respect is given to it by the people of the country; but by the Constitution it is limited to judicial functions, which would seem to exclude matters such as you ask about. A standing "Commission on Presidential Disability" could be set up by statute to be ready at all times. Either House could make the decision, if authorized by statute, but the Congress might not be in session. On the whole I come back to the idea that the Cabinet would be an appropriate body to perform this task.

Your fourth question, concerning constitutional difficulties, raises the most serious problem. "Inability" is so ill-provided for in the Constitution that the success of any system of supersession of the President, if made only by act of Congress, will depend on its acceptance by the officers of Government and the people. I am thinking of some national misfortune such as the suspected mental illness of a President. There might be two factions in the country, one favoring the President's continuance in his functions, the other opposing. The Constitution gives the President a 4-year term. Might not his supporters assert with much force that a nonconstitutional body was without constitutional power to displace the President?

I have already suggested the answer that on the whole seems to me wisest, for your fifth inquiry, as to the union in one agency of initiation and determination of the question. On the whole I think the Cabinet should perform both functions. This is not like a criminal prosecution, where an accusatory function may well be separate from the task of trial. The Cabinet will be sympathetic, not hostile. As to the sixth question, whether there should be a finding of the probable duration of the disability, I think the answer is in the negative. Could this have been determined in the cases of Presidents Garfield or Wilson?

Question 7, what happens when the disability ends? This raises the unpleasant picture of a Vice President clinging to office, supported by a clique; and if the termination of disability is left to the Cabinet, this hypothetical Vice President might have "packed" his Cabinet with his partisans. But this is not a realistic picture. Government cannot provide in advance for every conceivable set of unfortunate circumstances. And at the next session of the Congress that body would have a number of ways to circumvent any such unlikely activity as I suggest. I think I would leave termination of disability for determination by the Cabinet as well. But here again one has to assume acceptance by all concerned of the decision with reasonable cooperation, in the absence of a constitutional amendment.

As to the 8th and 9th questions, concerning the succession of the Vice President to duties, or to office, it seems to me that the Vice President should only become President in case of death, resignation, or removal. In case of disability the Vice President should merely perform the duties, because the disability may be removed. I know that there are difficulties of construction of the constitutional language here, but the sensible construction seems to me to be what I suggest.

The Constitution does not provide for an election to replace the President, in my opinion. I think the phrase "or a President shall be elected" refers to the next regular election.

Finally, as to your 11th inquiry, I think that legislation will depend for its effectiveness on voluntary acceptance, as any statute purporting to stop the functioning of a President elected for 4 years will run into constitutional obstacles. I am reassured by remembering that we have only twice had serious trouble of the sort you ask about—in the cases of President Garfield and Wilson, and those were handled without new constitutional or statutory provisions. . . .

Yours very sincerely,
Arthur E. Sutherland

PART IV

Constitutional Limitations on the Power of Government

INTRODUCTION

A central characteristic of a government of delegated powers, such as the national government under the United States Constitution, is that it is a government of limited power. Thus, the national government is limited in two ways: First, it has no affirmative authority to act save the enumerated powers conferred upon Congress and the express and inherent power of the President. This has been discussed in Parts II and III, *supra*. Second, there are a number of limitations expressly stated in the Constitution. To some extent these limitations are scattered throughout the entire document, but principally they are collected in section 9 of article I and in the amendments, especially the first ten.

The situation of state and local governments is in many respects the converse of that of the national government. While they may not act in a way inconsistent with action of the national government within its authorized sphere, still the entire residual power remains with the states. In the words of the tenth amendment:

"The powers not delegated to the United

States by the Constitution, nor prohibited
by it to the States, are reserved to the States
respectively, or to the people."

This also does not tell the entire story. The states,
too, are subject to some express limitations in the
Constitution itself. Part of these prohibitions against
state action are grouped together in section 10 of
article I. The most important, however, are contained
in the amendments. In the case of the states the
single most significant restriction is the group of restraints found in the fourteenth amendment. The
heart of these limitations appears in section 1 of that
amendment, as follows:

"No State shall make or enforce any law
which shall abridge the privileges or immunities of citizens of the United States; nor
shall any State deprive any person of life,
liberty, or property, without due process of
law; nor deny to any person within its jurisdiction the equal protection of the laws."

Before the adoption of the fourteenth amendment
in 1868, it had been accepted constitutional doctrine
that the first eight amendments to the Constitution,
the so-called Bill of Rights, applied as limitations
only upon the action of the national government, and
were not at all a restraint upon state action. *Barron*
v. *Baltimore,* 32 U.S. (7 Pet.) 243 (1833). Accordingly, before 1868 the extent to which freedom of
speech and press, for example, could be regulated by
the states, or the extent of state protection accorded
against unreasonable search and seizure was a matter exclusively for determination by the respective
states themselves. Even after the ratification of the
fourteenth amendment this concept did not change
until 1925 when the Court, in an almost offhand manner, announced that freedom of speech and of the
press "are among the fundamental personal rights
and 'liberties' protected by the due process clause of
the Fourteenth Amendment from impairment by the
States." *Gitlow* v. *New York,* 268 U.S. 652, 666
(1925). Thereafter, the argument was made to the

Court that the due process clause of the fourteenth amendment similarly "incorporated" the entire Bill of Rights as a limitation upon the states parallel to its restraining effect upon the national government. The argument had been at least preliminarily rejected in *Twining* v. *New Jersey*, 211 U.S. 78 (1908) and in *Palko* v. *Connecticut*, 302 U.S. 319 (1937). It was finally, definitively rejected in *Adamson* v. *California*, *infra*, despite an invocation of history by Mr. Justice Black, dissenting for the four-man minority.

ADAMSON v. CALIFORNIA
332 U.S. 46 (1947)

MR. JUSTICE REED delivered the opinion of the Court.

The appellant, Adamson, a citizen of the United States, was convicted, without recommendation for mercy, by a jury in a Superior Court of the State of California of murder in the first degree. After considering the same objections to the conviction that are pressed here, the sentence of death was affirmed by the Supreme Court of the state. 27 Cal. 2d 478, 165 P.2d 3. Review of that judgment by this Court was sought and allowed under Judicial Code § 237; 28 U.S.C. § 344. The provisions of California law which were challenged in the state proceedings as invalid under the Fourteenth Amendment to the Federal Constitution are those of the state constitution and penal code. . . . They permit the failure of a defendant to explain or to deny evidence against him to be commented upon by court and by counsel and to be considered by court and jury. The defendant did not testify. As the trial court gave its instructions and the District Attorney argued the case in accordance with the constitutional and statutory provisions just referred to, we have for decision the question of their constitutionality in these circumstances under the limitations of § 1 of the Fourteenth Amendment.

The appellant was charged in the information with former convictions for burglary, larceny and robbery and pursuant to § 1025, California Penal Code, answered that he had suffered the previous convictions. This answer barred allusion to these charges of convictions on the trial. Under California's interpretation of § 1025 of the Penal Code and § 2051 of the Code of Civil Procedure, however, if the defendant, after answering affirmatively charges alleging prior convictions, takes the witness stand to deny or explain away other evidence that has been introduced "the commission of these crimes could have been revealed to the jury on cross-examination to impeach his testimony." *People* v. *Adamson*, 27 Cal. 2d 478, 494, 165 P.2d 3, 11; *People* v. *Braun*, 14 Cal. 2d 1, 6, 92 P.2d 402, 405. This forces an accused who is a repeated offender to choose between the risk of having his prior offenses disclosed to the jury or of having it draw harmful inferences from uncontradicted evidence that can only be denied or explained by the defendant.

In the first place, appellant urges that the provision of the Fifth Amendment that no person "shall be compelled in any criminal case to be a witness against himself" is a fundamental national privilege or immunity protected against state abridgment by the Fourteenth Amendment or a privilege or immunity secured, through the Fourteenth Amendment, against deprivation by state action because it is a personal right, enumerated in the federal Bill of Rights.

Secondly, appellant relies upon the due process of law clause of the Fourteenth Amendment to invalidate the provisions of the California law, . . . and as applied (a) because comment on failure to testify is permitted, (b) because appellant was forced to forego testimony in person because of danger of disclosure of his past convictions through cross-examination, and (c) because the presumption of innocence was infringed by the shifting of the burden of proof to appellant in permitting comment on his failure to testify.

We shall assume, but without any intention thereby of ruling upon the issue, that permission by law to the court, counsel and jury to comment upon and consider the failure of defendant "to explain or to deny by his testimony any evidence or facts in the case against him" would infringe defendant's privilege against self-incrimination under the Fifth Amendment if this were a trial in a court of the United States under a similar law. Such an assumption does not determine appellant's rights under the Fourteenth Amendment. It is settled law that the clause of the Fifth Amendment, protecting a person against being compelled to be a witness against himself, is not made effective by the Fourteenth Amendment as a protection against state action on the ground that freedom from testimonial compulsion is a right of national citizenship, or because it is a personal privilege or immunity secured by the Federal Constitution as one of the rights of man that are listed in the Bill of Rights.

The reasoning that leads to those conclusions starts with the unquestioned premise that the Bill of Rights, when adopted, was for the protection of the individual against the federal government and its provisions were inapplicable to similar actions done by the states. *Barron* v. *Baltimore,* 7 Pet. 243; *Feldman* v. *United States,* 322 U.S. 487, 490. With the adoption of the Fourteenth Amendment, it was suggested that the dual citizenship recognized by its first sentence secured for citizens federal protection for their elemental privileges and immunities of state citizenship. The Slaughter-House Cases [16 Wall. 36, 21 L.Ed. 394] decided, contrary to the suggestion, that these rights, as privileges and immunities of state citizenship, remained under the sole protection of the state governments. This Court, without the expression of a contrary view upon that phase of the issues before the Court, has approved this determination. *Maxwell* v. *Bugbee,* 250 U.S. 525, 537; *Hamilton* v. *Regents,*

293 U.S. 245, 261. The power to free defendants in state trials from self-incrimination was specifically determined to be beyond the scope of the privileges and immunities clause of the Fourteenth Amendment in *Twining* v. *New Jersey*, 211 U.S. 78, 91-98. "The privilege against self-incrimination may be withdrawn and the accused put upon the stand as a witness for the state." The Twining case likewise disposed of the contention that freedom from testimonial compulsion, being specifically granted by the Bill of Rights, is a federal privilege or immunity that is protected by the Fourteenth Amendment against state invasion. This Court held that the inclusion in the Bill of Rights of this protection against the power of the national government did not make the privilege a federal privilege or immunity secured to citizens by the Constitution against state action. *Twining* v. *New Jersey, supra,* at 98-99; *Palko* v. *Connecticut, supra,* at 328. . . . We reaffirm the conclusion of the Twining and Palko cases that protection against self-incrimination is not a privilege or immunity of national citizenship.

Appellant secondly contends that if the privilege against self-incrimination is not a right protected by the privileges and immunities clause of the Fourteenth Amendment against state action, this privilege, to its full scope under the Fifth Amendment, inheres in the right to a fair trial. A right to a fair trial is a right admittedly protected by the due process clause of the Fourteenth Amendment. Therefore, appellant argues, the due process clause of the Fourteenth Amendment protects his privilege against self-incrimination. The due process clause of the Fourteenth Amendment, however, does not draw all the rights of the federal Bill of Rights under its protection. That contention was made and rejected in *Palko* v. *Connecticut*, 302 U.S. 319, 323. It was rejected with citation of the cases excluding several of the rights, protected by the Bill of Rights, against infringement by the National Government. Nothing has been called to our attention that either the framers of the Fourteenth Amendment or the states that adopted intended its due process clause to draw within its scope the earlier amendments to the Constitution. Palko held that such provisions of the Bill of Rights as were "implicit in the concept of ordered liberty," p. 325, became secure from state interference by the clause. But it held nothing more.

Specifically, the due process clause does not protect, by virtue of its mere existence, the accused's freedom from giving testimony by compulsion in state trials that is secured to him against federal interference by the Fifth Amendment. *Twining* v. *New Jersey*, 211 U.S. 78, 99-114; *Palko* v. *Connecticut, supra,* p. 323. For a state to require testimony from an accused is not necessarily a breach of a state's obligation to give a fair trial. Therefore, we must examine the effect of the California law applied in this trial to see whether the comment on failure to testify violates the protection against state action that the due process clause does grant to an accused. The due process clause forbids compulsion to testify by fear of hurt, torture or exhaustion. It forbids any other type of coercion that falls within the scope of due process. California follows Anglo-American legal tradition in excusing defendants in criminal prosecutions from compulsory testimony. Cf. VIII Wigmore on Evidence (3d ed.) § 2252. That is a matter of legal policy and not because of the requirements of due process under the Fourteenth Amendment. So our inquiry is directed, not at the broad question of the constitutionality of compulsory testimony from the accused under the due process clause, but to the constitutionality of the provision of the California law that permits comment upon his failure to testify. It is, of course, logically possible that while an accused might be required, under appropriate penalties, to submit himself as a witness without a violation of due process, comment by judge or jury on inferences to be drawn from his failure to testify in jurisdictions where an accused's privilege against self-incrimination is protected, might deny due process. For example, a statute might declare that a permitted refusal to testify would compel an acceptance of the truth of the prosecution's evidence. . . .

It is true that if comment were forbidden, an accused in this situation could remain silent and avoid evidence of former crimes and comment upon his failure to testify. We are of the view, however, that a state may control such a situation in accordance with its own ideas of the most efficient administration of criminal justice. The purpose of due process is not to protect an accused against a proper conviction but against an unfair conviction. When evidence is before a jury that threatens conviction, it does not seem unfair to require him to choose between leaving the adverse evidence unexplained and subjecting himself to impeachment through disclosure of former crimes. Indeed, this is a dilemma with which any defendant may be faced. If facts, adverse to the defendant, are proven by the prosecution, there may be no way to explain them favorably to the accused except by a witness who may be vulnerable to impeachment on cross-examination. The defendant must then decide whether or not to use such a witness. The fact that the witness may also be the defendant makes the choice more difficult but a denial of due process does not emerge from the circumstances. . . .

We find no other error that gives ground for our intervention in California's administration of criminal justice.

Affirmed.

MR. JUSTICE FRANKFURTER, concurring. . . .

The short answer to the suggestion that the provision of the Fourteenth Amendment, which ordains "nor shall any State deprive any person of life, liberty, or property, without due process of law," was a way of saying that every State must thereafter initiate prosecutions through indictment by a grand jury, must have a trial by a jury of twelve in criminal cases, and must have trial by such a jury in common law suits where the amount in controversy exceeds twenty dollars, is that it is a strange way of saying it. It would be extraordinarily strange for a Consti-

tution to convey such specific commands in such a
roundabout and inexplicit way. . . . The notion that
the Fourteenth Amendment was a covert way of imposing upon the States all the rules which it seemed
important to Eighteenth Century statesmen to write
into the Federal Amendments, was rejected by judges
who were themselves witnesses of the process by
which the Fourteenth Amendment became part of the
Constitution. Arguments that may now be adduced
to prove that the first eight Amendments were con-
cealed within the historic phrasing of the Fourteenth
Amendment were not unknown at the time of its
adoption. A surer estimate of their bearing was possible for judges at the time than distorting distance
is likely to vouchsafe. Any evidence of design or purpose not contemporaneously known could hardly
have influenced those who ratified the Amendment.
Remarks of a particular proponent of the Amendment, no matter how influential, are not to be deemed
part of the Amendment. What was submitted for
ratification was his proposal, not his speech. Thus, at
the time of the ratification of the Fourteenth Amendment the constitutions of nearly half of the ratifying
States did not have the rigorous requirements of the
Fifth Amendment for instituting criminal proceedings through a grand jury. . . . There is suggested
merely a selective incorporation of the first eight
Amendments into the Fourteenth Amendment. Some
are in and some are out, but we are left in the dark
as to which are in and which are out. Nor are we
given the calculus for determining which go in and
which stay out. If the basis of selection is merely that
those provisions of the first eight Amendments are incorporated which commend themselves to individual
justices as indispensable to the dignity and happiness
of a free man, we are thrown back to a merely subjective test. The protection against unreasonable
search and seizure might have primacy for one judge,
while trial by a jury of twelve for every claim above
twenty dollars might appear to another as an ultimate
need in a free society. In the history of thought

"natural law" has a much longer and much better founded meaning and justification than such subjective selection of the first eight Amendments for incorporation into the Fourteenth. . . .

And so, when, as in a case like the present, a conviction in a State court is here for review under a claim that a right protected by the Due Process Clause of the Fourteenth Amendment has been denied, the issue is not whether an infraction of one of the specific provisions of the first eight Amendments is disclosed by the record. The relevant question is whether the criminal proceedings which resulted in conviction deprived the accused of the due process of law to which the United States Constitution entitled him. Judicial review of that guaranty of the Fourteenth Amendment inescapably imposes upon this Court an exercise of judgment upon the whole course of the proceedings in order to ascertain whether they offend those canons of decency and fairness which express the notions of justice of English-speaking peoples even toward those charged with the most heinous offenses. These standards of justice are not authoritatively formulated anywhere as though they were prescriptions in a pharmacopoeia. But neither does the application of the Due Process Clause imply that judges are wholly at large. The judicial judgment in applying the Due Process Clause must move within the limits of accepted notions of justice and is not to be based upon the idiosyncrasies of a merely personal judgment. The fact that judges among themselves may differ whether in a particular case a trial offends accepted notions of justice is not disproof that general rather than idiosyncratic standards are applied. An important safeguard against such merely individual judgment is an alert deference to the judgment of the State court under review.

MR. JUSTICE BLACK, dissenting. . . .

The Court refuses to meet and decide the appellant's first contention. But while the Court's opinion, as I read it, strongly implies that the Fifth Amendment does not, of itself, bar comment upon failure to testify in federal courts, the Court nevertheless assumes that it does in order to reach the second constitutional question involved in appellant's case. I must consider the case on the same assumption that the Court does. For the discussion of the second contention turns out to be a decision which reaches far beyond the relatively narrow issues on which this case might have turned.

This decision reasserts a constitutional theory spelled out in *Twining* v. *New Jersey,* 211 U.S. 78, that this Court is endowed by the Constitution with boundless power under "natural law" periodically to expand and contract constitutional standards to conform to the Court's conception of what at a particular time constitutes "civilized decency" and "fundamental liberty and justice." Invoking this Twining rule, the Court concludes that although comment upon testimony in a federal court would violate the Fifth Amendment, identical comment in a state court does not violate today's fashion in civilized decency and fundamentals and is therefore not prohibited by the Federal Constitution as amended.

The Twining case was the first, as it is the only, decision of this Court which has squarely held that states were free, notwithstanding the Fifth and Fourteenth Amendments, to extort evidence from one accused of crime. I agree that if Twining be reaffirmed, the result reached might appropriately follow. But I would not reaffirm the Twining decision. I think that decision and the "natural law" theory of the Constitution upon which it relies degrade the constitutional safeguards of the Bill of Rights and simultaneously appropriate for this Court a broad power which we are not authorized by the Constitution to exercise. . . . My reasons for believing that the Twining decision should not be revitalized can best be understood by reference to the constitutional, judicial, and general history that preceded and followed the case. That reference must be abbreviated far more than is justified but for the necessary limitations of opinion-writing.

My study of the historical events that culminated in the Fourteenth Amendment, and the expressions of those who sponsored and favored, as well as those who opposed its submission and passage, persuades me that one of the chief objects that the provisions of the Amendment's first section, separately, and as a whole, were intended to accomplish was to make the Bill of Rights applicable to the states. With full knowledge of the import of the Barron [7 Pet. 243] decision, the framers and backers of the Fourteenth Amendment proclaimed its purpose to be to overturn the constitutional rule that case had announced. This historical purpose has never received full consideration or exposition in any opinion of this Court interpreting the Amendment. [An extensive analysis and discussion of decisions and opinions, from the Slaughter-House Cases onward, is omitted.]

I cannot consider the Bill of Rights to be an outworn 18th Century "strait jacket" as the Twining opinion did. Its provisions may be thought outdated abstractions by some. And it is true that they were designed to meet ancient evils. But they are the same kind of human evils that have emerged from century to century wherever excessive power is sought by the few at the expense of the many. In my judgment the people of no nation can lose their liberty so long as a Bill of Rights like ours survives and its basic purposes are conscientiously interpreted, enforced and respected so as to afford continuous protection against old, as well as new, devices and practices which might thwart those purposes. I fear to see the consequences of the Court's practice of substituting its own concepts of decency and fundamental justice for the language of the Bill of Rights as its point of departure in interpreting and enforcing that Bill of Rights. If the choice must be between the selective process of the Palko decision applying some of the Bill of Rights to the States, or the Twining rule applying none of them, I would choose the Palko selective process. But rather than accept either of these choices, I would follow what I believe was the original purpose of the Fourteenth Amendment—to extend to all the people of the nation the complete protection of the Bill of Rights. To hold that this Court can determine what, if any, provisions of the Bill of Rights will be enforced, and if so to what degree, is to frustrate the great design of a written Constitution. . . .

MR. JUSTICE DOUGLAS joins in this opinion.

MR. JUSTICE MURPHY, with whom MR. JUSTICE RUTLEDGE concurs, dissenting.

While in substantial agreement with the views of MR. JUSTICE BLACK, I have one reservation and one addition to make.

I agree that the specific guarantees of the Bill of Rights should be carried over intact into the first section of the Fourteenth Amendment. But I am not prepared to say that the latter is entirely and necessarily limited by the Bill of Rights. Occasions may arise where a proceeding falls so far short of conforming to fundamental standards of procedure as to warrant constitutional condemnation in terms of a lack of due process despite the absence of a specific provision in the Bill of Rights. . . .

FEDERALISM AND STATE CRIMINAL PROCEDURE†

(70 Harvard Law Review 1, 1956)

By Walter V. Schaefer*

The area in which the Constitution of the United States comes to grips with the procedure of state courts and the practices of state agencies in the administration of the criminal law is beset with problems that are matters of day-to-day concern to a judge of a state court of review. Such a court is responsible for the efficient administration of criminal justice within the state, and for its administration in accordance with the constitutions of the state and nation. From my own point of view, therefore, these problems are by no means academic; indeed, they have something of a "current events" flavor. . . .

The quality of newness that marks this field becomes apparent once we realize that many of those safeguards of criminal procedure which we now take for granted came surprisingly late. In England, although defendants accused of misdemeanors were permitted from early days to be represented by counsel, it was not until 1836 that this right was formally given to defendants in cases of felonies other than treason.[1] In our own country it was not until 1938 that the right to counsel in federal courts meant more than that a lawyer would be permitted to appear for the defendant if the defendant could afford to hire one.[2] And in some states it means no more than that today.[3]

Sir James Stephen tells us that in England until 1832 the accused "need not even be told the details of the charge against him till he appeared in the dock."[4] And again, "his theoretical right to 'challenge' the jury was (except in trials for treason) rendered nugatory by the fact, that he did not see the jury list until his trial."[5] . . .

The accused was everywhere disqualified as a witness in his own behalf until 1864, when the disqualification was first removed by statute in Maine.[6] In England the accused did not become a competent witness in all cases until 1898.[7] An adequate system of review did not exist in England before 1907.[8] And in our own federal courts there was no review at all until 1879, while serious crimes could not be reviewed as a matter of right before 1891.[9]

Superimposed upon the recency of many of our procedural safeguards is the novelty of federal intervention in the field. In a sense, of course, federal control over state criminal procedure is not new at all. The power to review state criminal convictions involving federal constitutional rights has existed from the beginning.[10] Until 1868, however, that power had little on which to operate, and it is the post-Civil War period that marks the real beginning of federal activity in this area—not only because the fourteenth amendment supplied a source of federally guaranteed procedural rights, but also because contemporaneous federal legislation was designed to implement such rights in other ways than by direct review. Congress created civil and criminal actions to enforce constitutional rights.[11] It even provided that certain classes of state criminal cases might be removed to federal courts for trial;[12] and, what is more important, in 1867 it extended the remedy of habeas corpus to prisoners in state custody "in violation of the constitution."[13]

This expansion of federal power produced an appreciable increase in the number of cases in the Supreme Court which presented challenges to state criminal procedures. But looking back on the half century following the ratification of the fourteenth amendment, one is struck by the absence of decisions in those areas which today seem of critical importance.

Cases involving the exclusion of Negroes from grand and petit juries, to be sure, came early, and the problem has remained an important and, to a degree, an unsolved one.[14] For the rest, however, we find that the Court was largely concerned with problems which today seem technical, or even insubstantial, such as the form and necessity of an indictment and the size of a jury.[15] Of course any question that has been settled tends in retrospect to look easier than those that are still with us. Still, the fact that those earlier problems were solved, in the main by single decisions which were rendered initially with a high degree of agreement within the Court and which were subsequently adhered to, suggests that no deep conflicts of social policy were involved.

But however we may characterize these older decisions, it is at least true that the problems which are vital today were not presented to the Court until recently: mob domination of a trial in 1915;[16] the right to counsel in 1932;[17] the effect of perjured testimony in 1935;[18] the admissibility of a coerced confession in 1936.[19] So far as the record discloses, the lateness of

these decisions cannot be explained on the theory
that the Court was originally reluctant to decide such
cases. Apparently the questions simply did not reach
the Court. Why this should be so is something of a
mystery; in part I think it may be explained by lack
of access to the courts, a factor to which I shall refer
later. In any event, it is appropriate to remember
that the present state of the law cannot be explained
simply as a conscious shift by the Supreme Court
from a policy of aloofness or indulgence to one of
strict standards and close supervision.

With these elements of newness it should not be
surprising that this area of the law is marked by uncertainty; that the measure of what is required of the
states is not always clear; or that the course of decision has not always been steady. This uncertainty
of course does not spring from novelty alone. It also
reflects the fact that a court is confronted here with
difficult problems whose resolution often demands a
choice between conflicting social policies. Of course
we know that not all the goals of our society are
wholly consistent with one another, and as lawyers
we should not be dismayed to find these conflicts ex-
hibited in judicial decisions. To point up problems
is as much a part of the judicial process as to solve
them.

There are unique difficulties in the field of criminal
law quite apart from the perplexities of federal-state
relations. Criminal law and its administration have
not engaged the active interest of the organized bar.
Able lawyers are constantly drawn away from the
practice of criminal law. That this should happen is
understandable, but it is unfortunate. Nor is there
significant concern beyond the legal profession. The
interest of the press and of the other media of communication starts and stops with the sensational. To
them, and to the public, details of procedure are dull.
That the rights we most cherish originated in procedural rules and depend upon them for survival has
not made these rules more glamorous. The public
rarely knows or cares about them. If it does, it is

because of the excitement generated by an individual case; and in that context rules of procedure are likely to be regarded as loopholes through which the criminal escapes.

When the supervision of state criminal procedure becomes a matter of federal concern, a new set of problems emerges. Here, as in other areas of federalism—the commerce clause, the supremacy clause, and the full faith and credit clause—there has been little significant congressional action. Solutions have been left to be worked out by the judicial process. The domains of federalism are ordinarily characterized by competing interests, and decision can be based upon an evaluation of those interests. The interest of the state can be measured against the interest of the nation or the competing interests of other states. In the field of criminal procedure, however, a strong local interest competes only against an ideal. Local interest is concerned with the particular case and with the guilt or innocence of the particular individual. We find counterpoised to it no interest of another state, for such extrastate sentiment as exists will, except in extraordinary cases, favor affirmance of the conviction. The counterbalance is only a general ideal of fair procedure which, if it is to prevail, must transcend the circumstances of the particular case.

Furthermore, the constitutional referent is principally the due process clause, which is of even greater generality than those provisions which govern the other areas of federalism. The restrictive content assigned to "privileges and immunities" has so far, at least, prevented this companion phrase from becoming significant,[20] while the equal protection clause—at least until [April 1956][21]—has been pretty largely confined to cases of jury exclusion. As for the due process clause itself, the suggestion that it crystallized the procedural incidents of English common law was early rejected, and the Court has likewise declined to view it as simply incorporating the specifics of the Bill of Rights.[22]

Due process cannot be confined to a particular set of existing procedures because due process speaks for the future as well as the present, and at any given time includes those procedures that are fair and feasible in the light of then existing values and capabilities. Some features of present procedures are now accepted by force of custom, or because no practical way has been found to improve them. Technological change or a refinement in our sense of justice may make their retention intolerable.

Definition of due process in terms of social values of course invites the question, "Who determines those values?"—and since in a practical sense it is the Supreme Court which does so, the inference may be, and on occasion has been, drawn that the Court's action in this area is purely creative, or even arbitrary. I do not think that decisions of the Court are arbitrary in the sense that they bear no relation to the prevailing standards of the society. That its decisions are creative seems to me unavoidable, particularly in a developing area of the law. To a court the common denominator of all cases is that they must be decided. The decision that lets a conviction stand may be quite as creative as that which strikes one down. It, too, becomes a precedent, and so shapes the law of the future.

In the common-law process, decided cases become fixed points from which boundaries are drawn and contours filled in. That is the process that has been used from the outset in giving meaning to the due process clause. The flexibility of this method of construing a constitution—a document designed for the ages—has its advantages, particularly in the application of a provision like the due process clause, which is the statement of an ideal for the future rather than a blueprint of the past. But it has its disadvantages as well. The materials with which any court works are the cases that come to it through the chances of litigation. While a broad discretionary jurisdiction gives a degree of control, it does not by any means guarantee that the casees will come to the court in the order best suited to the translation of the ideal into the actual. And ultimately the selection of principles depends heavily upon the character of the cases reaching the court and the order in which they get there. . . .

While the right of one accused of crime to have an attorney came late in England, it has existed in this country from the outset. The question which is alive today is whether or not a defendant who is unable to afford counsel is nonetheless entitled to be represented upon his arraignment and trial.

This question was late in emerging in the Supreme Court of the United States. It came first in 1932 in *Powell* v. *Alabama*,[24] where the Court held that due process required adequate representation by counsel in a state prosecution for a capital offense. But in that opinion the Court expressly refused to consider whether the failure to appoint counsel in criminal cases that did not involve the death penalty also violated due process. With respect to federal cases the Court went the full distance in *Johnson* v. *Zerbst*[25] in 1938, holding under the sixth amendment that in any criminal case a federal court lacks power and authority to deprive an accused of his life or liberty unless he has, or waives, the assistance of counsel. From the holding in *Johnson* v. *Zerbst* and the language used by the Court in subsequent state cases,[26] it was supposed that the same rule would be applied to state prosecutions.

In 1942, however, in *Betts* v. *Brady*,[27] a divided Court refused to apply to state prosecutions what it characterized as a rigid rule requiring that counsel be appointed unless waived, saying:

> [W]hile want of counsel in a particular case may result in a conviction lacking in . . . fundamental fairness, we cannot say that the Amendment embodies an inexorable command that no trial for any offense, or in any court, can be fairly conducted and justice accorded a defendant who is not represented by counsel.[28]

The "fair trial" doctrine of *Betts* v. *Brady* has never commanded the support of all of the members of the Court. Nevertheless, it is today the governing guide, and while the states are required to furnish counsel to an indigent defendant charged with a capital offense, determination as to whether due process requires the appointment of counsel in other cases depends upon the offense and a determination of the defendant's ability, in the light of his age, education, and the like, to defend himself without counsel.

Many of the states were recognizing a right to counsel going beyond the *Betts* v. *Brady* line before that case was decided.[29] Although not every state today offers counsel to the indigent defendant in the serious, but noncapital, criminal case, the trend is unmistakably in that direction. The story of the action taken within many of the states to ensure that every defendant knows that he can have counsel is too long to be told here. Representation has come officially from public defenders, from legal-aid societies, and from individual members of the bar. It is a story to be proud of.

To date the right-to-counsel cases have been presented under the due process clause. Another ground upon which the issue might be presented with different results is suggested both by the technique used in *Betts* v. *Brady* and by the decision in *Griffin* v. *Illinois*.[30] In *Betts* v. *Brady* the Court was confronted with earlier decisions which concededly lent "color to the argument" that every accused must be given an opportunity to be represented by counsel. Writing for the Court, Mr. Justice Roberts pointed out that in each of these earlier cases a state statute had required the appointment of counsel. As a basis of distinction under the due process clause, the reference to state statutes is mysterious. It has meaning, it seems to me, only in terms of equal protection of the law.

Griffin v. *Illinois* was based largely, if not entirely, upon the equal protection clause. Shortly stated, it held that since Illinois permits review of all aspects of a criminal case if, but only if, the defendant is able to put before the reviewing court a full transcript of the trial-court proceedings, it must furnish the same review to those who are unable to pay the court reporter for writing up the transcript.[31] The analogy to the right to counsel is close indeed: if a state allows one who can afford to retain a lawyer to be represented by counsel, and so to obtain a different kind of trial, it must furnish the same opportunity to those who are unable to hire a lawyer. Since indigence is constitutionally an irrelevance, it would seem that a successful argument might be based upon the proposition that the defendant by reason of his poverty is deprived of a right available to those who can afford to exercise it.

The second procedural standard which I shall touch upon relates to the use in evidence of a confession by the defendant. Unlike the question of right to counsel, the problem here relates not to what the state must affirmatively provide but to what its officers must refrain from doing. And the confession problem also differs in that the requirements of due process are here harder to define.

The basic fact is the third degree. Since the issuance of the Wickersham Report[32] in 1931, the third degree has aroused more concern than any other aspect of criminal procedure, and, while sharp differences have arisen over the cure, no one, I think, has ventured to defend the practice. The problem has engaged the attention of the Supreme Court since 1936, when *Brown* v. *Mississippi*[33] was decided.

The confession cases generally follow a rather set pattern. Following the commission of a crime the police take the accused into custody. During the course of his detention he is not permitted access to counsel and he is interrogated about the crime. The period of detention varies in length, but it is almost always longer than the local law allows. The interrogation terminates with his confession. He is then brought before a magistrate and formally charged with the offense. When the confession is offered at the trial the defendant does not usually deny having made it, but he repudiates it. Violence and threats on the part of the interrogating officers are alleged. These allegations are almost always denied. On rare occasions there will be objective evidence that the prisoner suffered injuries while in custody; in such cases there will be conflicting testimony as to how they were incurred. There will also be allegations as to the length and intensity of the interrogation. Unlike the charge of physical abuse, the length and frequency of interrogation is generally not disputed. . . .

Upon this factual situation, with all its unknowns, two partially overlapping legal doctrines are brought to bear. A third which might be thought to have a bearing, the privilege against self incrimination, has not been employed; indeed, in other contexts the Court has indicated that this privilege is not a part of due process.[34]

There is initially the common-law rule by which "involuntary" confessions are excluded from evidence. As generally stated, this rule goes to the trustworthiness of the evidence: while it may be improbable that an innocent man would confess a crime, the improbability rests on the assumption that he was not coerced into doing so.[35] This approach calls for a determination of what the police conduct was and also, except as to some kinds of conduct which are "presumed" to be coercive, for a determination of its actual effect upon the defendant. Its application is thus limited by the extent to which the ultimate facts are unknown or in dispute. But since the emphasis is upon trustworthiness, the logical consequence of this approach requires that the confession be received in evidence even though coerced, if its truthfulness can be established by other evidence. A typical case is that the gun is found where the defendant in his confession said he had hidden it.

The impropriety of admitting the confession has also been thought to rest on a quite different basis. If the defendant, at the pretrial stage, has been subjected to illegal confinement or violence, and if he has a right not to be so treated, then a confession which is the product of the mistreatment might be excluded from use at the trial on the same basis on which evidence obtained by unlawful search is excluded in some jurisdictions.[36] This second theory of exclusion also requires an inquiry into the character of the detention and interrogation and their effect on the prisoner. So far as physical violence is concerned, however, the inquiry would stop with a determination that the confession was in fact the product of the illegal treatment. Other evidence to show its truthfulness would be inadmissible. And when the theory is extended to cover illegally prolonged detention, the question tends to be reduced simply to whether the confession occurred during the detention.

It is this second theory which the Supreme Court, in *McNabb* v. *United States*,[37] announced as applicable to the federal courts. Although at one point it appeared that the *McNabb* rule might also come to be applied to state courts, the Supreme Court has not taken that step.[38] As with the right to counsel, the constitutional restraint that the Court imposes upon the states has been less rigorous than the rule that it applies in federal cases.

The rule that is in effect today with respect to state cases appears to be a blend. For while the Court has on occasion stated flatly that neither the common-law exclusionary rule nor a privilege against pretrial illegality governs its decisions, those decisions seem to contain elements, at least, of each doctrine.[39] Confessions extracted by force or threats of course present no problem. But ordinarily the use of force or threats is denied, and the Court, preferring to decide the case on the undisputed facts, must deal with the more debatable problems of police interrogation and illegally prolonged detention.

The simplicity of the *McNabb* rule and its prophylactic effect on undesirable police practices make it attractive. But it has its problems, too. Judges are trained to look at criminal cases in terms of guilt or innocence. The idea that the decision of the trial court should be evaluated in the light of the entire record is a significant factor. Indeed, the development of that point of view itself represents a major step in the reform of criminal procedure.[40] Probably it was the severity of the common law that moved courts to exalt minor technalities into grounds for reversal. Whatever its cause, the judicial attitude that could reverse a judgment because of a misplaced comma in an indictment only recently succumbed to the prevailing notion that only the error that actually prejudices the defendant will result in reversal. Despite occasional rear-guard skirmishes, the doctrine of harmless error has carried the field.

Even though the procedural requirements with which we are here concerned are by no means upon the same level with the hypertechnicalities of the recent past, and even though those requirements come with the ultimate sanction of a constitutional command, I can testify that it is not always easy to focus upon the procedural requirement and shut out considerations of guilt or innocence. And frequent references in the opinions of some of the Justices of the Supreme Court to the absence of a claim of innocence make it clear that the problem is not just a personal one.[41] The Court, however, has generally stated that a confession improperly admitted requires reversal regardless of other evidence of guilt.[42]

Thus far there has been no disposition on the part of the states to adopt the *McNabb* rule. State courts have been unwilling to disregard evidence of guilt in order to enforce police compliance with statutes requiring prompt arraignment.[43] Whether the constant concern which the Supreme Court has shown will produce a change in the practices of the police or the attitude of state courts cannot yet be stated.

In another area, that of search and seizure, some states have acted to increase the protection afforded even in the face of the Court's express refusal to impose on the states the most effective judicial deterrent. In *Wolf* v. *Colorado*[44] the Court held that while an unreasonable search and seizure violates the due process clause, the states are not required to exclude the evidence so obtained. The Court had held earlier, in *Weeks* v. *United States*,[45] that the contrary rule applied in federal courts. Shortly after the *Wolf* case the Court decided *Rochin* v. *California*.[46] In that case police officers forcibly extracted morphine capsules which the defendant had swallowed in an effort to destroy the evidence. The Court there held that a conviction based on a trial at which the capsules were used in evidence could not stand. In still a third case, *Irvine* v. *California*,[47] the Court upheld a conviction based on testimony obtained by secretly entering the defendant's home and installing a microphone.

The cases are, I think, hard to reconcile with each other and with the confession cases, except so far as physical violence is regarded as a more serious invasion of personal rights than is an illegal trespass or search and seizure. But what is of greater importance is the response among the states to the *Wolf* decision. The Court's earlier decision in the *Weeks* case had induced many states to adopt the exclusionary rule. At the time of the decision in *Wolf*, in 1949, sixteen states were said to have taken that position.[48] Although the decision in the *Wolf* case announced that the state courts were under no constitutional compulsion to follow the exclusionary rule, the states which had adopted that rule seem generally to be adhering to it.[49] And since the *Wolf* case was decided, California and Delaware have adopted the exclusionary rule by judicial decision[50] and North Carolina has done so by statute.[51]

The action of the California court is particularly interesting. Some of the leading cases, such as *Irvine* and *Rochin*, had come from that state. The opinion of the California court makes articulate its sense of frustration at continued and deliberate police violations of constitutional rights to which the court was made a party by admitting the fruits of the illegal action in evidence.[52] Judge Cardozo's expression, "The criminal is to go free because the constable has blundered,"[53] has no bearing upon the kind of deliberate and calculated illegality that had repeatedly confronted the California court. The California decision suggests that a line may be drawn between the casual and perhaps unintentional police violation of constitutional rights and that which is studied and deliberate.

There is another area in which it is at least arguable that the states have responded beyond the requirements actually laid down by the Supreme Court. It has been frequently stated, in opinions of Justices of the Supreme Court and elsewhere, that the decision in *Mooney* v. *Holohan*[54] laid down the requirement that each state must afford some corrective judicial process by which a claim of violation of constitutional right can be tested in the state court.[55] There have been references in the opinions to the "duty" resting upon the states to provide such a remedy.[56] But so far as I am aware, all such statements were made in cases that involved the doctrine that state remedies must be exhausted before there can be resort to federal habeas corpus, and so I venture to doubt that they are to be taken literally.

Nevertheless, most of the states have diligently attempted to provide a remedy. A variety of techniques has been employed by state courts and state legislatures. In state after state the scope of habeas corpus has been expanded so that claims of violation of constitutional rights may be heard,[57] as well as the jurisdictional objections to which habeas corpus was traditionally limited. Many states have proceeded by expanding the scope of the writ of error coram nobis to include constitutional claims.[58] In others, inherent judicial power has been relied upon to sanction a motion to vacate a conviction at any time upon constitutional grounds,[59] while in still others an extraordinary motion for new trial has been permitted long after judgment.[60] Statutory postconviction remedies have been adopted in some states,[61] and the Commission on Uniform Laws has recommended the adoption of a Uniform Post-Conviction Procedure Act.

Not all of the states have made the effort, and not all of those that have commenced the job have completed it.

Because the problems are new and complex, it is difficult at this stage to explain the different degrees of response by the states in these areas of criminal procedure. To some extent, of course, differences of opinion over the social goals involved may be important: the right to have counsel perhaps commands a greater recognition than the right not to be detained illegally by the police. But there is another factor, I think, which is operative here, and that is the ability of a state court to foresee clearly the consequences of the step to be taken and the degree to which the court can exercise a continuing control. In the case of the right to counsel, and in the shaping of a postconviction remedy, the end result can be pretty well known before the first step is taken. To the extent that it is not, such problems as arise will be within the immediate control of the court. The effects of the *McNabb* rule upon police efficiency, on the other hand, are not readily apparent, and its consequences are beyond the control of the court.

With these inconclusive observations, I should like to turn to a consideration of the relative roles of state and federal courts in dealing with these matters. Areas of federalism are always problem areas, and this one is no exception. Here the most acute problem is dissatisfaction with the habeas corpus jurisdiction of the federal courts. That dissatisfaction rests on several grounds. First, there has been a flood of frivolous attacks in the federal courts upon state-court convictions. In the population generally the new leisure that has come from technological advances has caused an outburst of "do it yourself" activity. That activity has spread to the penitentiaries, and there the "fixit" kit is the writ of habeas corpus. Second, there is a widespread feeling that it is unseemly for a single district judge to review the validity of a state-court conviction, especially if it has been approved by the highest court of the state with certiorari denied by the Supreme Court of the United States. And third, it has been urged that the use of federal habeas corpus has interfered unduly with the administration of state criminal law. Both the National Association of Attorneys General and the Conference of Chief Justices have expressed these objections.[62]

The jurisdiction of the United States courts to issue writs of habeas corpus in these cases stems from the Act of 1867.[63] The issuance of such a writ is authorized when a prisoner "is in custody in violation of the Constitution or laws or treaties of the United States."[64] One manifestation of the discontent of state officials took the form of an attack upon the constitutionality of the federal habeas corpus act on the grounds (1) that the proceeding was a suit against a state and so was prohibited by the eleventh amendment, and (2) that the habeas corpus proceeding involved a review of facts tried by a jury by a method unknown to the common law, and so violated the seventh amendment. The judges of the Court of Appeals for the Third Circuit, sitting en banc, unanimously rejected both contentions, and the Supreme Court of the United States denied certiorari.[65] But the attorneys general of forty-one states had joined in the brief that attacked the validity of this act.

In 1952 the Conference of Chief Justices adopted a resolution which stated that "orderly Federal procedure under our dual system of government should require that a final judgment of a State's highest court be subject to review or reversal only by the Supreme Court of the United States."[66] The Conference that year also appointed a committee to consider the habeas corpus problem and report its recommendations. The report of the committee suggested modifications in both state and federal procedure. It stated:

> Evidence and opinion from many responsible sources have convinced the committee that responsibility for the unfortunate conditions prevailing in habeas corpus litigation

rests upon the State as well as upon the
Federal judicial systems and that the evils
presently prevailing can be reduced substantially by action taken at the State level.[67]

The committee made many recommendations for the
improvement of state postconviction procedures. It
also recommended that the power of lower federal
courts to issue writs of habeas corpus be restricted to
those cases in which the prisoner had sought review
of the state-court proceedings in the Supreme Court
of the United States, and in which that Court had
expressly reserved to the prisoner the right to apply
for habeas corpus in a lower federal court.[68] The
Conference of Chief Justices approved the report of
its committee insofar as it recommended improvements in state postconviction remedies. The suggested modification of federal practice, however, did
not satisfy the Conference, which rejected the report
of its committee and reaffirmed its earlier resolution.[69] . . .

It is true that the federal district courts are flooded
with a large volume of worthless applications for
habeas corpus. Out of 4,849 federal-question habeas
corpus cases disposed of in the district courts during
the nine-year period 1946 through 1954, the petitioners were successful in 77, or 1.6 per cent of the
cases.[72] In 1955, 668 cases were disposed of, and the
petitioner was successful in 5, or 0.75 per cent.[73]

It has frequently been asserted that the increase in
the volume of federal habeas corpus cases is due to
a recent expansion of the scope of the writ by the
Supreme Court of the United States. In my opinion
that assertion is misleading, and I should like to say
why I think so. During its long history the writ of
habeas corpus had acquired basic characteristics, the
most important of which was that in the case of
prisoners held in custody pursuant to the judgment
of a court the writ was limited in scope to a consideration of the jurisdiction of the committing court over
the person and the subject matter. Those limitations
had been relaxed as early as 1833, so far as the fed-

eral courts were concerned, by an act which authorized the federal courts to grant the writ in all cases in which prisoners were committed for an act done or omitted to be done in pursuance of a law of the United States or the order of any judge or court thereof.[74] The Act of 1867 provided broadly that the federal courts should "have power to grant writs of habeas corpus in all cases where any person may be restrained of his or her liberty in violation of the constitution, or of any treaty or law of the United States."[75] The limits of federal concern with the civil and criminal law of the states were thus staked at the boundaries of the privileges and immunities, equal protection, and due process clauses, with the precise limits to be fixed as those clauses acquired specific meaning through the process of legislation and adjudication.

Despite the fact that under the Act of 1867 it was unmistakably clear that the scope of federal habeas corpus embraced all matters under the fourteenth amendment, the Supreme Court continued in many cases to speak in the language of jurisdiction, although it acted upon a much broader basis. For example, in *Wo Lee* v. *Hopkins*, the companion case to *Yick Wo* v. *Hopkins*,[76] decided in 1886, a prisoner was discharged from state custody on a federal writ of habeas corpus because the administration of the ordinance under which he had been convicted was discriminatory, and therefore unconstitutional. Of course it cannot be said that the state court lacked jurisdiction in the orthodox sense to determine that question, whether or not it decided correctly. The matter was set straight in 1889, when the Court held that "a party is entitled to a *habeas corpus*, not merely where the court is without jurisdiction of the cause, but where it has no constitutional authority or power to condemn the prisoner . . . ," and continued: "If we have seemed to hold the contrary in any case, it has been from inadvertence."[77] But even after that the Court from time to time lapsed into the language of jurisdiction.[78] . . .

The likelihood of interference with normal state procedure was lessened by the Supreme Court's decision in *Brown* v. *Allen*[84] in 1953. There the Court considered the effect to be given to state-court determinations of fact in subsequent federal habeas corpus cases. For federal courts to regard as conclusive the state court's determination of the facts on which depends a constitutional question would effect a drastic change in our constitutional system. On the other hand, it is unnecessary, and indeed impossible, for federal courts to try the facts de novo in every case. Shortly stated, *Brown* v. *Allen* authorized the federal court to look closely at the state-court determination of the facts and to accept that determination unless "a vital flaw [is] . . . found"[85] in the process of the state court's determination. The flexibility thus afforded had a dramatic effect upon practice in the federal district courts which is measurable quantitatively. The percentage of all habeas corpus cases in which evidence was actually heard was always small. From 1947 through 1952 evidence was heard in 8.5 per cent of the cases. Following *Brown* v. *Allen*, in the year 1954, evidence was heard in 3.3 per cent of the cases, a decline of 61 per cent.[86] . . .

The major problem is in the great number of unfounded petitions that have been filed. That they have depreciated the writ of habeas corpus cannot be doubted. I think that the remedy for this aspect of the problem lies in the establishment of a procedure by which the few meritorious petitions can be separated from the others. Apparently such a screening process cannot take place outside the judicial system, for a practice which contemplated examination of legal documents by a nonjudicial state official has been held invalid.[88] The initial determination could, however, be made by the district judge, or by a master or referee. To avoid the objection that determinations made by the highest state courts are being reviewed by a single federal judge, the statute could provide that further proceedings beyond the initial screening should take place before a statutory three-judge court which could hear evidence in the minimal number of cases in which it is appropriate to do so. Expense to the states could be curtailed by providing that the state need not appear except as directed by the court. This suggestion is not original. It was proposed in substance by the Conference of Senior Circuit Judges in 1943 and was temporarily set aside in 1947 to avoid delay in the enactment of the new Judicial Code.[89] It has far greater merit, it seems to me, than has the pending proposal.

It has been said of the habeas corpus cases that one who searches for a needle in a haystack is likely to conclude that the needle is not worth the effort.[90] That emphasis distorts the picture. Even with the narrowest focus it is not a needle we are looking for in these stacks of paper, but the rights of a human being. And if the perspective is broadened, even the significance of that single human being diminishes, and we begin to catch a glimpse of the full picture. The aim which justifies the existence of habeas corpus is not fundamentally different from that which informs our criminal law in general, that it is better that a guilty man go free than that an innocent one be punished. To the extent that the small number of meritorious petitions shows that the standards of due process are being honored in criminal trials we should be gratified; but the continuing availability of the federal remedy is in large part responsible for that result. What is involved, however, is not just the enforcement of defined standards. It is also the creative process of writing specific content into the highest of our ideals. So viewed, the burdensome test of sifting the meritorious from the worthless appears less futile, and there is less room for the emotions of federalism.

Considerations of federalism of course remain important. But in the world today they must be measured against the competing demands arising out of the relation of the United States to the rest of the world. The quality of a nation's civilization can be largely measured by the methods it uses in the enforcement of its criminal law. That measurement is not taken merely in retrospect by social historians of the future. It is taken from day to day by the peoples of the world, and to them the criminal procedure sanctioned by any of our states is the procedure sanctioned by the United States.

---

† The original version of this article was delivered in April 1956 as the Oliver Wendell Holmes Lecture at the Harvard Law School.

* Justice, Supreme Court of Illinois. Ph.B., Chicago, 1926, J.D., 1928.

The author is indebted to Mr. Roland D. Whitman of the Chicago Bar for his assistance.

1 BEANEY, THE RIGHT TO COUNSEL IN AMERICAN COURTS 9, 12 (1955).

2 See *Johnson* v. *Zerbst*, 304 U.S. 458 (1938).

3 BEANEY, *op. cit. supra* note 1, at 94.

4 STEPHEN, COMMENTARIES ON THE LAWS OF ENGLAND 526 (18th ed. 1925).

5 *Ibid.*

6 2 WIGMORE, EVIDENCE § 579 (3d ed. 1940).

7 *Ibid.*

8 See O'Halloran, *Development of the Right of Appeal in England in Criminal Cases*, 27 CAN. B. REV. 153 (1949).

9 The procedures of review were first instituted by the Act of March 3, 1879, c. 176, 20 STAT. 354, and the Act of March 3, 1891, c. 517, §§ 5, 6, 26 STAT. 827. See *United States* v. *Sanges*, 144 U.S. 310, 319-22 (1892).

10 Act of Sept. 24, 1789, c. 20, § 25, 1 STAT. 85; see *Twitchell* v. *Commonwealth*, 74 U.S. (7 Wall.) 321 (1868).

11 Act of April 9, 1866, c. 31, §§ 2, 3, 14 STAT. 27; Act of May 31, 1870, c. 114, §§ 17, 18, 16 STAT. 144; Act of April 20, 1871, c. 22, §§ 1, 2, 17 STAT. 13. The substance of these acts now appears in 18 U.S.C. §§ 241, 242 (1952) and REV. STAT. §§ 1979, 1980 (1875), 42 U.S.C. §§ 1983, 1985 (1952).

12 Act of April 9, 1866, c. 31, § 3, 14 STAT. 27; Act of May 11, 1866, c. 80, § 3, 14 STAT. 46; Act of May 31, 1870, c. 114, § 18, 16 STAT. 144. The substance of these acts now appears in 28 U.S.C. § 1443 (1952).

13 Act of Feb. 5, 1867, c. 28, § 1, 14 STAT. 385 (now 28 U.S.C. § 2241(c)(3) (1952)).

14 See *Strauder* v. *West Virginia*, 100 U.S. 303 (1879); *Virginia* v. *Rives*, 100 U.S. 313 (1879); *Ex parte* Virginia 100

U.S. 339 (1879); *Reece* v. *Georgia*, 350 U.S. 85 (1955); *Michel* v. *Louisiana*, 350 U.S. 91 (1955).

15 See, *e.g.*, *Hurtado* v. *California*, 110 U.S. 516 (1884); *Hayes* v. *Missouri*, 120 U.S. 68 (1887); *Leeper* v. *Texas*, 139 U.S. 462 (1891); *Davis* v. *Texas*, 139 U.S. 651 (1891); *Hallinger* v. *Davis*, 146 U.S. 314 (1892); *Hodgson* v. *Vermont*, 168 U.S. 262 (1897); *Brown* v. *New Jersey*, 175 U.S. 172 (1899); *Bolln* v. *Nebraska*, 176 U.S. 83 (1900); *Howard* v. *Fleming*, 191 U.S. 126 (1903).

16 *Frank* v. *Mangum*, 237 U.S. 309 (1915).

17 *Powell* v. *Alabama*, 287 U.S. 45 (1932).

18 *Mooney* v. *Holohan*, 294 U.S. 103 (1935).

19 *Brown* v. *Mississippi*, 297 U.S. 278 (1936).

20 See Slaughter-House Cases, 83 U.S. (16 Wall.) 36 (1873); *Twining* v. *New Jersey*, 211 U.S. 78 (1908); *Adamson* v. *California*, 332 U.S. 46 (1947).

21 See *Griffin* v. *Illinois*, 351 U.S. 12 (1956).

22 *Hurtado* v. *California*, 110 U.S. 516 (1884); *Twining* v. *New Jersey*, 211 U.S. 78 (1908); *Palko* v. *Connecticut*, 302 U.S. 319 (1937); *Adamson* v. *California*, 332 U.S. 46 (1947).

24 287 U.S. 45 (1932).

25 304 U.S. 458 (1938).

26 *Smith* v. *O'Grady*, 312 U.S. 329 (1941); *Avery* v. *Alabama*, 308 U.S. 444, 446-47 (1940) (dictum).

27 316 U.S. 455 (1942).

28 *Id.* at 473.

29 See BEANEY, *op. cit. supra* note 1, c. 4.

30 351 U.S. 12 (1956).

31 *Griffin* v. *Illinois* is important also because of the concurring opinion of Justice Frankfurter, *id.* at 20, which deals frankly with the problem of whether the Court's judgment should have retroactive effect. That problem is inherent in the application of due process as well as equal protection, unless those clauses are to become static. Although the question has not been explicitly faced in judicial opinions, there can be little doubt that the possibility of wholesale jail deliveries has retarded the development of procedural due process in criminal cases. . . .

32 4 NATIONAL COMMISSION ON LAW OBSERVANCE AND ENFORCEMENT, REPORTS (1931).

33 297 U.S. 278 (1936).

34 See *Adamson* v. *California*, 332 U.S. 46 (1947); *Twining* v. *New Jersey*, 211 U.S. 78 (1908). *But cf. Regan* v. *New York*, 349 U.S. 58 (1955).

35 See 3 WIGMORE, EVIDENCE §§ 822-26 (3d ed. 1940).

[36] See McCormick, *The Scope of Privilege in the Law of Evidence*, 16 TEXAS L. REV. 447, 450-57 (1938).

[37] 318 U.S. 332 (1943).

[38] See *Gallegos* v. *Nebraska*, 342 U.S. 55 (1951); *Watts* v. *Indiana*, 338 U.S. 49 (1949).

[39] See *Stroble* v. *California*, 343 U.S. 181 (1952); *Gallegos* v. *Nebraska, supra* note 38; *Malinski* v. *New York*, 324 U.S. 401 (1945); *Lisenba* v. *California*, 314 U.S. 219 (1941).

[40] See 1 WIGMORE, EVIDENCE § 21 (3d ed. 1940).

[41] See *Stein* v. *New York*, 346 U.S. 156, 188-94 (1953); *Gallegos v. Nebraska*, 342 U.S. 55, 68 (1951); *id.* at 71 (concurring opinion); *Watts* v. *Indiana*, 338 U.S. 49, 60 (1949) (concurring opinion); *Palmer* v. *Ashe*, 342 U.S. 134, 142 (1951) (dissenting opinion); *Haley* v. *Ohio*, 332 U.S. 596, 609 (1948) (dissenting opinion).

[42] *Malinski* v. *New York*, 324 U.S. 401 (1945); *Brown* v. *Allen*, 344 U.S. 443, 475 (1953) (dictum); *Stroble* v. *California*, 343 U.S. 181, 190 (1952) (dictum); *Gallegos* v. *Nebraska, supra* note 41, at 63 (dictum); *Lyons* v. *Oklahoma*, 322 U.S. 596, 597 n.1 (1944) (dictum). *But cf. Stein* v. *New York, supra* note 41.

[43] INBAU & REID, LIE DETECTION AND CRIMINAL INTERROGATION 210 (3d ed. 1953).

[44] 338 U.S. 25 (1949).

[45] 232 U.S. 383 (1914).

[46] 342 U.S. 165 (1952).

[47] 347 U.S. 128 (1954).

[48] *Wolf* v. *Colorado*, 338 U.S. 25, 29, 33-39 (1949).

[49] Iowa abandoned the rule before *Wolf. State* v. *Rowley*, 197 Iowa 977, 195 N.W. 881 (1923). States which have adhered to the exclusionary rule since the *Wolf* case are: Florida (*Byrd* v. *State*, 80 So. 2d 694 (Fla. 1955)); Idaho (*State* v. *Spencer*, 74 Idaho 173, 258 P.2d 1147 (1953) (by implication)); Illinois (*Chicago* v. *Lord*, 7 Ill. 2d 379, 130 N.E.2d 504 (1955)); Indiana (*Idol* v. *State*, 233 Ind. 307, 119 N.E. 2d 428 (1954)); Kentucky (*Ross* v. *Commonwealth*, 275 S.W. 2d 424 (Ky. 1955)); Michigan (*People* v. *Taylor*, 341 Mich. 570, 67 N.W.2d 698 (1954) (by implication)); Mississippi (*Thompson* v. *State*, 213 Miss. 325, 56 So. 2d 808 (1952)); Missouri (*State* v. *Clark*, 259 S.W.2d 813 (Mo. 1953)); Oklahoma (*Leason* v. *State*, 286 P.2d 288 (Okla. Crim. 1955)); Tennessee (*Reinhart* v. *State*, 193 Tenn. 15, 241 S.W.2d 854 (1951) (by implication)); Washington (*State* v. *Robbins*, 37 Wash. 2d 431, 432, 224 P.2d 345, 346 (1950) (dictum)); Wisconsin (*Potman* v. *State*, 259 Wis. 234, 242-43, 47 N.W. 2d 884, 888 (1951) (dictum)).

50 *People* v. *Cahan*, 44 Cal. 2d 434, 282 P.2d 905 (1955); *Rickards* v. *State*, 45 Del. (6 Terry) 573, 77 A.2d 199 (1950).

51 N.C. GEN. STAT. § 15-27 (1953).

52 See *People* v. *Cahan*, 44 Cal. 2d 434, 445, 282 P.2d 905; 911-12 (1955).

53 *People* v. *Defore*, 242 N.Y. 13, 21, 150 N.E. 585, 587 (1926).

54 294 U.S. 103 (1935).

55 *E.g.*, *Jennings* v. *Illinois*, 342 U.S. 104, 116 (1951) (dissenting opinion). See also SPECIAL COMMITTEE ON HABEAS CORPUS, REPORT TO THE CONFERENCE OF CHIEF JUSTICES, app. at 12 (Council of State Governments 1953), quoting from a memorandum of the Department of Justice of California:

> If any proposition can be stated dogmatically in this field it is this: the state courts must provide post-conviction corrective process which is at least as broad as the requirements which will be enforced by the federal courts in habeas corpus through the due process clause of the 14th amendment. A state can call this remedy whatever it wants, but it must provide some corrective process. Cf. *Mooney* v. *Holohan* (1935) 294 U.S. 103.

56 *E.g.*, *Jennings* v. *Illinois*, *supra* note 55, at 110; *Young* v. *Ragen*, 337 U.S. 235, 239 (1949).

57 See, *e.g.*, *People* v. *Adamson*, 34 Cal. 2d 320, 210 P.2d 13 (1949); *Sewell* v. *Lainson*, 244 Iowa 555, 57 N.W.2d 556 (1953); *Huffman* v. *Alexander*, 197 Ore. 283, 253 P.2d 289 (1953).

58 See *State ex rel. McManamon* v. *Blackford Circuit Court*, 229 Ind. 3, 95 N.E.2d. 556 (1950); *Bojinoff* v. *People*, 299 N.Y. 145, 85 N.E.2d 909 (1949). See also FRANK, CORAM NOBIS ¶ 2.02 (1953).

59 *Curan* v. *Woolley*, 48 Del. (9 Terry) 382, 104 A.2d 771 (1954); *State* v. *Magrum*, 76 N.D. 527, 38 N.W.2d 358 (1949).

60 *Fields* v. *Balkcom*, 211 Ga. 797, 89 S.E.2d 189 (1955); *People* v. *Henderson*, 343 Mich. 465, 72 N.W.2d 177 (1955).

61 ILL. REV. STAT. c. 38, §§ 826-32 (1955); N.C. GEN. STAT. §§ 15-217 to -222 (1953).

62 NATIONAL ASSOCIATION OF ATTORNEYS GENERAL, CONFERENCE PROCEEDINGS 170 (1954); Conference of Chief Justices Resolution on Habeas Corpus (Council of State Governments 1952).

63 Act. of Feb. 5, 1867, c. 28, § 1, 14 STAT. 385.

64 28 U.S.C. § 2241(c)(3) (1952).

65 *United States ex rel. Elliott* v. *Hendricks*, 213 F.2d 922 (3d Cir.), *cert. denied*, 348 U.S. 851 (1954).

⁶⁶ Conference of Chief Justices, Resolution on Habeas Corpus (Council of State Governments 1952).

⁶⁷ SPECIAL COMMITTEE ON HABEAS CORPUS, CONFERENCE OF CHIEF JUSTICES, REPORT 1 (Council of State Governments 1953).

⁶⁸ *Id.* at 3.

⁶⁹ See SPECIAL COMMITTEE ON HABEAS CORPUS, CONFERENCE OF CHIEF JUSTICES, REPORT 5-6 (Council of State Governments 1954).

⁷² *Hearings, supra* note 70, at 25.

⁷³ Letter from Henry P. Chandler, Director, Administrative Office of the United States Courts, to the author, April 23, 1956.

⁷⁴ Act of March 2, 1833, c. 57, § 7, 4 STAT. 634 (now 28 U.S.C. § 2241(c)(2) (1952)).

⁷⁵ Act. of Feb. 5, 1867, c. 28, § 1, 14 STAT. 385 (now 28 U.S.C. § 2241(c)(3) (1952)).

⁷⁶ 118 U.S. 356 (1886).

⁷⁷ Hans Nielsen, 131 U.S. 176, 184 (1889).

⁷⁸ *E.g.*, Matter of Moran, 203 U.S. 96 (1906); *Felts* v. *Murphy*, 201 U.S. 123 (1906).

⁸⁴ 344 U.S. 443 (1953).

⁸⁵ *Id.* at 506 (separate opinion of Frankfurter, J.).

⁸⁶ *Hearings, supra* note 70, at 24.

⁸⁸ *Ex parte* Hull, 312 U.S. 546 (1941).

⁸⁹ JUDICIAL CONFERENCE OF THE SENIOR CIRCUIT JUDGES, REPORT 22-24 (1943); JUDICIAL CONFERENCE OF THE SENIOR CIRCUIT JUDGES, REPORT 17, 18 (1947).

⁹⁰ Jackson, J., concurring in *Brown* v. *Allen*, 344 U.S. 443, 537 (1953).

FEDERAL CRIMINAL PROCEDURE AND
THE RIGHT OF CONFRONTATION

A matter of considerable importance in criminal, civil, and even administrative proceedings is the extent to which the right of confrontation, including opportunity for cross-examination, is guaranteed the accused in a criminal trial, the defendant in a civil action, the seeker of a privilege, or the government employee charged with being a security risk in an administrative hearing. Many administrative agencies have decided that considerations of national security forbid the disclosure of certain materials and even the identity of witnesses crucial to the establishment of the Government's position. This practice of nondisclosure has been upheld in a number of instances, particularly in connection with denial of, or discharge from, government employment. *E.g., Bailey* v. *Richardson,* 182 F. 2d 46 (D.C. Cir. 1950), affirmed by an equally divided Court, 341 U.S. 918 (1951). But compare *Parker* v. *Lester,* 227 F.2d 708 (9th Cir. 1955), where some confrontation was required in connection with the attempted discharge of merchant seamen under the Port Security Program; but how much confrontation was left undefined. See also *Boudin* v. *Dulles,* 235 F.2d 532 (D.C. Cir. 1956), where the court ordered the Secretary of State to state whether the findings on which he based the denial of a passport were based on evidence openly produced or in whole or in material part on secret information not disclosed to the applicant. A passport was issued by the Department of State, thus avoiding the necessity of passing squarely on the issue.

In criminal proceedings the necessity of confrontation is more apparent. Thus, in *Jencks* v. *United States,* 353 U.S. 657, 672 (1957), the Court held that in a federal criminal trial the defendant is entitled to demand that the Government produce "relevant statements or reports in its possession of government witnesses touching the subject matter of their testimony at the trial." Mr. Justice Clark sharply attacked the holding because it might allow the defendants "a Roman holiday for rummaging through confidential information as well as vital national secrets." *Id.* at 681-82. Congress acted promptly to clarify the misunderstandings that arose as to the nature of the decision, adding a new section 3500 to title 18 of the United States Code. The new section provides in substance that in any criminal prosecutions brought by the United States, after a government witness has testified on direct examination, the defendant shall be entitled to see any statement of the witness in the possession of the United States, to the extent relevant. If any portion is claimed by the United States to be irrelevant to the witness' testimony, the judge shall decide in camera, excising those portions which do not so relate, and making the remainder available to the defendant.

FREEDOM OF ENTERPRISE

In a Constitution which Chief Justice Marshall described as "intended to endure for ages to come," it should not be surprising to observe a flexible growth of the Constitution roughly paralleling the development of new forms and techniques of doing business. Perhaps the principal genius of the American economy has been its adaptability to new methods in science and new organizational structures to accommodate the changing needs of the business community. Even as these business forms to some extent found it necessary to conform to the strict letter of the Constitution where there was a fixed requirement or prohibition, probably more often the Constitution proved itself sufficiently fluid in concept so that it seldom hindered, and sometimes aided, the corporate form of doing business.

In a series of critical tests of the viability of the corporate form of business perhaps the most important was the first major encounter. In *Bank of Augusta* v. *Earle*, 38 U.S. (13 Pet.) 519 (1839), the ultimate issue was whether a corporation of one state could engage in business in another state. On one extreme it was argued by those interested in the growth of business enterprise that a corporation, like a citizen, could go wherever it wished to do business, without effective control by any state. Extremists on the other side insisted that a corporation should have no power outside the state of its creation. Happily for the development of business the latter position was rejected; and fortunately for the autonomy of the states, the former arguments were refused. Instead the Court took an essentially middle position, recognizing the power of the corporation to do business outside its home state, but subject to conditions of entry which might be imposed by foreign states where the corporation sought to do business. More recent decisions have added a further gloss to Chief Justice Taney's opinion, holding that the conditions upon which a foreign corporation is permitted to do business may not be "unreasonable," lest they be declared unconstitutional barriers to the doing of interstate business.

In the pre-Civil War period the most important clause in the Constitution for the protection of corporations, domestic as well as foreign, from hostile legislation by the states was the so-called contract clause, found in section 10 of article I.

"No State shall . . . pass any . . . Law impairing the Obligation of Contracts. . . ."

Although the clause had been designed primarily to prevent the state legislatures from relieving debtors of their obligations, the Court under Chief Justice Marshall gave it a much expanded meaning. In *Fletcher* v. *Peck*, 10 U.S. (6 Cr.) 87 (1810) the doctrine was extended to give protection to public grants of land involved in the infamous Yazoo Land Fraud. In *New Jersey* v. *Wilson*, 11 U.S. (7 Cr.) 164 (1812), corporate exemptions from taxation were brought within the clause. And in *Dartmouth College* v. *Woodward*, 17 U.S. (4 Wheat.) 518 (1819) charters to private corporations were assured substantial immunity from subsequent legislative reversals. Interpretation of the clause did not further expand its meaning; indeed its meaning was cut back somewhat by implied limitations later "discovered" by the Court. For example, the Court has since held that a state can not contract away its police power, that is, its power over the health, safety, and welfare of its citizens. *Stone* v. *Mississippi*, 101 U.S. 814 (1880). Moreover, by strict construction of legislative grants it has been said that "nothing passes by implication in public grants." *Charles River Bridge Co.* v. *Warren Bridge Co.*, 36 U.S. (11 Pet.) 420, 545-54 (1837). Even as to private contracts, where the clause has retained approximately its original interpretation, the Court has allowed a state, during the depression of the thirties, to extend the period for payment of mortgage obligations. *Home Building & Loan Ass'n* v. *Blaisdell*, 290 U.S. 398 (1934).

After the adoption of the fourteenth amendment in 1868, business enterprise quickly discovered in that amendment, particularly in the due process clause, a most important weapon. It was early held that "Corporations are persons within the meaning of the Fourteenth Amendment to the Constitution of the United States." *Santa Clara County* v. *Southern Pacific R.R.*, 118 U.S. 394 (1886). Thereafter, it was but a short step, under the predominantly *laissez faire* philosophy of the Court late in the nineteenth and early in the twentieth centuries, to a widespread judicial invalidation of legislation thought to be restrictive of free enterprise, whether in relation to individuals or corporations. Perhaps the most celebrated of these cases was *Lochner* v. *New York*, 198 U.S. 45 (1905), in which the Court held invalid as a deprivation of liberty without due process a New York statute limiting employment in bakeries to a maximum of sixty hours a week and ten hours a day. There were occasional inroads upon this severity of judgment, as in

Muller v. *Oregon*, 208 U.S. 412 (1908), where Louis Brandeis (later Mr. Justice) succeeded in persuading the Court to uphold an Oregon statute which forbade the employment of women in industry for more than ten hours in any one day. But it was not until 1937 that there was a real change of philosophy on the Court; thereafter the states have been essentially free to experiment with social and economic legislation bearing any reasonable relationship to the evil sought to be remedied. The turning point came in *Nebbia* v. *New York*, 291 U.S. 502 (1934), upholding a legislative program regulating milk production and pricing.

The First Amendment Freedoms

(The following excerpts are taken from pages 187-203 of *The Constitution and What It Means Today*, by Edward S. Corwin, 11th edition, 1954, Princeton University Press.)

AMENDMENT I

Congress shall make no law respecting an establishment of religion, or prohibiting the free exercise thereof; or abridging the freedom of speech or of the press; or the right of the people peaceably to assemble, and to petition the government for a redress of grievances.

In the case of *Gitlow* v. *New York*, decided in 1925,[1] the Court, while affirming a conviction for violation of a State statute prohibiting the advocacy of criminal anarchy, declared: "For present purposes we may and do assume that freedom of speech and of the press—which are protected by the First Amendment from abridgment by Congress—are among the fundamental personal rights and 'liberties' protected by the due process clause of the Fourteenth Amendment from impairment by the States."[2] This dictum became, two years later, accepted doctrine when the Court invalidated a State law on the ground that it abridged freedom of speech contrary to the due process clause of Amendment XIV.[3] Subsequent decisions have brought the other rights safeguarded by the First Amendment, freedom of religion,[4] freedom of the press,[5] and the right of peaceable assembly,[6] within the protection of the Fourteenth. In consequence of this development, cases dealing with the safeguarding of these rights against infringement by the States are at one or two points included in the ensuing discussion of the First Amendment, and especially those arising under the establishment of religion clause.

"An establishment of religion": Two theories regarding the meaning and intention of this clause have confronted each other in recent decisions of the Court. According to one, what the clause bans is the *preferential* treatment of any particular religion or sect by government in the United States. This theory has the support of Story, except for the fact that he regarded Congress as still free to prefer the Christian religion over other religions.[7] It is also supported by Cooley in his *Principles of Constitutional Law*, where it is said that the clause forbids "the setting up or recognition of a state church, or at least the conferring upon one church of special favors and advantages which are denied to others."[8] This conception of the clause is, moreover, foreshadowed in the Northwest Ordinance of 1787, the third article of which reads: "Religion, morality, and knowledge being necessary to good government, and the happiness of mankind, schools and the means of education shall forever be encouraged."[9] In short, religion as such is not excluded from the legitimate concerns of government, but quite the contrary.

The other theory was first voiced by Jefferson in a letter which he wrote a group of Baptists in Danbury, Connecticut in 1802. Here it is asserted that it was the purpose of the First Amendment to build "a wall of separation between Church and State."[10] Seventy-seven years later Chief Justice Waite, in speaking for the unanimous Court in the first Mormon Church case, in which the right of Congress to forbid polygamy in the territories was sustained, characterized this statement by Jefferson as "almost an authoritative declaration of the scope and effect of the amendment."[11]

In the first of a series of recent cases, a sharply divided Court, speaking by Justice Black, sustained, in 1947, the right of local authorities in New Jersey to provide free transportation for children attending parochial schools,[12] but accompanied its holding with these warning words, which appear to have had, at that time, the approval of most of the Justices: "The 'establishment of religion' clause of the First Amendment means at least this: Neither a state nor the Federal Government can set up a church. Neither can pass laws which aid one religion, aid all religions, or prefer one religion over another. Neither can force nor influence a person to go to or to remain away from church against his will or force him to profess a belief or disbelief in any religion. No person can be punished for entertaining or professing religious beliefs or disbeliefs, for church attendance or non-attendance. No tax in any amount, large or small, can be levied to support any religious activities or institutions, whatever they may be called, or whatever form they may adopt to teach or practice religion. Neither a state nor the Federal Government can, openly or secretly, participate in the affairs of any religious organizations or groups and *vice versa*."[13] And a year later a nearly unanimous Court overturned on the above grounds a "released time" arrangement under which the Champaign, Illinois, Board of Education agreed that religious instruction should be given in the local schools to pupils whose parents signed "request cards." By this plan the classes were to be conducted during regular school hours in the school building by outside teachers furnished by a religious council representing the various faiths, subject to the approval or supervision of the superintendent of schools. Attendance records were kept and reported to the school authorities in the same way as for other classes; and pupils not attending the religious-instruction classes were required to continue their regular secular studies.[14] Said Justice Black, speaking for the Court: "Here not only are the State's tax-supported public school buildings used for the dissemination of religious doctrines. The State also affords sectarian groups an invaluable aid in that it helps to provide pupils for their religious classes through use of the State's compulsory public school machinery. This is not separation of Church and State."[15]

Justice Frankfurter presented a supplementary, affirming opinion for himself and three other Justices, the purport of which was that public-supported education must be kept secular.[16] In a dissenting opinion, Justice Reed pointed out that "the Congress of the United States has a chaplain for each House who daily invokes divine blessings and guidance for the proceedings. The armed forces have commissioned chaplains from early days. They conduct the public services in accordance with the liturgical requirements of their respective faiths, ashore and afloat, employing for the purpose property belonging to the United States and dedicated to the services of religion. Under the Servicemen's Readjustment Act of 1944, eligible veterans may receive training at government expense for the ministry in denominational schools. The schools of the District of Columbia have opening exercises which 'include a reading from the Bible without note or comment, and the Lord's Prayer.' "[17]

Justice Reed's views were not without effect. In 1952 the Court, six Justices to three, sustained a New York City "released time" program under which religious instruction must take place off the school grounds and numerous other features of the Champaign model are avoided.[18] Speaking for the majority, Justice Douglas said: "We are a religious people whose institutions presuppose a Supreme Being. We guarantee the freedom to worship as one chooses. We make room for as wide a variety of beliefs and creeds as the spiritual needs of a man deem necessary. We sponsor an attitude on the part of government that shows no partiality to any one group and that lets each flourish according to the zeal of its adherents and the appeal of its dogma. When the state encourages religious instruction or cooperates with religious authorities by adjusting the schedule of public events to sectarian needs, it follows the best of our traditions. For it then respects the religious nature of our people and accommodates the public service to their spiritual needs. To hold that it may not would be to find in the Constitution a requirement that the government show a callous indifference to religious groups. That would be preferring those who believe in no religion over those who do believe. We find no constitutional requirement which makes it necessary for government to be hostile to religion and to throw its weight against efforts to widen the effective scope of religious influence."[19]

In 1899 the Court held that an agreement between the District of Columbia and the directors of a hospital chartered by Congress for erection of a building and treatment of poor patients at the expense of the District was valid despite the fact that the members of the corporation belonged to a monastic order or sisterhood of a particular church.[20] It has also sustained a contract made at the request of Indians to whom money was due as a matter of right, under a treaty, for the payment of such money by the Commissioner of Indian Affairs for the support of Indian Catholic schools.[21] In 1930 the use of public funds to furnish nonsectarian textbooks to pupils in parochial schools of Louisiana was sustained,[22] and in 1947, as we have seen, the use of public funds for the transportation of pupils attending such schools in New Jersey.[23] In the former case the Court cited the State's interest in secular education even when conducted in religious schools, in the latter its concern for the safety of school children on the highways; and

the National School Lunch Act,[24] which aids all
school children attending tax-exempt schools, can be
similarly justified. The most notable financial conces-
sion to religion, however, is not to be explained in
this way—the universal practice of exempting religious property from taxation. This unquestionably
traces back to the idea expressed in the Northwest
Ordinance that government has an interest in religion
as such.

"Free exercise thereof": The religious freedom here
envisaged has two aspects. It "forestalls compulsion
by law of the acceptance of any creed or the practice
of any form of worship," and conversely it "safeguards
the free exercise of the chosen form of religion."[25]
But "the free exercise thereof" does not embrace actions which are "in violation of social duties or subversive of good order"; hence it was within Congress's
power to prohibit polygamy in the territories.[26] So it
was held in 1878, and sixty-two years later the Court
added these words of qualification to a decision setting aside a State enactment as violative of religious
freedom: "Nothing we have said is intended even re-
motely to imply that, under the cloak of religion, persons may, with impunity, commit frauds upon the
public."[27] Yet four years later, when the promoters
of a religious sect, whose founder had at different
times identified himself as Saint Germain, Jesus,
George Washington, and Godfre Ray King, were convicted of using the mails to defraud by obtaining
money on the strength of having supernaturally healed
hundreds of persons, they found the Court in a soft-
ened frame of mind. Although the trial judge, carefully discriminating between the question of the truth
of defendants' pretensions and that of their good faith
in advancing them, had charged the jury that it could
pass on the latter but not the former, this caution did
not avail with the Court, which contrived on another
ground ultimately to upset the verdict of "guilty."
The late Chief Justice Stone, speaking for himself and
Justices Roberts and Frankfurter, dissented: "I cannot say that freedom of thought and worship includes

freedom to procure money by making knowingly false statements about one's religious experiences"—which sounds uncommonly like common sense.[28]

"Freedom of speech or of the press": According to Blackstone, who was the oracle of the common law when the First Amendment was framed, "liberty of the press consists in laying no *previous* restraints upon publications, and not in freedom from censure for criminal matter when published. Every freeman," he asserted, "has an undoubted right to lay what sentiments he pleases before the public; to forbid this is to destroy the freedom of the press; but if he publishes what is improper, mischievous, and illegal, he must take the consequences of his own temerity. . . . To punish (as the law does at present) any dangerous or offensive writings, which, when published, shall on a fair and impartial trial be adjudged of a pernicious tendency, is necessary for the preservation of peace and good order, of government and religion, the only solid foundations of civil liberty."[29] Also, as the law stood at that time, the question whether a publication or oral utterance was of "a pernicious tendency" was, in a criminal trial, a question not for the jury but for the judge; nor was the truth of the utterance a defense.

While it was originally no intention of the authors of Amendment I to revise the common law, as set forth by Blackstone, on the subject of freedom of the press,[30] there was one feature of it which early ran afoul of the facts of life in America. This was the common law of "seditious libel," which operated to put persons in authority beyond the reach of public criticism. The first step was taken in the famous, or infamous, Sedition Act of 1798, which admitted the defense of truth in prosecutions brought under it, and submitted the general issue of defendant's guilt to the jury.[31] But the substantive doctrine of "seditious libel" the Act of 1798 still retained, a circumstance which put several critics of President Adams in jail, and thereby considerably aided Jefferson's election as President in 1800. Once in office, nevertheless, Jefferson himself appealed to the discredited principle against partisan critics. Writing his friend Governor McKean of Pennsylvania in 1803 anent such critics, Jefferson said: "The federalists having failed in destroying freedom of the press by their gag-law, seem to have attacked it in an opposite direction; that is by pushing its licentiousness and its lying to such a degree of prostitution as to deprive it of all credit. . . . This is a dangerous state of things, and the press ought to be restored to its credibility if possible. The restraints provided by the laws of the States are sufficient for this, if applied. And I have, therefore, long thought that a few prosecutions of the most prominent offenders would have a wholesome effect in restoring the integrity of the presses. Not a general prosecution, for that would look like persecution; but a selected one."[32]

The sober truth is that it was that archenemy of Jefferson and of democracy, Alexander Hamilton, who made the greatest single contribution toward rescuing this particular freedom as a political weapon from the coils and toils of the common law, and that in connection with one of Jefferson's "selected prosecutions." The reference is to Hamilton's many-times-quoted formula in the Croswell case in 1804: "The liberty of the press is the right to publish with impunity, truth, with good motives, for justifiable ends though reflecting on government, magistracy, or individuals."[33] Equipped with this brocard, which is today embodied in twenty-four State constitutions, our State courts working in co-operation with juries, whose attitude usually reflected the robustiousness of American political discussion before the Civil War, gradually wrote into the common law of the States the principle of "qualified privilege," which is a notification to plaintiffs in libel suits that if they are unlucky enough to be office holders or office seekers, they must be prepared to shoulder the almost impossible burden of showing defendant's "special malice."[34]

In 1907 the Court, speaking by Justice Holmes, rejected the contention that the Fourteenth Amendment rendered applicable against the States "a prohibition similar to that in the First," and at the same time endorsed Blackstone, in words drawn from an early Massachusetts case: "The preliminary freedom[i.e., from censorship] extends as well to the false as to the true; the subsequent punishment may extend to the true as to the false."[35] Even as late as 1922 Justice Pitney, speaking for the Court, said: "Neither the Fourteenth Amendment nor any other provision of the Constitution of the United States imposes upon the States any restriction about 'freedom of speech' or the 'liberty of silence.' . . ."[36] *Gitlow* v. *New York,* in which this position was abandoned, came three years later.

And meantime the so-called "clear and present danger doctrine" had made its appearance. This formula lays down the requirement that before an utterance can be penalized by government it must, ordinarily, have occurred "in such circumstances or have been of such a nature as to create a clear and present danger" that it would bring about "substantive evils" within the power of government to prevent.[37] The question whether these conditions exist is one of law for the courts, and ultimately for the Supreme Court, in enforcement of the First and/or the Fourteenth Amendment;[38] and in exercise of its power of review in these premises the Court is entitled to review broadly findings of facts of lower courts, whether State or federal.[39]

The formula emerged in the course of a decision in 1919, holding that the circulation of certain documents constituted an "attempt," in the sense of the Espionage Act of 1917, to cause insubordination in the armed forces and to obstruct their recruitment.[40] Said Justice Holmes, speaking for the Court: "We admit that in many places and in ordinary times the defendants in saying all that was said in the circular would have been within their constitutional rights. But the character of every act depends upon the circumstances in which it is done. . . . The most stringent protection of free speech would not protect a man in falsely shouting fire in a theatre and causing a panic. It does not even protect a man from an injunction against uttering words that have all the effect of force. . . . The question in every case is whether the words used are used in such circumstances and are of such a nature as to create a clear and present danger that they will bring about the substantive evils that Congress has a right to prevent. It is a question of proximity and degree."[41]

Whether Justice Holmes actually intended here to add a new dimension to constitutional freedom of speech and press may be seriously questioned, inasmuch as in two similar cases following shortly after, in which he again spoke for the Court, and in which prosecutions under the Espionage Act were sustained, he did not allude to the formula.[42] Moreover, when a case did arise in which the formula might have made a difference, seven Justices declined to follow it.[43] This time, however, Justice Holmes, accompanied by Justice Brandeis, dissented on the ground that defendants' utterances did not create a clear and present danger of substantive evils. From this time forth in the course of the next twenty years, these two Justices filed numerous opinions, sometimes in dissent, sometimes in affirmation, of rulings of the Court in freedom of speech cases in which the "clear and present danger" test was urged, but without convincing any of their brethren of its soundness.[44] Then suddenly in 1940, the stone rejected of the builders suddenly appeared at the head of the column, and along with it the further tenet that freedom of speech and press occupied "a preferred position" in the scale of constitutional values.[45]

In the national field, where Amendment I operates directly, and without assistance from the due process clause of Amendment XIV, "clear and present danger" has played a negligible role in defining freedom of speech and press and of religion. In 1890, in *Davis v. Beason*,[46] a conviction for "advocating" polygamy was sustained without the question being raised whether there had been "imminent danger" of the advocacy succeeding. That, to be sure, was fifty years before the Court's adoption of the "clear and present danger" doctrine. But the application to newspapers of the Anti-Trust Acts, the National Labor Relations Act, and the Fair Labor Standards Act in 1945, 1937, and 1946, respectively, was similarly unembarrassed.[47] So also has been that of the Hatch Acts, limiting the political activities of employees of the government;[48] and of legislation punishing utterances intended to obstruct recruitment of the armed services or to encourage insubordination in them.[49]

"Clear and present danger" was first thrust forward aggressively, in resistance to provisions of the Labor Management Relations (Taft-Hartley) Act of 1947, which require, as a condition of a union's utilizing the opportunities afforded by the act, each of its officers to file an affidavit with the National Labor Relations Board (1) that he is not a member of the Communist Party or affiliated with such party, and (2) that he does not believe in, and is not a member of, nor does he support "any organization that believes in or teaches the overthrow of the United States Government by force or by any illegal or unconstitutional methods." The statute also makes it a criminal offense to make willfully or knowingly any false statement in such an affidavit.[50] In two cases decided in 1950 these provisions were sustained, in one instance by an evenly divided Court.[51] The main proposition of the Court, as stated by the late Chief Justice Vinson, was that, "not the relative certainty that evil conduct will result from speech in the immediate future, but the extent and gravity of the substantive evil must be measured by the 'test' laid down in the *Schenck Case*."[52] In thus balancing the importance of the interest protected by legislation from harmful speech against the demands of the clear and present danger rule the Court paved the way for its decision a year later in *Dennis* v. *United States*.[53]

Here the Court sustained, by a vote of 7 to 2, the

conviction, under the Smith Act of 1940,[54] of eleven leaders of the Communist Party on the charge of "knowingly and willfully" advocating and teaching the overthrow of government in the United States by force and violence and of willfully and knowingly conspiring to advocate and teach the same. Emphasizing the substantial character of the government's interest in preventing its own overthrow by force, the late Chief Justice, speaking for the majority, adopted the following statement from Chief Judge Learned Hand's opinion for the Circuit Court of Appeals in the same case: "'In each case [courts] must ask whether the gravity of the evil, discounted by its improbability, justifies such invasion of free speech as is necessary to avoid the danger.'"[55] This formula, comments the Chief Justice, "is as succinct and inclusive as any other we might devise at this time. It takes into consideration those factors which we deem relevant, and relates their significances. More we cannot expect from words."[56]

In the second place, the Chief Justice emphasizes the conspiratorial nature of defendant's activities. "It is," he declares, "the existence of the conspiracy which creates the danger";[57] and Justices Frankfurter and Jackson also dwell upon this aspect of the case in their concurring opinions;[58] while Justices Black and Douglas, in their dissents, significantly ignore it. For if the conspiracy was a danger at all, it was certainly a "clear and present" one, in which connection it is pertinent to note that under the common law acts which, when performed by a single individual are at worst private torts, may become indictable when performed by a combination of persons.[59]

It can probably be safely said, on the basis of the Dennis holding, that the "clear and present danger" formula will never be successfully invoked in behalf of persons shown to have conspired to incite to a breach of federal law. On the other hand, as Justice Jackson suggests, the formula may still be applicable in cases essentially trivial and in cases where the intent of the speaker is innocent or ambiguous but other circumstances create a real danger of violence, or other substantive evil.[60] The common law, properly charged, would probably do quite as well in such cases without an assist from "clear and present danger."[61]

Congress's control over the newspaper press is reinforced by its control of the mails. Few newspapers or periodicals can profitably circulate except locally unless they enjoy the "second class privilege" that is, the privilege of specially low rates—and this privilege, being a gratuity, is under the nearly absolute control of Congress, notwithstanding which Congress's delegate in the matter, the Postmaster General, may not, in carrying out Congress's expressed will that the privilege be confined to publications "originated and published for the dissemination of information of a public character, or devoted to literature, the sciences, arts, or some special industry," set himself up as a censor, for if he does the Court will over-rule him and bring his decrees to naught.[62] Moreover, Congress may banish from the mails altogether, as well as from the channels of interstate commerce, indecent, fraudulent, and seditious matter.[63] For there can be no right to circulate what there is no right to publish, circulation indeed being only an incident of publication. Nor, as we have seen, is it an invasion of freedom of the press to require a newsgathering agency to treat its employees in the same way as other employers are required to treat theirs; or to subject it to the anti-monopoly provisions of the Sherman Anti-Trust Act.[64]

Historically, the right of petition is the primary right, the right peaceably to assemble a subordinate and instrumental right, as if Amendment I read: "the right of the people peaceably to assemble" *in order to* "petition the government."[65] Today, however, the right of peaceable assembly is, in the language of the Court, "cognate to those of free speech and free press and is equally fundamental.

". . . [It] is one that cannot be denied without violating those fundamental principles of liberty and justice which lie at the base of all civil and political institutions—principles which the Fourteenth Amendment embodies in the general terms of its due process clause. . . . The holding of meetings for peaceable political action cannot be proscribed. Those who assist in the conduct of such meetings cannot be branded as criminals on that score. The question . . . is not as to the auspices under which the meeting is held but as to its purposes; not as to the relations of the speakers, but whether their utterances transcend the bounds of the freedom of speech which the Constitution protects."[66] Even so, the right is not unlimited. Under the common law any assemblage was unlawful which aroused the apprehensions of "men of firm and rational minds with families and property there," and it is not unlikely that the First Amendment takes this principle into account.[67]

Furthermore, the right of petition too has expanded. It is no longer confined to demands for "a redress of grievances," in any accurate meaning of these words, but comprehends demands for an exercise by the government of its powers in furtherance of the interests and prosperity of the petitioners, and of their views on politically contentious matters. On this ground, two recent decisions of lower federal courts sitting in the District of Columbia have cast doubt on the constitutionality of the Federal Regulation of Lobbying Act of 1946, under which more than 2,000 lobbyists have registered and 495 organizations report lobbying contributions and expenditures.[68] In disposing of the second of these cases the Supreme Court indicated that while Congress undoubtedly possesses power to investigate the *modus operandi* of lobbying activities and their influence on public opinion, such inquiries may conceivably take such a range as to encounter the prohibitions of Amendment I.[69]

1 268 U.S. 652 (1925).

2 Ibid. 666.

3 *Fiske* v. *Kan.*, 274 U.S. 380 (1927).

4 *Cantwell* v. *Conn.*, 310 U.S. 296 (1940).

5 *Near* v. *Minn.*, 283 U.S. 697 (1931).

6 *DeJonge* v. *Ore.*, 299 U.S. 353 (1937).

7 2 Story, *Comms.*, §§1870-1879 (1833).

8 Cooley, *Principles*, 224-225 (ed. of 1898).

9 H. S. Commager (ed.), *Documents of American History*, 128, 131 (3rd Ed., 1947).

10 Saul K. Padover (ed.), *The Complete Jefferson*, 518-519 (1943).

11 *Reynolds* v. *U.S.*, 98 U.S. 145, 164 (1879). In his 2nd Inaugural Address, Jefferson expressed a very different, and presumably more carefully considered, opinion upon the purpose of Amendment I: "In matters of religion, I have considered that its free exercise is placed by the Constitution independent of the powers of the general government." This was said three years after the Danbury letter. 1 Richardson, *Messages and Papers of the Presidents*, 379 (Ed. of 1909).

12 *Everson* v. *Board of Education*, 330 U.S. 1 (1947).

13 *Ibid.*, 15, 16.

14 *McCollum* v. *Board of Education*, 333 U.S. 203 (1948).

15 *Ibid.* 212.

16 *Ibid.* 212ff.

17 *Ibid.* 253-254.

18 *Zorach* v. *Clauson*, 343 U.S. 306 (1952).

19 *Ibid.* 313-314. JJ. Black, Frankfurter and Jackson dissented.

20 *Bradfield* v. *Roberts*, 175 U.S. 291 (1899).

21 *Quick Bear* v. *Leupp*, 210 U.S. 50 (1908).

22 *Cochran* v. *Louisiana State Board of Education*, 281 U.S. 370 (1930).

23 *Everson* v. *Board of Education*, 330 U.S. 1 (1947).

24 60 Stat. 230 (1946).

25 J. Roberts for the Court in *Cantwell* v. *Conn.*, 310 U.S. 296 at 303 (1940).

26 *Reynolds* v. *U.S.*, 98 U.S. 145 (1878). *See also Davis* v. *Beason*, 133 U.S. 333 (1890); and *Mormon Church* v. *U.S.*, 136 U.S. 1 (1890). It was never intended that the First Amendment to the Constitution "could be invoked as a protection against legislation for the punishment of acts inimical to the peace, good order and morals of society." 133 U.S. at 342.

27 310 U.S. at 306. Nor does the Constitution protect one in

uttering obscene, profane, or libelous words, even with pious intent. *Chaplinsky* v. *N.H.*, 315 U.S. 568 (1942).

[28] *United States* v. *Ballard*, 322 U.S. 78 (1944). The interstate transportation of plural wives by polygamous Fundamentalists is punishable under the Mann Act. *Cleveland* v. *U.S.*, 329 U.S. 14 (1946); U.S. Code, tit. 18, §398. Nor is it a violation of religious freedom to deny conscientious objectors the right to practice law. *Re Summers*, 325 U.S. 561 (1945). *Kedroff* v. *St. Nicholas Cathedral of the Russian Orthodox Church in N.A.*, 344 U.S. 94 (1952) involved a dispute between the Archbishop in New York by appointment of the Patriarch in Moscow and a corporation created by the State to take over the Church's property in New York for the benefit and use of an American separatist movement in the Orthodox Church. The Court held that, in thus attempting to regulate church administration, New York had violated the "free exercise" of religion clause. Considering the probable relationship of the Patriarch in Moscow to the political powers that be in that city, the holding seems unrealistic. Indeed, the New York act set aside appears on its face to advance the free exercise by its beneficiaries of their religion, which is still, it is agreed, that of the Orthodox Church. For a similar controversy between branches of the Presbyterian Church which was similarly disposed of on the basis of "general principles of law," *see Watson* v. *Jones*, 13 Wall. 679 (1879). This occurred of course before the Court had recalled *Swift* v. *Tyson*.

[29] 4 *Blackstone Comms.*, 151.

[30] *See* J. Frankfurter's opinion in *Dennis* v. *U.S.*, 341 U.S. 494, 521-525 (1951); citing *Robertson* v. *Baldwin*, 165 U.S. 275, 281 (1897).

[31] These two improvements upon the common law were, in fact, adopted from Fox's Libel Act, passed by Parliament in 1792.

[32] 9 *Writings of Thomas Jefferson*, 451-452 (Ford ed., 1905).

[33] *People* v. *Croswell*, 3 Johns. (N.Y.), 337.

[34] *See* Edward S. Corwin, *Liberty against Government*, 157-159n. (Louisiana State Univ. Press, 1948); Cooley, *Constitutional Limitations*, ch. 12; Samuel A. Dawson, *Freedom of the Press, A Study of the Doctrine of "Qualified Privilege"* (Columbia Univ. Press, 1924).

[35] *Patterson* v. *Colo.*, 205 U.S. 454, 461-462 (1907).

[36] *Prudential Life Ins. Co.* v. *Cheek*, 259 U.S. 530, 543 (1922).

[37] *Schenck* v. *United States*, 249 U.S. 47 (1919).

38 *See* Justice Brandeis' concurring opinion in *Whitney* v. *Calif.*, 274 U.S. 357 (1927); and cases reviewed below.

39 *Fiske* v. *Kansas*, 274 U.S. 380 (1927).

40 Note 37 above.

41 249 U.S. at 52.

42 The reference is to *Frohwerk* v. *U.S.*, 249 U.S. 204; *and Debs* v. *U.S.*, 249 U.S. 211.

43 *Abrams* v. *U.S.*, 250 U.S. 616 (1919).

44 *See Schaefer* v. *U.S.*, 251 U.S. 466 (1920); *Gitlow* v. *N.Y.*, 268 U.S. 652 (1925); *Whitney* v. *Calif.*, 274 U.S. 357 (1927).

45 *Thornhill* v. *Ala.*, 310 U.S. 88, and *Cantwell* v. *Conn.*, 310 U.S. 296 are especially referred to. *Cf. Herndon* v. *Lowry*, 301 U.S. 242 (1937).

46 133 U.S. 333, 345 (1890). *See also Fox* v. *Wash.*, 236 U.S. 273 (1915).

47 *See Associated Press* v. *U.S.*, 326 U.S. 1 (1945); *Associated Press* v. *N.L.R.B.*, 301 U.S. 103, 133 (1937); *Oklahoma Press Pub. Co.* v. *Walling*, 327 U.S. 186 (1946).

48 *United Public Workers* v. *Mitchell*, 330 U.S. 75 (1947).

49 *Schenck* v. *U.S.*, 249 U.S. 47 (1919); *Frohwerk* v. *U.S.*, 249 U.S. 204 (1919); *Debs* v. *U.S.*, 249 U.S. 211 (1919); *Abrams* v. *U.S.*, 250 U.S. 616 (1919); *Schaefer* v. *U.S.*, 251 U.S. 466 (1919); *Pierce* v. *U.S.*, 252 U.S. 239 (1920); *cf. Gilbert* v. *Minn.*, 254 U.S. 325 (1920); *Hartzel* v. *U.S.*, 322 U.S. 680 (1944).

50 61 Stat. 136, 146 (1947).

51 *C.I.O. et al* v. *Douds*, 339 U.S. 382 (1950); *Osman* v. *Douds*, 339 U.S. 846 (1950).

52 339 U.S. 382, 394, 397.

53 341 U.S. 494 (1951).

54 54 Stat. 670 (1940).

55 341 U.S. at 509, citing 183 F. (2nd) at 212.

56 *Ibid.*

57 341 U.S. at 510-511.

58 341 U.S. at 542 and 572.

59 Bouvier's *Law Dictionary*, 216 (Baldwin, Ed., N.Y., 1928).

60 341 U.S. at 568-569.

61 In a series of cases in which certain organizations sued the Attorney General for declaratory or injunctive relief looking to the deletion of their names from a list of organizations designated by him to be subversive, the Court reversed holdings of the courts below which had denied relief. Two Justices thought the order not within the President's Executive Order No. 9835, which lays down a procedure for the determination of the loyalty of federal employees or would-be-em-

ployees. Justice Black thought the Attorney General had violated Amendment I and that the President's order constituted a Bill of Attainder. He and Justices Frankfurter and Jackson also held that the Attorney General had violated due process of law in having failed to give the petitioners notice and hearing. Justice Reed, with the concurrence of the Chief Justice and Justice Minton, dissented, asserting that the action of the Court constituted an interference with the discretion of the executive in the premises. See *Anti-Fascist Committee* v. *McGrath*, 341 U.S. 123 (1951). The subject of freedom of speech and press with collateral issues is further considered in connection with the due process of law clause of Amendment XIV.

62 *United States ex rel. Milwaukee Soc. Dem. Pub. Co.* v. *Burleson*, 255 U.S. 407 (1921), and cases there cited; *Hannegan* v. *Esquire, Inc.*, 327 U.S. 146 (1946); U.S. Code, tit. 39 §226.

63 *In re Rapier*, 143 U.S. 110 (1892); *Public Clearing House* v. *Coyne*, 194 U.S. 497 (1904); *Lewis Pub. Co.* v. *Morgan*, 229 U.S. 288 (1913).

64 *Associated Press* v. *N.L.R.B.*, 301 U.S. 103 (1937); *Associated Press* v. *U.S.*, 326 U.S. 1 (1945).

65 *United States* v. *Cruikshank*, 92 U.S. 542, 552 (1876).

66 *De Jonge* v. *Ore.*, 299 U.S. 353, 364-365 (1937). See also *Hague* v. *Com. for Indust'l Organization*, 307 U.S. 496 (1939).

67 See a valuable article by J. M. Jarrett and V. A. Mund, "The Right of Assembly," 9 *New York University Law Quarterly Review*, 1-38 (1931), *People* v. *Kerrick*, 261 Pac. Rep. (Calif.) 756 (1927); and *State* v. *Butterworth*, 104 N.J.L. 579 (1928), are two modern cases on the subject which were thoroughly argued and carefully decided.

68 U.S. Code, tit. 2, §§ 261-270; *National Asso. of Manufacturers* v. *McGrath*, 103 F. Supp. 510 (1952); *Rumely* v. *U.S.*, 197 F. (2nd) 166, 174-175 (1952).

69 *United States* v. *Rumely*, 345 U.S. 41, 46 (1953). See *also*: General Interim Report of the House Select Committee on Lobbying Activities, 81st Cong., 2nd Sess. (United States Government Printing Office, Washington, 1950): *also* 9 *Encyclopedia of the Social Sciences*, 567, "Lobbying." For the details of J. Q. Adams' famous fight for the right of petition in the early 1830's, *see* A. C. McLaughlin, *A Constitutional History of the United States*, 478-481 (N.Y., 1935).

ADDENDUM TO THE FIRST AMENDMENT FREEDOMS

Since Professor Corwin wrote in 1953, there have been important developments, particularly in relation to the continuing struggle against subversion and in the regulation of obscenity.

The most important new federal legislation in this connection is the Communist Control Act of 1954. 68 Stat. 775 (1954), 50 U.S.C. §§ 841-44 (Supp. 1954). Although designed like its predecessors to control subversion, the 1954 act for the first time purported to outlaw the Communist Party directly. This is premised in part upon the following findings of fact:

> "The Congress hereby finds and declares that the Communist Party of the United States, although purportedly a political party, is in fact an instrumentality of a conspiracy to overthrow the Government of the United States."

In view of this and other and more detailed findings Congress concluded that "the Communist Party should be outlawed." The act is not without its anomalies, perhaps resulting from the intense legislative confusion surrounding its course through Congress. Thus, while section 3 of the act purports to deprive the Communist Party of the normal privileges accorded other political parties, the same section also provides "That nothing in this section shall be construed as amending the Internal Security Act of 1950, as amended." The earlier act, however, provided that the Communist Party should not be outlawed. Moreover, section 4 of the 1954 act provides that knowing membership in the Communist Party shall subject such a person to all the penalties of the Internal Security Act specified for a member of a "Communist-action" organization. However, this seems to travel in a circle, since members of "Com-

munist-action" organizations are subjected to penalties under the 1950 act only after registration by such
an organization (none has so registered) or a final
order by the Subversive Activities Control Board requiring such registration (no "final" order in this
sense had been made effective as of the end of 1957,
nor does such an order appear likely in the near
future). And of course such a determination would
in any event invoke the Internal Security Act penalties. If that is all the new section means, it may mean
nothing.

In 1953, after a fourteen-month hearing in which a
15,000-page record was accumulated, the Subversive
Activities Control Board held that the Communist
Party was required to register as a "Communist-action" or "Communist-front" organization. In December 1954 this determination was upheld by the Court
of Appeals for the District of Columbia in a two-to-
one decision. *Communist Party* v. *Subversive Activities Control Board*, 223 F.2d 531 (D.C. Cir. 1954).
The limitation on free speech was justified as follows:

> "The activities of a World Communist
> movement such as that described in this
> statute and of organizations in this country
> devoted to its objectives constitute a clear
> and present danger within the meaning of
> any definition of the point at which freedom
> of speech gives way to the requirements of
> government security." *Id.* at 544.

However, the Supreme Court reversed and remanded
to the Control Board for reconsideration in view of
the fact that three of the government witnesses were
under charges of false swearing. 351 U.S. 115 (1956).
The Control Board expunged from the record the
challenged testimony and again recommended that
the Communist Party be required to register. *N.Y.
Times*, p. 7, col. 3, Dec. 19, 1956. And there the matter still stands at the end of 1957, seven years after
the enactment of the Internal Security Act. There is
still no order finally declared by the Supreme Court

to require registration of the Communist Party as a
"Communist-action" organization.

Meanwhile, what had been widely thought to be
the impact of the *Dennis* case was somewhat diluted
by *Yates* v. *United States,* 354 U.S. 298 (1957), in
which the Court reversed the conviction of several
second-string Communists and remanded for a new
trial. The Government and the accused were agreed
on one thing only—that conviction at a second trial
would be more difficult under the standards announced by the Court. At the same term the Court
called for reargument of the cases in which the Government had sought convictions under section 2 of
the Smith Act for mere "knowing" membership in the
Communist Party. *Lightfoot* v. *United States* and
Scales v. *United States,* 353 U.S. 936 (1957). However, this, too, must be retried for failure to give access to Government records required by the decision
in the *Jencks* case, *supra.*

Finally, the Court announced significant limitations
upon Congress and the states in the conduct of legislative investigations. *Watkins* v. *United States, infra,*
and *Sweezy* v. *New Hampshire,* 354 U.S. 234 (1957).

Watkins v. United States
354 U.S. 178 (1957)

Mr. Chief Justice Warren delivered the opinion
of the Court.

This is a review by certiorari of a conviction under
2 U. S. C. § 192 for "contempt of Congress." The
misdemeanor is alleged to have been committed during a hearing before a congressional investigating
committee. It is not the case of a truculent or con-
tumacious witness who refuses to answer all questions or who, by boisterous or discourteous conduct,
disturbs the decorum of the committee room. Petitioner was prosecuted for refusing to make certain
disclosures which he asserted to be beyond the

authority of the committee to demand. The controversy thus rests upon fundamental principles of the power of the Congress and the limitations upon that power. We approach the questions presented with conscious awareness of the far-reaching ramifications that can follow from a decision of this nature.

On April 29, 1954, petitioner appeared as a witness in compliance with a subpoena issued by a Subcommittee of the Committee on Un-American Activities of the House of Representatives. The Subcommittee elicited from petitioner a description of his background in labor union activities. He had been an employee of the International Harvester Company between 1935 and 1953. During the last eleven of those years, he had been on leave of absence to serve as an official of the Farm Equipment Workers International Union, later merged into the United Electrical, Radio and Machine Workers. He rose to the position of President of District No. 2 of the Farm Equipment Workers, a district defined geographically to include generally Canton and Rock Falls, Illinois, and Dubuque, Iowa. In 1953, petitioner joined the United Auto Workers International Union as a labor organizer.

Petitioner's name had been mentioned by two witnesses who testified before the Committee at prior hearings. . . .

Petitioner answered these allegations freely and without reservation. His attitude toward the inquiry is clearly revealed from the statement he made when the questioning turned to the subject of his past conduct, associations and predilections:

"I am not now nor have I ever been a card-carrying member of the Communist Party.

. . .

"I would like to make it clear that for a period of time from approximately 1942 to 1947 I cooperated with the Communist Party and participated in Communist activities to such a degree that some persons may honestly believe that I was a member of the party.

"I have made contributions upon occasions to Communist causes. I have signed petitions for Communist causes. I attended caucuses at an FE convention at which Communist Party officials were present.

"Since I freely cooperated with the Communist Party I have no motive for making the distinction between cooperation and membership except the simple fact that it is the truth. I never carried a Communist Party card. I never accepted discipline and indeed on several occasions I opposed their position. . . ."

[In response to committee questions about the Communist Party affiliations of other persons, he said:]

"I am not going to plead the fifth amendment, but I refuse to answer certain questions that I believe are outside the proper scope of your committee's activities. I will answer any questions which this committee puts to me about myself. I will also answer questions about those persons whom I knew to be members of the Communist Party and whom I believe still are. I will not, however, answer any questions with respect to others with whom I associated in the past. I do not believe that any law in this country requires me to testify about persons who may in the past have been Communist Party members or otherwise engaged in Communist Party activity but who to my best knowledge and belief have long since removed themselves from the Communist movement.

"I do not believe that such questions are relevant to the work of this committee nor do I believe that this committee has the right to undertake the public exposure of persons because of their past activities. I may be wrong, and the committee may have this power, but until and unless a court of law so holds and directs me to answer, I most firmly refuse to discuss the political activities of my past associates."

The Chairman of the Committee submitted a report of petitioner's refusal to answer questions to the House of Representatives. H. R. Rep. No. 1579, 83d Cong., 2d Sess. The House directed the Speaker to certify the Committee's report to the United States Attorney for initiation of criminal prosecution. H. Res. 534, 83d Cong., 2d Sess. A seven-count indictment was returned. Petitioner waived his right to jury trial and was found guilty on all counts by the court. The sentence, a fine of $100 and one year in prison, was suspended, and petitioner was placed on probation.

An appeal was taken to the Court of Appeals for the District of Columbia. The conviction was reversed by a three-judge panel, one member dissenting. Upon rehearing *en banc,* the full bench affirmed the conviction with the judges of the original majority in dissent. We granted certiorari because of the very important questions of constitutional law presented. 352 U.S. 822.

We start with several basic premises on which there is general agreement. The power of the Congress to conduct investigations is inherent in the legislative process. That power is broad. It encompasses inquiries concerning the administration of existing laws as well as proposed or possibly needed statutes. It includes surveys of defects in our social, economic or political system for the purpose of enabling the Congress to remedy them. It comprehends probes into departments of the Federal Government to expose corruption, inefficiency or waste. But broad as is this power of inquiry, it is not unlimited. There is no general authority to expose the private affairs of individuals without justification in terms of the functions of the Congress. This was freely conceded by the Solicitor General in his argument of this case. Nor is the Congress a law enforcement or trial agency. These are functions of the executive and judicial departments of government. No inquiry is an end in itself; it must be related to and in furtherance of a legitimate task of the Congress. Investigations conducted solely for the personal aggrandizement of the investigators or to "punish" those investigated are indefensible. . . .

The history of contempt of the legislature in this country is notably different from that of England. In the early days of the United States, there lingered the direct knowledge of the evil effects of absolute power. Most of the instances of use of compulsory process by the first Congresses concerned matters affecting the qualification or integrity of their members or came about in inquiries dealing with suspected corruption or mismanagement of government officials. Unlike the English practice, from the very outset the use of contempt power by the legislature was deemed subject to judicial review.

There was very little use of the power of compulsory process in early years to enable the Congress to obtain facts pertinent to the enactment of new statutes or the administration of existing laws. The first occasion for such an investigation arose in 1827 when the House of Representatives was considering a revision of the tariff laws. In the Senate, there was no use of a fact-finding investigation in aid of legislation until 1859. In the Legislative Reorganization Act, the Committee on Un-American Activities is the only standing committee of the House of Representatives that was given the power to compel disclosures.

It is not surprising, from the fact that the Houses of Congress so sparingly employed the power to conduct investigations, that there have been few cases requiring judicial review of the power. The nation was almost one hundred years old before the first case reached this Court to challenge the use of compulsory process as a legislative device, rather than in inquiries concerning the elections or privileges of

Congressmen. In *Kilbourn* v. *Thompson,* 103 U.S. 168, decided in 1881, an investigation had been authorized by the House of Representatives to learn the circumstances surrounding the bankruptcy of Jay Cooke & Company, in which the United States had deposited funds. The committee became particularly interested in a private real estate pool that was a part of the financial structure. The Court found that the subject matter of the inquiry was "in its nature clearly judicial and therefore one in respect to which no valid legislation could be enacted." The House had thereby exceeded the limits of its own authority.

Subsequent to the decision in *Kilbourn,* until recent times, there were very few cases dealing with the investigative power. The matter came to the fore again when the Senate undertook to study the corruption in handling of oil leases in the 1920's. In *McGrain* v. *Daugherty,* 273 U.S. 135, and *Sinclair* v. *United States,* 279 U.S. 263, the Court applied the precepts of *Kilbourn* to uphold the authority of the Congress to conduct the challenged investigations. The Court recognized the danger to effective and honest conduct of the Government if the legislature's power to probe corruption in the executive branch were unduly hampered.

Following these important decisions, there was another lull in judicial review of investigations. The absence of challenge, however, was not indicative of the absence of inquiries. To the contrary, there was vigorous use of the investigative process by a Congress bent upon harnessing and directing the vast economic and social forces of the times. Only one case came before this Court, and the authority of the Congress was affirmed.

In the decade following World War II, there appeared a new kind of congressional inquiry unknown in prior periods of American history. Principally this was the result of the various investigations into the threat of subversion of the United States Government, but other subjects of congressional interest also contributed to the changed scene. This new phase of legislative inquiry involved a broad-scale intrusion into the lives and affairs of private citizens. It brought before the courts novel questions of the appropriate limits of congressional inquiry. Prior cases, like *Kilbourn, McGrain* and *Sinclair,* had defined the scope of investigative power in terms of the inherent limitations of the sources of that power. In the more recent cases, the emphasis shifted to problems of accommodating the interest of the Government with the rights and privileges of individuals. The central theme was the application of the Bill of Rights as a restraint upon the assertion of governmental power in this form.

It was during this period that the Fifth Amendment privilege against self-incrimination was frequently invoked and recognized as a legal limit upon the authority of a committee to require that a witness answer its questions. Some early doubts as to the applicability of that privilege before a legislative committee never matured. When the matter reached this Court, the Government did not challenge in any way that the Fifth Amendment protection was available to the witness, and such a challenge could not have prevailed. It confined its argument to the character of the answers sought and to the adequacy of the claim of privilege. *Quinn* v. *United States,* 349 U.S. 155; *Emspak* v. *United States,* 349 U.S. 190; *Bart* v. *United States,* 349 U.S. 219.

A far more difficult task evolved from the claim by witnesses that the committees' interrogations were infringements upon the freedoms of the First Amendment. Clearly, an investigation is subject to the command that the Congress shall make no law abridging freedom of speech or press or assembly. While it is true that there is no statute to be reviewed, and that an investigation is not a law, nevertheless an investigation is part of law-making. It is justified solely as an adjunct to the legislative process. The First Amendment may be invoked against infringement of the protected freedoms by law or by law-making.

Abuses of the investigative process may imperceptibly lead to abridgment of protected freedoms. The mere summoning of a witness and compelling him to testify, against his will, about his beliefs, expressions or associations is a measure of governmental interference. And when those forced revelations concern matters that are unorthodox, unpopular, or even hateful to the general public, the reaction in the life of the witness may be disastrous. This effect is even more harsh when it is past beliefs, expressions or associations that are disclosed and judged by current standards rather than those contemporary with the matters exposed. Nor does the witness alone suffer the consequences. Those who are identified by witnesses and thereby placed in the same glare of publicity are equally subject to public stigma, scorn and obloquy. Beyond that, there is the more subtle and immeasurable effect upon those who tend to adhere to the most orthodox and uncontroversial views and associations in order to avoid a similar fate at some future time. That this impact is partly the result of non-governmental activity by private persons cannot relieve the investigators of their responsibility for initiating the reaction. . . .

We have no doubt that there is no congressional power to expose for the sake of exposure. The public is, of course, entitled to be informed concerning the workings of its government. That cannot be inflated into a general power to expose where the predominant result can only be an invasion of the private rights of individuals. But a solution to our problem is not to be found in testing the motives of committee members for this purpose. Such is not our function. Their motives alone would not vitiate an investigation which had been instituted by a House of Congress if that assembly's legislative purpose is being served. . . .

[The majority examined the Committee authority and the information given petitioner, then concluded that the questions asked of petitioner were not pertinent to the "subject under inquiry." Accordingly, the judgment was reversed and remanded with instructions to dismiss the indictment.]

MR. JUSTICE FRANKFURTER, concurring.

I deem it important to state what I understand to be the Court's holding. Agreeing with its holding, I join its opinion.

The power of the Congress to punish for contempt of its authority is, as the Court points out, rooted in history. It has been acknowledged by this Court since 1821. *Anderson* v. *Dunn*, 6 Wheat. 204. Until 1857, Congress was content to punish for contempt through its own process. By the Act of January 24, 1857, 11 Stat. 155, as amended by the Act of January 24, 1862, 12 Stat. 333, Congress provided that, "in addition to the pains and penalties now existing" (referring of course to the power of Congress itself to punish for contempt), "contumacy in a witness called to testify in a matter properly under consideration by either House, and deliberately refusing to answer questions pertinent thereto, shall be a misdemeanor against the United States." *In re Chapman*, 166 U.S. 661, 672. This legislation is now 2 U. S. C. § 192. By thus making the federal judiciary the affirmative agency for enforcing the authority that underlies the congressional power to punish for contempt, Congress necessarily brings into play the specific provisions of the Constitution relating to the prosecution of offenses and those implied restrictions under which courts function.

To turn to the immediate problem before us, the scope of inquiry that a committee is authorized to pursue must be defined with sufficiently unambiguous clarity to safeguard a witness from the hazards of vagueness in the enforcement of the criminal process against which the Due Process Clause protects. The questions must be put with relevance and definiteness sufficient to enable the witness to know whether his refusal to answer may lead to conviction for criminal contempt and to enable both the trial and the appellate courts readily to determine whether the particular circumstances justify a finding of guilt.

While implied authority for the questioning by the Committee, sweeping as was its inquiry, may be squeezed out of the repeated acquiescence by Congress in the Committee's inquiries, the basis for determining petitioner's guilt is not thereby laid. Prosecution for contempt of Congress presupposes an adequate opportunity for the defendant to have awareness of the pertinency of the information that he has denied to Congress. And the basis of such awareness must be contemporaneous with the witness' refusal to answer and not at the trial for it. Accordingly, the actual scope of the inquiry that the Committee was authorized to conduct and the relevance of the questions to that inquiry must be shown to have been luminous at the time when asked and not left, at best, in cloudiness. The circumstances of this case were wanting in these essentials.

MR. JUSTICE CLARK, dissenting.

As I see it the chief fault in the majority opinion is its mischievous curbing of the informing function of the Congress. While I am not versed in its procedures, my experience in the executive branch of the Government leads me to believe that the requirements laid down in the opinion for the operation of the committee system of inquiry are both unnecessary and unworkable. . . .

REGULATION OF OBSCENITY

The United States Supreme Court has often hinted that obscenity is not within the area of protected speech and press. *E.g., Near* v. *Minnesota*, 283 U.S. 697, 716 (1931); *Chaplinsky* v. *New Hampshire*, 315 U.S. 568, 572 (1942). However, not until 1957 was there a square holding to that effect in *Roth* v. *United States* and *Alberts* v. *California*, 354 U.S. 476 (1957). In those companion cases the Court affirmed two convictions, one for the violation of a federal statute making punishable the mailing of material that is "obscene, lewd, lascivious, or filthy," and the other for violation of a California statute making punishable the keeping for sale or advertising of material that is "obscene or indecent." From that starting point the Court went on to an even more troublesome issue in *Kingsley Books, Inc.* v. *Brown*, 354 U.S. 436 (1957). The issue there was the constitutionality of section 22-a of the New York Code of Criminal Procedure which provides for injunction against the sale or distribution of written and printed matter found upon trial to be obscene, and for seizure and destruction of the publications thus condemned. Because it was conceded that the offending publications were obscene, it was generally assumed that the case presented for decision the question whether the injunctive relief provided for was a prior restraint forbidden by the first amendment as incorporated into the fourteenth. However, Mr. Justice Frankfurter, speaking for the five-man majority, never quite reached that issue. Rather he suggested that the injunction should work no greater hardship on the publisher than the alternatively permitted sanction of criminal punishment for offering for sale lewd or obscene publications.

The dissenters took issue with the majority in three separate opinions. Chief Justice Warren and Justices Black and Douglas thought the statute operated as a prior restraint violative of the first amendment because the law "places the book on trial," instead of subjecting the conduct of each individual defendant to the test of a separate criminal trial. Mr. Justice Brennan thought the statute constitutionally defective because there was no provision for a jury trial. In any event, it appears that the act of Congress and the statutes of California and New York which were upheld in these cases offer the federal government a variety of methods for the future control of obscenity.

Freedom from Discrimination

There is no clear historical evidence that the fourteenth amendment, when adopted, was intended to apply to jury service, voting rights, or even segregation. As Chief Justice Warren said in the *School Segregation Cases*, in reference to the historical sources, "At best, they are inconclusive." In any event, public education, after the adoption of the fourteenth amendment, continued on the same segregated basis as had been the pre-Civil War practice, often in the North as well as in the South. Thus, the general acceptance of the permissibility of segregation was not established, but rather merely confirmed, in *Plessy* v. *Ferguson*, 163 U.S. 537 (1896), whence came the constitutional mainstay of segregation, the doctrine of "separate but equal."

Had the fourteenth amendment's requirement of the equal protection of the laws been embodied in a statute rather than in a constitutional provision, there would seem little doubt that the judicial construction in the *Plessy* case was a correct interpretation of the original intention. And there the matter would rest, at least in the absence of amendment or repeal. However, one must recall the prophetic warning of Chief Justice Marshall from the *McCulloch* case, *supra*, that "we must never forget that it is a *constitution* we are expounding." This, then, was the spirit in which the *School Segregation Cases* were decided. The principal case, *Brown* v. *Board of Education*, is reproduced below. Its companion case, *Bolling* v. *Sharpe*, 347 U.S. 497 (1954), held segregation in the public schools of the District of Columbia a denial of due process.

BROWN v. BOARD OF EDUCATION
347 U.S. 483 (1954)

MR. CHIEF JUSTICE WARREN delivered the opinion of the Court.

These cases come to us from the States of Kansas, South Carolina, Virginia, and Delaware. They are premised on different facts and different local conditions but a common legal question justifies their consideration together in this consolidated opinion.

In each of the cases, minors of the Negro race, through their legal representatives, seek the aid of the courts in obtaining admission to the public schools of their community on a nonsegregated basis. In each instance, they had been denied admission to schools attended by white children under laws requiring or permitting segregation according to race. This segregation was alleged to deprive the plaintiffs of the equal protection of the laws under the Fourteenth Amendment. In each of the cases other than the Delaware case, a three-judge federal district court denied relief to the plaintiffs on the so-called "separate but equal" doctrine announced by this Court in *Plessy* v. *Ferguson*, 163 U.S. 537, 16 S.Ct. 1138, 41 L.Ed. 256. Under that doctrine, equality of treatment is accorded when the races are provided substantially equal facilities, even though these facilities be separate. In the Delaware case, the Supreme Court of Delaware adhered to that doctrine, but ordered that the plaintiffs be admitted to the white schools because of their superiority to the Negro schools.

The plaintiffs contend that segregated public schools are not "equal" and cannot be made "equal," and that hence they are deprived of the equal protection of the laws. Because of the obvious importance of the question presented, the Court took jurisdiction. Argument was heard in the 1952 Term, and reargument was heard this Term on certain questions propounded by the Court.

Reargument was largely devoted to the circumstances surrounding the adoption of the Fourteenth Amendment in 1868. It covered exhaustively consideration of the Amendment in Congress, ratification by the states, then existing practices in racial segregation, and the views of proponents and opponents of the Amendment. This discussion and our own investigation convince us that, although these sources cast some light, it is not enough to resolve the problem with which we are faced. At best, they are inconclusive. The most avid proponents of the post-War Amendments undoubtedly intended them to remove all legal distinctions among "all persons born or naturalized in the United States." Their opponents, just as certainly, were antagonistic to both the letter and the spirit of the Amendments and wished them to have the most limited effect. What others in Congress and the state legislatures had in mind cannot be determined with any degree of certainty.

An additional reason for the inconclusive nature of the Amendment's history, with respect to segregated schools, is the status of public education at that time. In the South, the movement toward free common schools supported by general taxation, had not yet taken hold. Education of white children was largely in the hands of private groups. Education of Negroes was almost nonexistent, and practically all of the race were illiterate. In fact, any education of Negroes was forbidden by law in some states. Today, in contrast, many Negroes have achieved outstanding success in the arts and sciences as well as in the business and professional world. It is true that public education had already advanced further in the North, but the effect of the Amendment on Northern States was generally ignored in the congressional debates. Even in the North, the conditions of public education did not approximate those existing today. The curriculum was usually rudimentary; ungraded schools were common in rural areas; the school term was but three months a year in many states; and compulsory school attendance was virtually unknown. As a consequence, it is not surprising that there should be so little in the history of the Fourteenth Amendment relating to its intended effect on public education.

In the first cases in this Court construing the Fourteenth Amendment, decided shortly after its adoption, the Court interpreted it as proscribing all state-imposed discriminations against the Negro race. The doctrine of "separate but equal" did not make its appearance in this Court until 1896 in the case of *Plessy* v. *Ferguson, supra,* involving not education but transportation. American courts have since labored with the doctrine for over half a century. In this Court, there have been six cases involving the "separate but equal" doctrine in the field of public education. In *Cumming* v. *Board of Education of Richmond County,* 175 U.S. 528, 20 S.Ct. 197, 44 L.Ed. 262, and *Gong Lum* v. *Rice,* 275 U.S. 78, 48 S.Ct. 91, 72 L.Ed. 172, the validity of the doctrine itself was not challenged. In more recent cases, all on the graduate school level, inequality was found in that specific benefits enjoyed by white students were denied to Negro students of the same educational qualifications. *State of Missouri* ex rel. *Gaines* v. *Canada,* 305 U.S. 337, 59 S.Ct. 232, 83 L.Ed. 208; *Sipuel* v. *Board of Regents of University of Oklahoma,* 332 U.S. 631, 68 S.Ct. 299, 92 L.Ed. 247; *Sweatt* v. *Painter,* 339 U.S. 629, 70 S.Ct. 848, 94 L.Ed. 1114; *McLaurin* v. *Oklahoma State Regents,* 339 U.S. 637, 70 S.Ct. 851, 94 L.Ed. 1149. In none of these cases was it necessary to reexamine the doctrine to grant relief to the Negro plaintiff. And in *Sweatt* v. *Painter, supra,* the Court expressly reserved decision on the question whether *Plessy* v. *Ferguson* should be held inapplicable to public education.

In the instant cases, that question is directly presented. Here, unlike *Sweatt* v. *Painter,* there are findings below that the Negro and white schools involved have been equalized, or are being equalized, with respect to buildings, curricula, qualifications and salaries of teachers, and other "tangible" factors. Our decision, therefore, cannot turn on merely a comparison of these tangible factors in the Negro and white schools involved in each of the cases. We must look instead to the effect of segregation itself on public education.

In approaching this problem, we cannot turn the clock back to 1868 when the amendment was adopted, or even to 1896 when *Plessy* v. *Ferguson* was written. We must consider public education in the light of its full development and its present place in American life throughout the Nation. Only in this way can it be determined if segregation in public schools deprives these plaintiffs of the equal protection of the laws.

Today, education is perhaps the most important function of state and local governments. Compulsory school attendance laws and the great expenditures for education both demonstrate our recognition of the importance of education to our democratic society. It is required in the performance of our most basic public responsibilities, even service in the armed forces. It is the very foundation of good citizenship. Today it is a principal instrument in awakening the child to cultural values, in preparing him for later professional training, and in helping him to adjust normally to his environment. In these days, it is doubtful that any child may reasonably be expected to succeed in life if he is denied the opportunity of an education. Such an opportunity, where the state has undertaken to provide it, is a right which must be made available to all on equal terms.

We come then to the question presented: Does segregation of children in public schools solely on the basis of race, even though the physical facilities and other "tangible" factors may be equal, deprive the children of the minority group of equal educational opportunities? We believe that it does.

In *Sweatt* v. *Painter, supra* [339 U.S. 629, 70 S.Ct. 850], in finding that a segregated law school for Negroes could not provide them equal educational opportunities, this Court relied in large part on "those qualities which are incapable of objective measurement but which make for greatness in a law school." In *McLaurin* v. *Oklahoma State Regents, supra* [339 U.S. 637, 70 S.Ct. 853], the Court, in requiring that a Negro admitted to a white graduate school be treated like all other students, again resorted to intangible considerations: ". . . his ability to study, to engage in discussions and exchange views with other students, and, in general, to learn his profession." Such considerations apply with added force to children in grade and high schools. To separate them from others of similar age and qualifications solely because of their race generates a feeling of inferiority as to their status in the community that may affect their hearts and minds in a way unlikely ever to be undone. The effect of this separation on their educational opportunities was well stated by a finding in the Kansas case by a court which nevertheless felt compelled to rule against the Negro plaintiffs:

"Segregation of white and colored children in public schools has a detrimental effect upon the colored children. The impact is greater when it has the sanction of the law; for the policy of separating the races is usually interpreted as denoting the inferiority of the Negro group. A sense of inferiority affects the motivation of a child to learn. Segregation with the sanction of law, therefore, has a tendency to retard the educational and mental development of Negro children and to deprive them of some of the benefits they would receive in a racially integrated school system."

Whatever may have been the extent of psychological knowledge at the time of *Plessy* v. *Ferguson*, this finding is amply supported by modern authority.[11]

---

[11] K. B. Clark, Effect of Prejudice and Discrimination on Personality Development (Midcentury White House Conference on Children and Youth, 1950); Witmer and Kotinsky, Personality in the Making (1952), c. VI; Deutscher and Chein, The Psychological Effects of Enforced Segregation: A Survey

Any language in *Plessy* v. *Ferguson* contrary to this finding is rejected.

We conclude that in the field of public education the doctrine of "separate but equal" has no place. Separate educational facilities are inherently unequal. Therefore, we hold that the plaintiffs and others similarly situated for whom the actions have been brought are, by reason of the segregation complained of, deprived of the equal protection of the laws guaranteed by the Fourteenth Amendment. This disposition makes unnecessary any discussion whether such segregation also violates the Due Process Clause of the Fourteenth Amendment.

Because these are class actions, because of the wide applicability of this decision, and because of the great variety of local conditions, the formulation of decrees in these cases presents problems of considerable complexity. On reargument, the consideration of appropriate relief was necessarily subordinated to the primary question—the constitutionality of segregation in public education. We have now announced that such segregation is a denial of the equal protection of the laws. In order that we may have the full assistance of the parties in formulating decrees, the cases will be restored to the docket, and the parties are requested to present further argument on Questions 4 and 5 previously propounded by the Court for the reargument this Term.[18] The Attorney General of the

---

of Social Science Opinion, 26 J. Psychol. 259 (1948); Chein, What are the Psychological Effects of Segregation Under Conditions of Equal Facilities?, 3 Int. J. Opinion and Attitude Res. 229 (1949); Brameld, Educational Costs, in Discrimination and National Welfare (McIver, ed., 1949), 44-48; Frazier, The Negro in the United States (1949), 674-681. And see generally Myrdal, An American Dilemma (1944). [Footnote by the Court.]

[18] "4. Assuming it is decided that segregation in public schools violates the Fourteenth Amendment.

"(a) would a decree necessarily follow providing that, within the limits set by normal geographic school districting, Negro

United States is again invited to participate. The Attorneys General of the states requiring or permitting segregation in public education will also be permitted to appear as amici curiae upon request to do so by September 15, 1954, and submission of briefs by October 1, 1954.

It is so ordered.

BROWN v. BOARD OF EDUCATION
349 U.S. 294 (1955)

MR. CHIEF JUSTICE WARREN delivered the opinion of the Court.

These cases were decided on May 17, 1954. The opinions of that date, declaring the fundamental principle that racial discrimination in public education is unconstitutional, are incorporated herein by reference. All provisions of federal, state, or local law requiring or permitting such discrimination must yield

---

children should forthwith be admitted to schools of their choice, or

"(b) may this Court, in the exercise of its equity powers, permit an effective gradual adjustment to be brought about from existing segregated systems to a system not based on color distinctions?

"5. On the assumption on which questions 4(a) and (b) are based, and assuming further that this Court will exercise its equity powers to the end described in question 4(b),

"(a) should this Court formulate detailed decrees in these cases;

"(b) if so, what specific issues should the decrees reach;

"(c) should this Court appoint a special master to hear evidence with a view to recommending specific terms for such decrees;

"(d) should this Court remand to the courts of first instance with directions to frame decrees in these cases, and if so, what general directions should the decrees of this Court include and what procedure should the courts of first instance follow in arriving at the specific terms of more detailed decrees?"
[Footnote by the Court.]

to this principle. There remains for consideration the manner in which relief is to be accorded.

Because these cases arose under different local conditions and their disposition will involve a variety of local problems, we requested further argument on the question of relief. In view of the nationwide importance of the decision, we invited the Attorney General of the United States and the Attorneys General of all states requiring or permitting racial discrimination in public education to present their views on that question. The parties, the United States, and the States of Florida, North Carolina, Arkansas, Oklahoma, Maryland, and Texas filed briefs and participated in the oral argument.

These presentations were informative and helpful to the Court in its consideration of the complexities arising from the transition to a system of public education freed of racial discrimination. The presentations also demonstrated that substantial steps to eliminate racial discrimination in public schools have already been taken, not only in some of the communities in which these cases arose, but in some of the states appearing as *amici curiae,* and in other states as well. Substantial progress has been made in the District of Columbia and in the communities in Kansas and Delaware involved in this litigation. The defendants in the cases coming to us from South Carolina and Virginia are awaiting the decision of this Court concerning relief.

Full implementation of these constitutional principles may require solution of varied local school problems. School authorities have the primary responsibility for elucidating, assessing, and solving these problems; courts will have to consider whether the action of school authorities constitutes good faith implementation of the governing constitutional principles. Because of their proximity to local conditions and the possible need for further hearings, the courts which originally heard these cases can best perform this judicial appraisal. Accordingly, we believe it appropriate to remand the cases to those courts.

In fashioning and effectuating the decrees, the courts will be guided by equitable principles. Traditionally, equity has been characterized by a practical flexibility in shaping its remedies and by a facility for adjusting and reconciling public and private needs. These cases call for the exercise of these traditional attributes of equity power. At stake is the personal interest of the plaintiffs in admission to public schools as soon as practicable on a nondiscriminatory basis. To effectuate this interest may call for elimination of a variety of obstacles in making the transition to school systems operated in accordance with the constitutional principles set forth in our May 17, 1954, decision. Courts of equity may properly take into account the public interest in the elimination of such obstacles in a systematic and effective manner. But it should go without saying that the vitality of these constitutional principles cannot be allowed to yield simply because of disagreement with them.

While giving weight to these public and private considerations, the courts will require that the defendants make a prompt and reasonable start toward full compliance with our May 17, 1954, ruling. Once such a start has been made, the courts may find that additional time is necessary to carry out the ruling in an effective manner. The burden rests upon the defendants to establish that such time is necessary in the public interest and is consistent with good faith compliance at the earliest practicable date. To that end, the courts may consider problems related to administration, arising from the physical condition of the school plant, the school transportation system, personnel, revision of school districts and attendance areas into compact units to achieve a system of determining admission to the public schools on a nonracial basis, and revision of local laws and regulations which may be necessary in solving the foregoing problems. They will also consider the adequacy of any plans the defendants may propose to meet these problems and to effectuate a transition to a racially nondiscriminatory school system. During this period of transition, the courts will retain jurisdiction of these cases.

The judgments below, except that in the Delaware case, are accordingly reversed and remanded to the District Courts to take such proceedings and enter such orders and decrees consistent with this opinion as are necessary and proper to admit to public schools on a racially nondiscriminatory basis with all deliberate speed the parties to these cases. The judgment in the Delaware case—ordering the immediate admission of the plaintiffs to schools previously attended only by white children—is affirmed on the basis of the principles stated in our May 17, 1954, opinion, but the case is remanded to the Supreme Court of Delaware for such further proceedings as that court may deem necessary in light of this opinion.

It is so ordered.

The original decision in 1954 and the issuance of the decree in 1955 in the *School Segregation Cases* can be said to represent an ending and a beginning. The decision was the culmination of a long trend from which this important decision may well have been forecast. Thus, it had been the established rule since 1880 that selection for jury duty cannot be made on the basis of race. *Strauder* v. *West Virginia*, 100 U.S. 303 (1880). It has also long been settled that the right of franchise may not be restricted in any way because of race. *Guinn* v. *United States*, 238 U.S. 347 (1915); *Smith* v. *Allwright*, 321 U.S. 649 (1944). Judicial enforcement has been denied to restrictive covenants even between private persons where segregated housing was the objective. *Shelley* v. *Kraemer*, 334 U.S. 1 (1948); *Barrows* v. *Jackson*, 346 U.S. 249 (1953). Segregated transportation has been condemned, *Gayle* v. *Browder*, 142 F. Supp. 707 (M.D. Ala. 1956), *aff'd*, 352 U.S. 903 (1956), as has been segregation in recreation, *Mayor and City Council* v. *Dawson,* 350 U.S. 877 (1955). But most important of all were the cases in which the Court gradually eroded away much of the concept of separate but equal as it had been understood to apply to higher education. *Missouri ex rel. Gaines* v. *Canada,* 305 U.S. 337 (1938); *Sweatt* v. *Painter,* 339 U.S. 629 (1950); *McLaurin* v. *Oklahoma State Regents,* 339 U.S. 637 (1950). The case of *Plessy* v. *Ferguson, supra,* and the concept of "separate but equal" seem now to have been finally rejected by the Supreme Court.

The decision in the *School Segregation Cases* was also a beginning, for the difficult task of completing the process of desegregation was not to be completed at once, but, in the words of the Court, "with all deliberate speed." In different states this meant various things. By the opening of the fall school term in 1957 the District of Columbia public schools had been completely desegregated, as had most of the school districts in Kentucky, Maryland, Missouri, and Oklahoma. Desegregation had been effected in some districts in the states of Arkansas, Delaware, North Carolina, Tennessee, and Texas. There remained, then, only seven states in which there was no desegregation at the public school level: Alabama, Florida, Georgia, Louisiana, Mississippi, South Carolina, and Virginia. The opposition in the resisting states is, however, intense, characterized by defiant resolutions of so-called "interposition," elaborate school assignment plans designed to preserve segregated schools, and the establishment of legislative and judicial barriers to the successful functioning of the National Association for the Advancement of Colored People.

Not directly related to the controversy over school segregation, but a part of the total picture of civil rights ferment was the enactment, after intense congressional debate, of the Civil Rights Act of 1957. That act provided for the establishment of a Commission on Civil Rights to investigate allegations of voting deprivations based on race, color, or national origin, to study legal developments constituting a denial of equal protection of the laws, and to appraise federal laws and policies in that connection. In addition, the act authorized the creation of a Civil Rights Division in the Department of Justice. But most importantly, the act authorized the Attorney General to proceed in the name of the United States for preventive relief against any person reasonably believed to be about to deny another person the exercise of his right to vote. Violators of injunctions so secured are in most instances assured jury trial of any criminal contempt brought against them.

THE SELF-INCRIMINATION CLAUSE

(42 American Bar Association Journal 935, 1956)

By Beecher N. Claflin

"No person . . . shall be compelled in any criminal case to be a witness against himself. . . ."

Until recent years, the above clause, which is only a portion of the Fifth Amendment to the Constitution of the United States, received scant attention from laymen. Probably most people who gave the clause any thought at all had the general impression that it had something to do with a criminal not being required to take the witness stand. However, particularly since the end of World War II, the widely publicized congressional committee investigations of crime and of Communist infiltration and influence in this country have focused attention upon the self-incrimination clause of the Fifth Amendment and it has become a subject of heated controversy.

Because the clause seems to serve as an effective shield not only against disclosure by a notorious witness of his own activities, but also against disclosure of the activities of the witness' associates, the self-incrimination clause is an enigma, if not an anathema, to many laymen already impatient and distrustful of procedural aspects of the law. On the other hand, there are those who feel that the self-incrimination clause is only a minimum protection, that the courts have permitted congressional committees too wide an area of investigation, and that the general public has not been properly tolerant of those who have invoked the self-incrimination clause.

The principle that a person should not be compelled to accuse himself came into being in the English common law following the agitation in the seventeenth century over the coercive, inquisitorial procedure of the English church courts. Thereafter, during the latter half of the seventeenth century, the privilege against self-incrimination became firmly established in the English common law courts with respect to an accused on trial, and it was extended during this period to other witnesses.[1] At the same time, the Massachusetts colony permitted compulsory self-incrimination as late as 1685.[2]

As pointed out by one modern court,[3] the privilege against self-incrimination is not to be found in any English or American charter or constitution until 1776. In that year it was included in the Virginia Declaration of Rights. Subsequently, it was included in the Federal Constitution as one of the individual safeguards demanded by those who feared oppressive federal authority.

We are here concerned only with the language and policy of the federal constitutional provision. We shall not examine similar state provisions, the question of court or administrative jurisdiction, or the question of the legal scope of congressional investigations. Let us, then, examine closely the component parts of the clause.

1. "No person . . ."

The federal constitutional provision against compulsory self-incrimination, viewed in light of its historical background, is one designed for protection of the *individual* against oppression. As such, it does not prevent the compulsory disclosure of organizational documents which may result in a criminal prosecution of an organization. Thus it is well established that a collective group such as a corporation, a union, or a political party has no standing to invoke the privilege.[4]

However, this exception extends further. Relying upon the very personal nature of the privilege and upon the necessity for governmental regulation of collective groups, the courts have held that a witness appearing in a representative capacity cannot refuse to produce documents belonging to an organization even though those documents may ultimately lead to the individual's prosecution.[5] This exception seems justified as a matter of policy, since the potential danger to society of non-punishment of unlawful acts by a collective group, potentially at least wielding greater power than an individual, overbalances the potential oppression of a representative or officer of the organization. Further, a person becoming an official of an organization has a higher responsibility to society in that representative capacity than in an individual capacity.

The concept of the very personal nature of the privilege has been extended so as to require a sole proprietor to produce personally incriminating records of a quasi-public nature, without protection of the self-incrimination clause. A case of this type in the Supreme Court[6] involved the production of O.P.A. records which, under the law, the businessman was required to keep in order to assist the government in policing the enforcement of the economic control measure. The conclusion of the courts as to quasi-public records is justified as a matter of policy. The point is, however, that the self-incrimination clause is not so sacrosanct that it has not been molded to fit a particular governmental need.

2. ". . . shall be compelled . . ."

It is clear that a natural individual has, under this

clause, a *privilege* against self-incrimination, not a *right* against self-incrimination. The clause is concerned with disclosure under compulsion, not a complete freedom from disclosure under any circumstances.

If an individual gives a voluntary statement to a court, administrative board, or legislative committee and makes no claim of privilege he cannot, in the absence of an applicable immunity statute, claim that he should not have been subsequently convicted of a federal crime based upon his testimony previously given.[7] The reverse is also true. A witness cannot refuse to testify at all before any questions are asked of him.[8]

In short, the witness must invoke the privilege, and he must invoke it at the time the question or questions are put to him.

Granted that a witness, in order to invoke the privilege, is not required to use particular words or a pat formula, yet there must be an affirmative claim of privilege. In *Quinn* v. *United States*,[9] and *Emspak* v. *United States*,[10] companion cases decided in 1955, a majority of the Supreme Court found such an affirmative claim in what seemed to be an ambiguous assertion. In each of those cases, the witness asserted the First Amendment, supplemented by the Fifth Amendment, as grounds for refusing to answer certain questions. Although represented by counsel, the witness at no point mentioned "self-incrimination" or "tend to incriminate." A reading of the portion of the transcript quoted in the Supreme Court report indicates that the witness may well have been avoiding a precise claim of the privilege against self-incrimination. The First Amendment relates to freedom of speech and religion, and the Fifth Amendment relates to a number of subjects in addition to self-incrimination. The breadth of the majority's construction becomes apparent upon the reading of Justice Reed's dissenting opinion.[11] Justice Reed concluded that the witness had not met the burden of advising his interrogators in understandable terms of the claim of privilege against self-incrimination, and that the assertion smacked strongly of a due process claim under the Fifth Amendment. . . .

We now come to the basic question as to the type of protection the self-incrimination clause was designed to afford the individual. The privilege which the clause incorporates resulted from a reaction to legally constituted authority exacting incriminating statements from witnesses. Historically, the clause is a protection only against compulsion by legal authority.

Consistent with this historical purpose, considerable legal precedent limits the clause to protection of an individual against successful *prosecution* based upon testimony unwillingly given.

Thus sixty years ago, in *Brown* v. *Walker*,[12] the Supreme Court concluded that it is only a legal detriment with which the constitutional provision is concerned; that such provision does not grant immunity against personal disgrace or opprobrium. Therefore, held the Court, an immunity statute which gave complete protection from prosecution in return for incriminating testimony was constitutional.

Ten years later, the Supreme Court said:

> The object of the amendment is to establish in express language and upon a firm basis the general principle of English and American jurisprudence, that no one shall be compelled to give testimony which may expose him to prosecution for crime. It is not declared that he may not be compelled to testify to facts which may impair his reputation for probity, or even tend to disgrace him, but the line is drawn at testimony that may expose him to prosecution. If the testimony relates to criminal acts long since past, and against the prosecution of which the statute of limitations has run, or for which he has already received a pardon or is guar-

anteed an immunity, the amendment does not apply.[13]

In 1948, the Supreme Court in reviewing the policy of the self-incrimination clause said:

> If a witness could not be prosecuted on facts concerning which he testified, the witness could not fairly say he had been compelled in a criminal case to be a witness against himself. He might suffer disgrace and humiliation but such unfortunate results to him are outside of constitutional protection.[14]

On the economic side, it has been held that the self-incrimination clause does not guarantee that the person invoking it shall be continued in private employment.[15]

On the other hand, the Supreme Court recently gave recognition to the factor of private pressures at least in an indirect way with this language in the *Emspak* case:

> Second, if it is true that in these times a stigma may somehow result from a witness' reliance on the Self-Incrimination Clause, a committee should be all the more ready to recognize a veiled claim of the privilege. Otherwise, the great right which the Clause was intended to secure might be effectively frustrated by private pressures.[16]

While we find the contention of social and economic compulsion frequently made, it would seem that it has been put to rest by *In re Ullman*.[17] In that case, the defendant urged that no matter how broad an immunity statute might be, it could not be co-extensive with the constitutional privilege because of the governmental sanctions against employment and other privileges, and because of the social and economic consequences which follow self-exposure under a grant of immunity. The District Court rejected this contention, saying that the authority of *Brown* v. *Walker* remains unimpaired and that the principle of that case is "firmly imbedded in our constitutional law." The Second Circuit Court of Appeals affirmed on the authority of that case, but indicated that its views might have been different if the law were not so well settled. A majority of the Supreme Court on March 26, 1956, affirmed the decision in the *Ullman* case and reaffirmed the authority of *Brown* v. *Walker*. The Court upheld the constitutionality of the Immunity Act of 1954[18] which grants immunity from prosecution under certain conditions in cases involving national security.

We now come to the concept of waiver. The witness is not *compelled* to testify if he in fact waives the privilege against incrimination.

The simplest example is that of the defendant in a criminal case who, by taking the stand, waives the privilege as to all of his testimony.[19]

A more difficult case is presented by a non-defendant witness before a court or government body who freely answers some questions, but then stops short. The question is, of course, whether the witness has waived the privilege by the testimony already given.

In *United States* v. *St. Pierre*[20] it was held that at least after a witness has confessed all the elements of a crime in a general way, he may not withhold the details. The Court said that while it must be conceded that the privilege suppresses the truth, it is not a privilege to garble the truth.

The leading case on this subject of waiver is *Rogers* v. *United States*,[21] decided by the Supreme Court in 1951. In that case, the petitioner voluntarily testified to the fact that she had been Treasurer of the Communist Party of Denver, but invoked the privilege when asked to name the person to whom she turned over party records. The Court laid down a test, and its application to the facts, in the following language:

> . . . the court was required to determine,
> as it must whenever the privilege is claimed,

whether the question presented a reasonable danger of further crimination in light of all the circumstances, including any previous disclosures. As to each question to which a claim of privilege is directed, the court must determine whether the answer to that particular question would subject the witness to a "real danger" of further crimination. After petitioner's admission that she held the office of Treasurer of the Communist Party of Denver, disclosure of acquaintance with her successor presents no more than a "mere imaginary possibility" of increasing the danger of prosecution.[22]

A still different case is presented when the witness unambiguously asserts the privilege before proceeding to testify under the protection of an immunity statute. In such case, the Supreme Court has ruled that for a witness' statements thereafter to constitute a waiver, there must be a clear and unequivocal expression of intent to waive the privilege.[23]

3. ". . . in any criminal case . . ."

Counselman v. *Hitchcock*,[24] decided by the Supreme Court in 1892, set at rest any doubt as to the breadth of meaning contained in the above four words. There the Court said:

It is impossible that the meaning of the constitutional provision can only be, that a person shall not be compelled to be a witness against himself in a criminal prosecution against himself. It would doubtless cover such cases; but it is not limited to them. The object was to insure that a person should not be compelled, when acting as a witness in any investigation, to give testimony which might tend to show that he himself had committed a crime. The privilege is limited to criminal matters, but it is as broad as the mischief against which it seeks to guard.[25]

4. ". . . to be a witness against himself . . ."

The words "against himself" mean that the clause gives no protection to disclosure of facts which tend to incriminate only third parties.[26] The difficulty, however, is that quite frequently answers to questions about third parties will also involve the witness at least indirectly. Therefore, as a practical matter, this limitation seems to have little effect as a brake on the application of the clause.

Being a witness against himself includes not only personal papers and oral testimony but also, in theory at least, silence. That is, no inference of guilt, from a legal standpoint, is to be made from a defendant remaining silent.[27]

As to documentary evidence, we have seen that the privilege does not extend to papers belonging to an organization or to quasi-public records. Today with much of business being carried on in corporate form and with the Federal Government requiring so much in the way of detailed records, there is much documentary evidence which is outside of the privilege.

As to oral testimony, there remain for consideration the questions (1) who makes the determination whether a question is incriminatory, and (2) what are the tests of an incriminatory question.

As to the first question, it was established by Chief Justice Marshall in *United States* v. *Burr*[28] that it is the province of the court to judge whether any direct answer to the question proposed will furnish evidence against the witness. Thus, simply asserting the privilege is not sufficient. The witness himself is not the sole and ultimate judge of the incriminating nature of the question. But, as Chief Justice Marshall pointed out, a witness is not required to prove that the answer will in fact incriminate him, because if such were the case, the very purpose of the privilege would be defeated, because in the course of such proof, incriminating facts would be disclosed.

How then does a court judge whether a question is incriminatory?

A possible answer need not admit the crime or even an element of the crime for the question to be incriminatory. The concept of "link in a chain" was set forth by Chief Justice Marshall in the following language of *United States* v. *Burr*:

> If such answer may disclose a fact which furnishes a necessary and essential link in a chain of testimony, which would be sufficient to convict him of any crime, he is not bound to answer it so as to furnish matter for that conviction. . . . [29]

From the modern cases it appears that "link in a chain" includes testimony once removed, *i.e.*, testimony which may reveal sources from which evidence could be obtained that would lead to conviction or prosecution. In *Counselman* v. *Hitchcock*,[30] the Supreme Court considered an immunity statute as not being co-extensive with the constitutional guarantee because the statute, among other things, afforded no protection against the use of compelled testimony to search out other evidence to be used against the witness. And more recently, this concept of testimony once removed was given specific recognition by a district court in a case not involving an immunity statute.[31] Finally, in a dissenting opinion in the *Emspak* case Justice Harlan recognized the concept of an incriminating answer as follows:

> The concept of an incriminating answer includes not only those answers which constitute an admission of guilt, but also those which may furnish evidence of guilt or merely supply a lead to obtaining such evidence. *Counselman* v. *Hitchcock*, 142 U.S. 547 (1892).[32]

Following the concept of a link in a chain to its logical conclusion, the answer to the most innocuous question could conceivably tend to incriminate. However, the Supreme Court in *Hoffman* v. *United States*[33] gives us this test:

> To sustain the privilege, it need only be evident from the implications of the question, in the setting in which it is asked, that a responsive answer to the question or an explanation of why it cannot be answered might be dangerous because injurious disclosure could result. The trial judge in appraising the claim "must be governed as much by his personal perception of the peculiarities of the case as by the facts actually in evidence." See Taft, J., in Ex parte Irvine, 74 F. 954, 960 (C. C. S. D. Ohio, 1896).[34]

The setting or circumstances in which a particular question is asked seems to be of utmost importance when a question innocent on its face is asked. The Courts have given consideration to other questions put to the witness, the notoriety of the witness as disclosed by newspaper reports or past record, statements made by members of the investigative body to the witness, publicity given to the hearings, and the fact that some incriminatory information concerning the witness is already in the possession of the investigative body.[35] The result is that a person of good repute has much less chance of successfully invoking the privilege, at least as to apparently innocent questions, than a person of ill repute.

After having been reversed several times in upholding contempt convictions of witnesses for refusal to answer questions, the Third Circuit Court of Appeals in *United States* v. *Coffey*[36] undertook a reappraisal of the Supreme Court's present position as to incriminatory questions. It came to the conclusion that *Mason* v. *United States*,[37] decided in 1917, would not be followed today. In the *Mason* case, the Court held that a man might be required to answer a question whether cards were being played at a table where he had been sitting in an Alaskan billiard parlor. The Third Circuit Court had regarded the *Mason* case as being particularly striking, even extreme, in its insistence upon an affirmative showing that an answer innocent on its face had sinister implications, for, said the court, "the normal connotation of a card game in a frontier saloon is not that of a game of Old Maid on a supervised public playground."

The Third Circuit in the *Coffey* case concluded by re-interpreting the *Hoffman* case as follows:

> It is enough (1) that the trial court be shown by argument how conceivably a prosecutor, building on the seemingly harmless answer, might proceed step by step to link the witness with some crime against the United States, and (2) that this suggested course and scheme of linkage not seem incredible in the circumstances of the particular case. It is in this latter connection, the credibility of the suggested connecting chain, that the reputation and known history of the witness may be significant.[38]

In a dissenting opinion in the *Emspak* case, Justice Harlan re-examines the standard for judging the character of a question and the application of the standard to two types of questions, those innocent on their face and those which are dangerous questions.[39] He notes a tendency of the Supreme Court in recent *per curiam* reversals of contempt convictions to stray from the application of the traditional standard of "real danger v. imaginary possibility." As to questions innocent on their face, he states that where the background facts are not known to the court, the witness is required to open the door wide enough for the court to see that there is substance to his claim. He points out that if the background facts are known or suspected to exist, this problem of opening the door a crack disappears, for all the witness has to do is point to such facts or suspicions. However, he makes the further point that if background facts can make an innocent question dangerous, they can also make a dangerous question innocent, and that in deciding whether the privilege is available, the court must take into account all the facts—not just those tending to make the question dangerous. . . .

1 8 WIGMORE ON EVIDENCE (3d Ed.), Sec. 2250; *Quinn* v. *United States,* 349 U.S. 155, 161 (1955); *In re Watson,* 293 Mich. 263, 291 N.W. 652 (1940).

2 8 WIGMORE ON EVIDENCE (3d Ed.), Sec. 2250.

3 *In re Watson,* 293 Mich. 263, 291 N.W. 652 (1940).

4 *Wilson* v. *United States,* 221 U.S. 361 (1911), corporation; *United States* v. *White,* 322 U.S. 644 (1944), labor union; *Rogers* v. *United States,* 340 U.S. 367 (1951), Communist Party.

5 Cases cited in note 4.

6 *Shapiro* v. *United States,* 335 U.S. 1 (1948).

7 *United States* v. *Monia,* 317 U.S. 424, 427 (1943); *May* v. *United States,* 175 F. 2d 994 (D.C. Cir. 1949), *cert. den.* 338 U.S. 830 (1949).

8 *Enrichi* v. *United States,* 212 F. 2d 702 (10th Cir., 1954).

9 349 U.S. 155 (1955).

10 349 U.S. 190 (1955).

11 *Quinn* v. *United States,* 349 U.S. 155 (1955), at page 171 *et seq.*

12 161 U.S. 591 (1896).

13 *Hale* v. *Henkel,* 201 U.S. 43, 66 (1906).

14 *Smith* v. *United States,* 337 U.S. 137, 147 (1949).

15 *United Electrical Radio and Machine Workers of America* v. *General Electric Company,* 127 F. Supp. 934 (D.Ct., District of Columbia 1954), affirmed by Court of Appeals for District of Columbia Circuit on March 22, 1956.

16 349 U.S. 190, 195 (1955).

17 128 F. Supp. 617 (D.Ct., S.D., N.Y. 1955); affirmed in *United States* v. *Ullman,* 221 F. 2d 760 (2d Cir., 1955); affirmed by Supreme Court of the United States on March 26, 1956. THE NEW YORK TIMES, March 27, 1956, page 1, column 8.

18 18 U.S.C. §3486.

19 See discussion in *Johnson* v. *United States,* 318 U. S. 189 (1943).

20 132 F. 2d 837 (2d Cir., 1942), writ of certiorari dismissed, 319 U.S. 41 (1943).

21 340 U.S. 367 (1951).

22 340 U.S. 367, 374, 375 (1951).

23 Smith v. United States, 337 U.S. 137 (1949).

24 142 U.S. 547 (1892).

25 142 U.S. 547, 562 (1892). It has been held that the clause is designed as a protection against *federal* prosecution and that apprehension of state prosecution alone is insufficient ground for invoking the clause. United States v. Murdock, 284 U.S. 141 (1931). However, a federal immunity statute may be broad enough to preclude state prosecution based upon evidence given at a federal inquiry. Adams v. Maryland, 347 U.S. 179 (1954).

26 Saffo v. United States, 213 F. 2d 131 (8th Cir., 1954).

27 Helton v. United States, 221 F. 2d 338 (5th Cir., 1955).

28 25 Fed. Cases 38, Case No. 14,692e (Circ. Ct., D. Va. 1807).

29 25 Fed. Cases 38, 41, Case No. 14,692e (Circ. Ct., D. Va. 1807).

30 142 U.S. 547 (1892).

31 United States v. Raley, 96 F. Supp. 495 (D. Ct., D.C. 1951).

32 349 U.S. 190, 204, 205 (1955).

33 341 U. S. 479 (1951).

34 341 U.S. 479, 486, 487 (1951).

35 Hoffman v. United States, 341 U.S. 479 (1951); United States v. Doto, 205 F. 2d 416 (2d Cir., 1953), cert. den. 350 U.S. 847; United States v. Jaffe, 96 F. Supp. 191 (D. Ct., D.C. 1951); United States v. Fischetti, 103 F. Supp. 796 (D. Ct., D.C. 1952); United States v. Pechart, 103 F. Supp. 417 (D. Ct. N.D. Calif., 1952).

36 198 F. 2d 438 (3d Cir., 1952).

37 244 U.S. 362 (1917).

38 198 F. 2d 438, 440 (3d Cir., 1952).

39 349 U.S. 190, 204 to 213 (1955).

The Constitution Of The United States Of America

WE THE PEOPLE of the United States, in Order to form a more perfect Union, establish Justice, insure domestic Tranquility, provide for the common defence, promote the general Welfare, and secure the Blessings of Liberty to ourselves and our Posterity, do ordain and establish this CONSTITUTION for the United States of America.

ARTICLE I.

SECTION 1. All legislative Powers herein granted shall be vested in a Congress of the United States, which shall consist of a Senate and House of Representatives.

SECTION 2. The House of Representatives shall be composed of Members chosen every second Year by the People of the several States, and the Electors in each State shall have the Qualifications requisite for Electors of the most numerous Branch of the State Legislature.

No Person shall be a Representative who shall not have attained to the Age of twenty-five Years, and been seven Years a Citizen of the United States, and who shall not, when elected, be an Inhabitant of that State in which he shall be chosen.

[Representatives and direct Taxes shall be apportioned among the several States which may be included within this Union, according to their respective Numbers, which shall be determined by adding to the whole Number of free Persons, including those bound to Service for a Term of Years, and excluding Indians not taxed, three fifths of all other Persons.] The actual Enumeration shall be made within three Years after the first Meeting of the Congress of the United States, and within every subsequent Term of ten Years, in such Manner as they shall by Law direct. The Number of Representatives shall not exceed one for every thirty Thousand, but each State shall have at Least one Representative; and until such enumeration shall be made, the State of New Hampshire shall be entitled to chuse three, Massachusetts eight, Rhode-Island and Providence Plantations one, Connecticut five, New-York six, New Jersey four, Pennsylvania eight, Delaware one, Maryland six, Virginia ten, North Carolina five, South Carolina five, and Georgia three.

When vacancies happen in the Representation from any State, the Executive Authority thereof shall issue Writs of Election to fill such Vacancies.

The House of Representatives shall chuse their Speaker and other Officers; and shall have the sole Power of Impeachment.

SECTION 3. The Senate of the United States shall be composed of two Senators from each State, chosen by the Legislature thereof, for six Years; and each Senator shall have one Vote.

Immediately after they shall be assembled in Consequence of the first Election, they shall be divided as equally as may be into three Classes. The Seats of the Senators of the first Class shall be vacated at the Expiration of the second Year, of the second Class at the Expiration of the fourth Year, and of the third Class at the Expiration of the sixth Year, so that one-third may be chosen every second Year; and if Vacancies happen by Resignation, or otherwise, during the Recess of the Legislature of any State, the Executive thereof may make temporary Appointments until the next Meeting of the Legislature, which shall then fill such Vacancies.

No Person shall be a Senator who shall not have attained to the Age of thirty Years, and been nine Years a Citizen of the United States, and who shall not, when elected, be an Inhabitant of that State for which he shall be chosen.

The Vice President of the United States shall be President of the Senate, but shall have no Vote, unless they be equally divided.

The Senate shall chuse their other Officers, and also a President pro tempore, in the absence of the Vice President, or when he shall exercise the Office of President of the United States.

The Senate shall have the sole Power to try all Impeachments. When sitting for that Purpose, they shall be on Oath or Affirmation. When the President of the United States is tried, the Chief Justice shall preside: And no Person shall be convicted without the Concurrence of two thirds of the Members present.

Judgment in Cases of Impeachment shall not extend further than to removal from Office, and disqualification to hold and enjoy any Office of honor, Trust or Profit under the United States: but the Party convicted shall nevertheless be liable and subject to Indictment, Trial, Judgment and Punishment, according to Law.

SECTION 4. The Times, Places and Manner of holding Elections for Senators and Representatives, shall be prescribed in each State by the Legislature thereof; but the Congress may at any time by Law make or alter such Regulations, except as to the Place of Chusing Senators.

The Congress shall assemble at least once in every Year, and such Meeting shall be on the first Monday in December, unless they shall by Law appoint a different Day.

SECTION 5. Each House shall be the Judge of the Elections, Returns and Qualifications of its own Members, and a Majority of each shall constitute a Quorum to do Business; but a smaller number may adjourn from day to day, and may be authorized to compel the Attendance of absent Members, in such Manner, and under such Penalties as each House may provide.

Each House may determine the Rules of its Proceedings, punish its Members for disorderly Behavior, and, with the Concurrence of two thirds, expel a Member.

Each House shall keep a Journal of its Procedings, and from time to time publish the same, excepting such Parts as may in their Judgment require Secrecy; and the Yeas and Nays of the Members of either House on any question shall, at the Desire of one fifth of those Present, be entered on the Journal.

Neither House, during the Session of Congress, shall, without the Consent of the other, adjourn for more than three days, nor to any other Place than that in which the two Houses shall be sitting.

SECTION 6. The Senators and Representatives shall receive a Compensation for their Services, to be ascertained by Law, and paid out of the Treasury of the United States. They shall in all Cases, except Treason, Felony and Breach of the Peace, be privileged from Arrest during their Attendance at the Session of their respective Houses, and in going to and returning from the same; and for any Speech or Debate in either House, they shall not be questioned in any other Place.

No Senator or Representative shall, during the Time for which he was elected, be appointed to any civil Office under the Authority of the United States, which shall have been created, or the Emoluments whereof shall have been encreased during such time; and no Person holding any Office under the United States, shall be a Member of either House during his Continuance in Office.

SECTION 7. All Bills for raising Revenue shall originate in

the House of Representatives; but the Senate may propose or concur with Amendments as on other Bills.

Every Bill which shall have passed the House of Representatives and the Senate, shall, before it become a Law, be presented to the President of the United States; If he approves he shall sign it, but if not he shall return it, with his Objections to that House in which it shall have originated, who shall enter the Objections at large on their Journal, and proceed to reconsider it. If after such Reconsideration two thirds of that House shall agree to pass the Bill, it shall be sent, together with the Objections, to the other House, by which it shall likewise be reconsidered, and if approved by two thirds of that House, it shall become a Law. But in all such Cases the Votes of both Houses shall be determined by Yeas and Nays, and the Names of the Persons voting for and against the Bill shall be entered on the Journal of each House respectively. If any Bill shall not be returned by the President within ten Days (Sundays excepted) after it shall have been presented to him, the Same shall be a Law, in like Manner as if he had signed it, unless the Congress by their Adjournment prevent its Return, in which Case it shall not be a Law.

Every Order, Resolution, or Vote to which the Concurrence of the Senate and House of Representatives may be necessary (except on a question of Adjournment) shall be presented to the President of the United States; and before the Same shall take Effect, shall be approved by him, or being disapproved by him, shall be repassed by two thirds of the Senate and House of Representatives, according to the Rules and Limitations prescribed in the Case of a Bill.

SECTION 8. The Congress shall have Power To lay and collect Taxes, Duties, Imposts and Excises, to pay the Debts and provide for the common Defence and general Welfare of the United States; but all Duties, Imposts and Excises shall be uniform throughout the United States;

To borrow money on the credit of the United States;

To regulate Commerce with foreign Nations, and among the several States, and with the Indian Tribes;

To establish an uniform Rule of Naturalization, and uniform Laws on the subject of Bankruptcies throughout the United States;

To coin Money, regulate the Value thereof, and of foreign Coin, and fix the Standard of Weights and Measures;

To provide for the Punishment of counterfeiting the Securities and current Coin of the United States;

To establish Post Offices and post Roads;

To promote the Progress of Science and useful Arts, by securing for limited Times to Authors and Inventors the exclusive Right to their respective Writings and Discoveries;

To constitute Tribunals inferior to the supreme Court;

To define and punish Piracies and Felonies committed on the high Seas, and Offenses against the Law of Nations;

To declare War, grant Letters of Marque and Reprisal, and make Rules concerning Captures on Land and Water;

To raise and support Armies, but no Appropriation of Money to that Use shall be for a longer Term than two Years;

To provide and maintain a Navy;

To make Rules for the Government and Regulation of the land and naval Forces;

To provide for calling forth the Militia to execute the Laws of the Union, suppress Insurrections and repel Invasions;

To provide for organizing, arming, and disciplining the Militia, and for governing such Part of them as may be employed in the Service of the United States, reserving to the States respectively, the Appointment of the Officers, and the Authority of training the Militia according to the discipline prescribed by Congress;

To exercise exclusive Legislation in all Cases whatsoever, over such District (not exceeding ten Miles square) as may, by Cession of particular States, and the acceptance of Congress, become the Seat of the Government of the United States, and to exercise like Authority over all Places purchased by the Consent of the Legislature of the State in which the Same shall be, for the Erection of Forts, Magazines, Arsenals, dock-Yards, and other needful Buildings;—And

To make all Laws which shall be necessary and proper for carrying into Execution the foregoing Powers, and all other Powers vested by this Constitution in the Government of the United States, or in any Department or Officer thereof.

SECTION 9. The Migration or Importation of such Persons as any of the States now existing shall think proper to admit, shall not be prohibited by the Congress prior to the Year one thousand eight hundred and eight, but a tax or duty may be imposed on such Importation, not exceeding ten dollars for each Person.

The privilege of the Writ of Habeas Corpus shall not be suspended, unless when in Cases of Rebellion or Invasion the public Safety may require it.

No Bill of Attainder or ex post facto Law shall be passed.

No capitation, or other direct, Tax shall be laid, unless in

Proportion to the Census or Enumeration herein before directed to be taken.

No Tax or Duty shall be laid on Articles exported from any State.

No Preference shall be given by any Regulation of Commerce or Revenue to the Ports of one State over those of another: nor shall Vessels bound to, or from, one State, be obliged to enter, clear, or pay Duties in another.

No Money shall be drawn from the Treasury, but in Consequence of Appropriations made by Law; and a regular Statement and Account of the Receipts and Expenditures of all public Money shall be published from time to time.

No Title of Nobility shall be granted by the United States: And no Person holding any Office of Profit or Trust under them, shall, without the Consent of the Congress, accept of any present, Emolument, Office, or Title, of any kind whatever, from any King, Prince, or foreign State.

SECTION 10. No State shall enter into any Treaty, Alliance, or Confederation; grant Letters of Marque and Reprisal; coin Money; emit Bills of Credit; make any Thing but gold and silver Coin a Tender in Payment of Debts; pass any Bill of Attainder, ex post facto Law, or Law impairing the Obligation of Contracts, or grant any Title of Nobility.

No State shall, without the Consent of the Congress, lay any Imposts or Duties on Imports or Exports, except what may be absolutely necessary for executing it's inspection Laws: and the net Produce of all Duties and Imposts, laid by any State on Imports or Exports, shall be for the Use of the Treasury of the United States; and all such Laws shall be subject to the Revision and Controul of the Congress.

No State shall, without the Consent of Congress, lay any duty of Tonnage, keep Troops, or Ships of War in time of Peace, enter into any Agreement or Compact with another State, or with a foreign Power, or engage in War, unless actually invaded, or in such imminent Danger as will not admit of delay.

ARTICLE II.

SECTION 1. The executive Power shall be vested in a President of the United States of America. He shall hold his Office during the Term of four Years, and, together with the Vice-President, chosen for the same Term, be elected, as follows

Each State shall appoint, in such Manner as the Legislature thereof may direct, a Number of Electors, equal to the whole Number of Senators and Representatives to which the State may be entitled in the Congress: but no Senator or Representative, or Person holding an Office of Trust or Profit under the United States, shall be appointed an Elector.

[The Electors shall meet in their respective States, and vote by Ballot for two persons, of whom one at least shall not be an Inhabitant of the same State with themselves. And they shall make a List of all the Persons voted for, and of the Number of Votes for each; which List they shall sign and certify, and transmit sealed to the Seat of the Government of the United States, directed to the President of the Senate. The President of the Senate shall, in the Presence of the Senate and House of Representatives, open all the Certificates, and the Votes shall then be counted. The Person having the greatest Number of Votes shall be the President, if such Number be a Majority of the whole Number of Electors appointed; and if there be more than one who have such Majority, and have an equal Number of Votes, then the House of Representatives shall immediately chuse by Ballot one of them for President; and if no Person have a Majority, then from the five highest on the List the said House shall in like Manner chuse the President. But in chusing the President, the Votes shall be taken by States, the Representation from each State having one Vote; A quorum for this Purpose shall consist of a Member or Members from two-thirds of the States, and a Majority of all the States shall be necessary to a Choice. In every Case, after the Choice of the President, the Person having the greatest Number of Votes of the Electors shall be the Vice President. But if there should remain two or more who have equal Votes, the Senate shall chuse from them by Ballot the Vice-President.]

The Congress may determine the Time of chusing the Electors, and the Day on which they shall give their Votes; which Day shall be the same throughout the United States.

No person except a natural born Citizen, or a Citizen of the United States, at the time of the Adoption of this Constitution, shall be eligible to the Office of President; neither shall any Person be eligible to that Office who shall not have attained to the Age of thirty-five Years, and been fourteen Years a Resident within the United States.

In Case of the Removal of the President from Office, or of his Death, Resignation, or Inability to discharge the Powers and Duties of the said Office, the same shall devolve on the Vice President, and the Congress may by Law provide for the Case of Removal, Death, Resignation or Inability, both of the President and Vice President, declaring what Officer shall then act as President, and such Officer shall act accordingly, until the Disability be removed, or a President shall be elected.

The President shall, at stated Times, receive for his Services, a Compensation, which shall neither be encreased nor diminished during the Period for which he shall have been elected, and he shall not receive within that Period any other Emolument from the United States, or any of them.

Before he enter on the Execution of his Office, he shall take the following Oath or Affirmation:—"I do solemnly swear (or affirm) that I will faithfully execute the Office of President of the United States, and will to the best of my Ability, preserve, protect and defend the Constitution of the United States."

Section 2. The President shall be Commander in Chief of the Army and Navy of the United States, and of the Militia of the several States, when called into the actual Service of the United States; he may require the Opinion in writing, of the principal Officer in each of the executive Departments, upon any subject relating to the Duties of their respective Offices, and he shall have Power to Grant Reprieves and Pardons for Offenses against the United States, except in Cases of Impeachment.

He shall have Power, by and with the Advice and Consent of the Senate, to make Treaties, provided two-thirds of the Senators present concur; and he shall nominate, and by and with the Advice and Consent of the Senate, shall appoint Ambassadors, other public Ministers and Consuls, Judges of the supreme Court, and all other Officers of the United States, whose Appointments are not herein otherwise provided for, and which shall be established by Law: but the Congress may by Law vest the Appointment of such inferior Officers, as they think proper, in the President alone, in the Courts of Law, or in the Heads of Departments.

The President shall have Power to fill up all Vacancies that may happen during the Recess of the Senate, by granting Commissions which shall expire at the End of their next Session.

Section 3. He shall from time to time give to the Congress Information of the State of the Union, and recommend to their Consideration such Measures as he shall judge necessary and expedient; he may, on extraordinary Occasions, convene both Houses, or either of them, and in Case of Disagreement between them, with Respect to the Time of Adjournment, he may adjourn them to such Time as he shall think proper; he shall receive Ambassadors and other public Ministers; he shall take Care that the Laws be faithfully executed, and shall Commission all the Officers of the United States.

Section 4. The President, Vice President and all civil Officers of the United States, shall be removed from Office on Impeachment for, and Conviction of, Treason, Bribery, or other high Crimes and Misdemeanors.

ARTICLE III.

SECTION 1. The judicial Power of the United States, shall be vested in one supreme Court, and in such inferior Courts as the Congress may from time to time ordain and establish. The Judges, both of the supreme and inferior Courts, shall hold their Offices during good Behaviour, and shall, at stated Times, receive for their Services a Compensation which shall not be diminished during their Continuance in Office.

SECTION 2. The judicial Power shall extend to all Cases, in Law and Equity, arising under this Constitution, the Laws of the United States, and Treaties made, or which shall be made, under their Authority;—to all Cases affecting Ambassadors, other public Ministers and Consuls;—to all Cases of admiralty and maritime Jurisdiction;—to Controversies to which the United States shall be a Party;—to Controversies between two or more States;—between a State and Citizens of another State;—between Citizens of different States;—between Citizens of the same State claiming Lands under Grants of different States, and between a State, or the Citizens thereof, and foreign States, Citizens or Subjects.

In all Cases affecting Ambassadors, other public Ministers and Consuls, and those in which a State shall be Party, the supreme Court shall have original Jurisdiction. In all the other Cases before mentioned, the supreme Court shall have appellate Jurisdiction, both as to Law and Fact, with such Exceptions, and under such Regulations as the Congress shall make.

The trial of all Crimes, except in Cases of Impeachment, shall be by Jury; and such Trial shall be held in the State where the said Crimes shall have been committed; but when not committed within any State, the Trial shall be at such Place or Places as the Congress may by Law have directed.

SECTION 3. Treason against the United States, shall consist only in levying War against them, or in adhering to their Enemies, giving them Aid and Comfort. No Person shall be convicted of Treason unless on the Testimony of two Witnesses to the same overt Act, or on Confession in open Court.

The Congress shall have power to declare the Punishment of Treason, but no Attainder of Treason shall work Corruption of Blood, or Forfeiture except during the Life of the Person attainted.

ARTICLE IV.

SECTION 1. Full Faith and Credit shall be given in each State to the public Acts, Records, and judicial Proceedings of every other State. And the Congress may by general Laws prescribe the Manner in which such Acts, Records and Proceedings shall be proved, and the Effect thereof.

SECTION 2. The Citizens of each State shall be entitled to all Privileges and Immunities of Citizens in the several States.

A Person charged in any State with Treason, Felony, or other Crime, who shall flee from Justice, and be found in another State, shall on demand of the executive Authority of the State from which he fled, be delivered up, to be removed to the State having Jurisdiction of the Crime.

No Person held to Service or Labour in one State, under the Laws thereof, escaping into another, shall, in Consequence of any Law or Regulation therein, be discharged from such Service or Labour, but shall be delivered up on Claim of the Party to whom such Service or Labour may be due.

SECTION 3. New States may be admitted by the Congress into this Union; but no new State shall be formed or erected within the Jurisdiction of any other State; nor any State be formed by the Junction of two or more States, or parts of States, without the Consent of the Legislatures of the States concerned as well as of the Congress.

The Congress shall have Power to dispose of and make all needful Rules and Regulations respecting the Territory or other Property belonging to the United States; and nothing in this Constitution shall be so construed as to Prejudice any Claims of the United States, or of any particular State.

SECTION 4. The United States shall guarantee to every State in this Union a Republican Form of Government, and shall protect each of them against Invasion; and on Application of the Legislature, or of the Executive (when the Legislature cannot be convened) against domestic Violence.

ARTICLE V.

The Congress, whenever two-thirds of both Houses shall deem it necessary, shall propose Amendments to this Constitution, or, on the Application of the Legislatures of two-thirds of the several States, shall call a Convention for proposing Amendments, which, in either Case, shall be valid to all Intents and Purposes, as part of this Constitution, when ratified by the Legislatures of three-fourths of the several States, or by Conventions in three-fourths thereof, as the one or the other

Mode of Ratification may be proposed by the Congress; Provided that no Amendment which may be made prior to the Year One thousand eight hundred and eight shall in any Manner affect the first and fourth Clauses in the Ninth Section of the first Article; and that no State, without its Consent, shall be deprived of its equal Suffrage in the Senate.

ARTICLE VI.

All Debts contracted and Engagements entered into, before the Adoption of this Constitution, shall be as valid against the United States under this Constitution, as under the Confederation.

This Constitution, and the Laws of the United States which shall be made in Pursuance thereof; and all Treaties made, or which shall be made, under the Authority of the United States, shall be the supreme Law of the Land; and the Judges in every State shall be bound thereby, any Thing in the Constitution or Laws of any State to the Contrary notwithstanding.

The Senators and Representatives before mentioned, and the Members of the several State Legislatures, and all executive and judicial Officers, both of the United States and of the several States, shall be bound by Oath or Affirmation, to support this Constitution; but no religious Test shall ever be required as a Qualification to any Office or public Trust under the United States.

ARTICLE VII.

The Ratification of the Conventions of nine States shall be sufficient for the Establishment of this Constitution between the States so ratifying the Same.

DONE in Convention by the Unanimous Consent of the States present the Seventeenth Day of September in the Year of our Lord one thousand seven hundred and Eighty seven and of the Independence of the United States of America the Twelfth. In Witness whereof We have hereunto subscribed our Names.

Go. WASHINGTON
Presidt and deputy from Virginia

New Hampshire.
JOHN LANGDON
NICHOLAS GILMAN

Massachusetts.
NATHANIEL GORHAM
RUFUS KING

Connecticut.
WM SAML JOHNSON
ROGER SHERMAN

New York.
ALEXANDER HAMILTON

New Jersey.
WIL: LIVINGSTON
DAVID BREARLEY.
WM PATTERSON
JONA: DAYTON

Pennsylvania.
B. FRANKLIN
ROBT. MORRIS
THOS. FITZSIMONS
JAMES WILSON
THOMAS MIFFLIN
GEO. CLYMER
JARED INGERSOLL
GOUV MORRIS

Delaware.
GEO: READ
JOHN DICKINSON
JACO: BROOM
GUNNING BEDFORD jun
RICHARD BASSETT

Maryland.
JAMES MCHENRY
DANL CARROLL
DAN: OF ST THOS JENIFER

Virginia.
JOHN BLAIR—
JAMES MADISON JR.

North Carolina.
WM BLOUNT
HU WILLIAMSON
RICHD DOBBS SPAIGHT,

South Carolina.
J. RUTLEDGE
CHARLES PINCKNEY

CHARLES COTESWORTH PINCKNEY
PIERCE BUTLER.

Georgia.

WILLIAM FEW
ABR BALDWIN

Attest:

WILLIAM JACKSON, Secretary.

ARTICLES IN ADDITION TO, AND AMENDMENT OF, THE CON-
STITUTION OF THE UNITED STATES OF AMERICA, PROPOSED
BY CONGRESS, AND RATIFIED BY THE LEGISLATURES OF THE
SEVERAL STATES, PURSUANT TO THE FIFTH ARTICLE OF THE
ORIGINAL CONSTITUTION.

[ARTICLE I.]

Congress shall make no law respecting an establishment of
religion, or prohibiting the free exercise thereof; or abridging
the freedom of speech, or of the press; or of the right of the
people peaceably to assemble, and to petition the Government
for a redress of grievances.

[ARTICLE II.]

A well regulated Militia, being necessary to the security of
a free State, the right of the people to keep and bear Arms,
shall not be infringed.

[ARTICLE III.]

No Soldier shall, in time of peace be quartered in any
house, without the consent of the Owner, nor in time of war,
but in a manner to be prescribed by law.

[ARTICLE IV.]

The right of the people to be secure in their persons, houses,
papers, and effects, against unreasonable searches and seizures,
shall not be violated, and no Warrants shall issue, but upon
probable cause, supported by Oath or affirmation, and particularly describing the place to be searched, and the persons
or things to be seized.

[ARTICLE V.]

No person shall be held to answer for a capital, or otherwise infamous crime, unless on a presentment or indictment
of a Grand Jury, except in cases arising in the land or naval

forces, or in the Militia, when in actual service in time of War or public danger; nor shall any person be subject for the same offence to be twice put in jeopardy of life or limb; nor shall be compelled in any criminal case to be a witness against himself, nor be deprived of life, liberty, or property, without due process of law; nor shall private property be taken for public use, without just compensation.

[ARTICLE VI.]

In all criminal prosecutions, the accused shall enjoy the right to a speedy and public trial, by an impartial jury of the State and district wherein the crime shall have been committed, which district shall have been previously ascertained by law, and to be informed of the nature and cause of the accusation; to be confronted with the witnesses against him; to have compulsory process for obtaining witnesses in his favor, and to have the Assistance of Counsel for his defence.

[ARTICLE VII.]

In suits at common law, where the value in controversy shall exceed twenty dollars, the right of trial by jury shall be preserved, and no fact tried by a jury, shall be otherwise reexamined in any Court of the United States, than according to the rules of the common law.

[ARTICLE VIII.]

Excessive bail shall not be required, nor excessive fines imposed, nor cruel and unusual punishments inflicted.

[ARTICLE IX.]

The enumeration in the Constitution, of certain rights, shall not be construed to deny or disparage others retained by the people.

[ARTICLE X.]

The powers not delegated to the United States by the Constitution, nor prohibited by it to the States, are reserved to the States respectively, or to the people.

ARTICLE XI.

The Judicial power of the United States shall not be construed to extend to any suit in law or equity, commenced or prosecuted against one of the United States by Citizens of another State, or by Citizens or Subjects of any Foreign State.

ARTICLE XII.

The Electors shall meet in their respective states and vote by ballot for President and Vice-President, one of whom, at least, shall not be an inhabitant of the same state with themselves; they shall name in their ballots the person voted for as President, and in distinct ballots the person voted for as Vice-President, and they shall make distinct lists of all persons voted for as President, and of all persons voted for as Vice-President, and of the number of votes for each, which lists they shall sign and certify, and transmit sealed to the seat of the government of the United States, directed to the President of the Senate;—The President of the Senate shall, in presence of the Senate and House of Representatives, open all the certificates and the votes shall then be counted;—The person having the greatest number of votes for President, shall be the President, if such number be a majority of the whole number of Electors appointed; and if no person have such majority, then from the persons having the highest numbers not exceeding three on the list of those voted for as President, the House of Representatives shall choose immediately, by ballot, the President. But in choosing the President, the votes shall be taken by states, the representation from each state having one vote; a quorum for this purpose shall consist of a member or members from two-thirds of the states, and a majority of all the states shall be necessary to a choice. And if the House of Representatives shall not choose a President whenever the right of choice shall devolve upon them, before the fourth day of March next following, then the Vice-President shall act as President, as in the case of the death or other constitutional disability of the President.—The person having the greatest number of votes as Vice-President, shall be the Vice-President, if such number be a majority of the whole number of Electors appointed, and if no person have a majority, then from the two highest numbers on the list, the Senate shall choose the Vice-President; a quorum for the purpose shall consist of two-thirds of the whole number of Senators, and a majority of the whole number shall be necessary to a choice. But no person constitutionally ineligible to the office of President shall be eligible to that of Vice-President of the United States.

ARTICLE XIII.

SECTION 1. Neither slavery nor involuntary servitude, except as a punishment for crime whereof the party shall have been duly convicted, shall exist within the United States, or any place subject to their jurisdiction.

SECTION 2. Congress shall have power to enforce this article by appropriate legislation.

ARTICLE XIV.

SECTION 1. All persons born or naturalized in the United States, and subject to the jurisdiction thereof, are citizens of the United States and of the State wherein they reside. No State shall make or enforce any law which shall abridge the privileges or immunities of citizens of the United States; nor shall any State deprive any person of life, liberty, or property, without due process of law; nor deny to any person within its jurisdiction the equal protection of the laws.

SECTION 2. Representatives shall be apportioned among the several States according to their respective numbers, counting the whole number of persons in each State, excluding Indians not taxed. But when the right to vote at any election for the choice of electors for President and Vice-President of the United States, Representatives in Congress, the Executive and Judicial officers of a State, or the members of the Legislature thereof, is denied to any of the male inhabitants of such State, being twenty-one years of age, and citizens of the United States, or in any way abridged, except for participation in rebellion, or other crime, the basis of representation therein shall be reduced in the proportion which the number of such male citizens shall bear to the whole number of male citizens twenty-one years of age in such State.

SECTION 3. No person shall be a Senator or Representative in Congress, or elector of President and Vice-President, or hold any office, civil or military, under the United States, or under any State, who, having previously taken an oath, as a member of Congress, or as an officer of the United States, or as a member of any State legislature, or as an executive or judicial officer of any State, to support the Constitution of the United States, shall have engaged in insurrection or rebellion against the same, or given aid or comfort to the enemies thereof. But Congress may by a vote of two-thirds of each House, remove such disability.

SECTION 4. The validity of the public debt of the United States, authorized by law, including debts incurred for payment of pensions and bounties for services in suppressing insurrection or rebellion, shall not be questioned. But neither the United States nor any State shall assume or pay any debt or obligation incurred in aid of insurrection or rebellion against the United States, or any claim for the loss or emancipation of any slave; but all such debts, obligations and claims shall be held illegal and void.

SECTION 5. The Congress shall have power to enforce, by appropriate legislation, the provisions of this article.

ARTICLE XV.

SECTION 1. The right of citizens of the United States to vote shall not be denied or abridged by the United States or by any State on account of race, color, or previous condition of servitude—

SECTION 2. The Congress shall have power to enforce this article by appropriate legislation.

ARTICLE XVI.

The Congress shall have power to lay and collect taxes on incomes, from whatever source derived, without apportionment among the several States, and without regard to any census or enumeration.

ARTICLE XVII.

The Senate of the United States shall be composed of two Senators from each State, elected by the people thereof, for six years; and each Senator shall have one vote. The electors in each State shall have the qualifications requisite for electors of the most numerous branch of the State legislatures.

When vacancies happen in the representation of any State in the Senate, the executive authority of such State shall issue writs of election to fill such vacancies: *Provided,* That the legislature of any State may empower the executive thereof to make temporary appointments until the people fill the vacancies by election as the legislature may direct.

This amendment shall not be so construed as to affect the election or term of any Senator chosen before it becomes valid as part of the Constitution.

ARTICLE XVIII.

SECTION 1. After one year from the ratification of this article the manufacture, sale, or transportation of intoxicating liquors within, the importation thereof into, or the exportation thereof from the United States and all territory subject to the jurisdiction thereof for beverage purposes is hereby prohibited.

SECTION 2. The Congress and the several States shall have concurrent power to enforce this article by appropriate legislation.

SECTION 3. This article shall be inoperative unless it shall have been ratified as an amendment to the Constitution by the legislatures of the several States, as provided in the Constitution, within seven years from the date of the submission hereof to the States by the Congress.

ARTICLE XIX.

The right of citizens of the United States to vote shall not be denied or abridged by the United States or by any State on account of sex.

Congress shall have power to enforce this article by appropriate legislation.

ARTICLE XX.

SECTION 1. The terms of the President and Vice President shall end at noon on the 20th day of January, and the terms of Senators and Representatives at noon on the 3d day of January, of the years in which such terms would have ended if this article had not been ratified; and the terms of their successors shall then begin.

SECTION 2. The Congress shall assemble at least once in every year, and such meeting shall begin at noon on the 3d day of January, unless they shall by law appoint a different day.

SECTION 3. If, at the time fixed for the beginning of the term of the President, the President elect shall have died, the Vice President elect shall become President. If a President shall not have been chosen before the time fixed for the beginning of his term, or if the President elect shall have failed to qualify, then the Vice President elect shall act as President until a President shall have qualified; and the Congress may by law provide for the case wherein neither a President elect nor a Vice President elect shall have qualified, declaring who shall then act as President, or the manner in which one who is to act shall be selected, and such person shall act accordingly until a President or Vice President shall have qualified.

SECTION 4. The Congress may by law provide for the case of the death of any of the persons from whom the House of Representatives may choose a President whenever the right of choice shall have devolved upon them, and for the case of the death of any of the persons from whom the Senate may choose a Vice President whenever the right of choice shall have devolved upon them.

SECTION 5. Sections 1 and 2 shall take effect on the 15th day of October following the ratification of this article.

SECTION 6. This article shall be inoperative unless it shall have been ratified as an amendment to the Constitution by the legislatures of three-fourths of the several States within seven years from the date of its submission.

ARTICLE XXI.

SECTION 1. The eighteenth article of amendment to the Constitution of the United States is hereby repealed.

SECTION 2. The transportation or importation into any State, Territory, or possession of the United States for delivery or use therein of intoxicating liquors, in violation of the laws thereof, is hereby prohibited.

SECTION 3. This article shall be inoperative unless it shall have been ratified as an amendment to the Constitution by conventions in the several States, as provided in the Constitution, within seven years from the date of the submission hereof to the States by the Congress.

ARTICLE XXII.

SECTION 1. No person shall be elected to the office of the President more than twice, and no person who has held the office of President, or acted as President, for more than two years of a term to which some other person was elected President shall be elected to the office of the President more than once. But this Article shall not apply to any person holding the office of President when this Article was proposed by the Congress, and shall not prevent any person who may be holding the office of President, or acting as President, during the term within which this Article becomes operative from holding the office of President or acting as President during the remainder of such term.

SECTION 2. This article shall be inoperative unless it shall have been ratified as an amendment to the Constitution by the legislatures of three-fourths of the several States within seven years from the date of its submission to the States by the Congress.

TABLE OF JUSTICES OF THE
UNITED STATES SUPREME COURT

(Chief Justices are in **bold-faced** type.)

	State from Which App.	App. by President	Period of Service		Born	Died
JOHN JAY	New York	Washington	1789	1795	1745	1829
John Rutledge1	S. Carolina	Washington	1789	1791	1739	1800
William Cushing	Mass.	Washington	1789	1810	1732	1810
James Wilson	Penna.	Washington	1789	1798	1724	1798
John Blair	Virginia	Washington	1789	1796	1732	1800
James Iredell	N. Carolina	Washington	1790	1799	1750	1799
Thomas Johnson	Maryland	Washington	1791	1793	1732	1819
William Paterson	New Jersey	Washington	1793	1806	1745	1806
JOHN RUTLEDGE2	S. Carolina	Washington	1795	1795	1739	1800
Samuel Chase	Maryland	Washington	1796	1811	1741	1811
OLIVER ELLSWORTH	Conn.	Washington	1796	1800	1745	1807
Bushrod Washington	Virginia	J. Adams	1798	1829	1762	1829
Alfred Moore	N. Carolina	J. Adams	1799	1804	1755	1810
JOHN MARSHALL	Virginia	J. Adams	1801	1835	1755	1835
William Johnson	S. Carolina	Jefferson	1804	1834	1771	1834
Brockholst Livingston	New York	Jefferson	1806	1823	1757	1823
Thomas Todd	Kentucky	Jefferson	1807	1826	1765	1826
Gabriel Duval	Maryland	Madison	1811	1835	1752	1844
Joseph Story	Mass.	Madison	1811	1845	1779	1845
Smith Thompson	New York	Monroe	1823	1843	1768	1843
Robert Trimble	Kentucky	J. Q. Adams	1826	1828	1777	1828
John McLean	Ohio	Jackson	1829	1861	1785	1861
Henry Baldwin	Penna.	Jackson	1830	1844	1780	1844
James M. Wayne	Georgia	Jackson	1835	1867	1790	1867
ROGER B. TANEY	Maryland	Jackson	1836	1864	1777	1864
Philip P. Barbour	Virginia	Jackson	1836	1841	1783	1841
John Catron	Tennessee	Van Buren	1837	1865	1786	1865
John McKinley	Alabama	Van Buren	1837	1852	1780	1852
Peter V. Daniel	Virginia	Van Buren	1841	1860	1784	1860
Samuel Nelson	New York	Tyler	1845	1872	1792	1873
Levi Woodbury	New Hamp.	Polk	1845	1851	1789	1851
Robert C. Grier	Penna.	Polk	1846	1870	1794	1870
Benjamin R. Curtis	Mass.	Fillmore	1851	1857	1809	1874
John A. Campbell	Alabama	Pierce	1853	1861	1811	1889
Nathan Clifford	Maine	Buchanan	1858	1881	1803	1881
Noah H. Swayne	Ohio	Lincoln	1862	1881	1804	1884
Samuel F. Miller	Iowa	Lincoln	1862	1890	1816	1890
David Davis	Illinois	Lincoln	1862	1877	1815	1886
Stephen J. Field	California	Lincoln	1863	1897	1816	1899
SALMON P. CHASE	Ohio	Lincoln	1864	1873	1808	1873
William Strong	Penna.	Grant	1870	1880	1808	1895
Joseph P. Bradley	New Jersey	Grant	1870	1892	1813	1892
Ward Hunt	New York	Grant	1872	1882	1810	1886
MORRISON R. WAITE	Ohio	Grant	1874	1888	1816	1888
John Marshall Harlan	Kentucky	Hayes	1877	1911	1833	1911

	State from Which App.	App. by President	Period of Service		Born	Died
William B. Woods	Georgia	Hayes	1880	1887	1824	1887
Stanley Matthews	Ohio	Garfield	1881	1889	1824	1889
Horace Gray	Mass.	Arthur	1881	1902	1828	1902
Samuel Blatchford	New York	Arthur	1882	1893	1820	1893
Lucius Q. C. Lamar	Mississippi	Cleveland	1888	1893	1825	1893
MELVILLE W. FULLER	Illinois	Cleveland	1888	1910	1833	1910
David J. Brewer	Kansas	Harrison	1889	1910	1837	1910
Henry B. Brown	Michigan	Harrison	1890	1906	1836	1913
George Shiras	Penna.	Harrison	1892	1903	1832	1924
Howell E. Jackson	Tennessee	Harrison	1893	1895	1832	1895
Edward D. White	Louisiana	Cleveland	1894	1910	1845	1921
Rufus W. Peckham	New York	Cleveland	1895	1909	1838	1909
Joseph McKenna	California	McKinley	1898	1925	1843	1926
Oliver Wendell Holmes	Mass.	Roosevelt	1902	1932	1841	1935
William R. Day	Ohio	Roosevelt	1903	1922	1849	1923
William H. Moody	Mass.	Roosevelt	1906	1910	1853	1917
Horace H. Lurton	Tennessee	Taft	1910	1914	1844	1914
Charles E. Hughes	New York	Taft	1910	1916	1862	1948
EDWARD D. WHITE	Louisiana	Taft	1910	1921	1845	1921
Willis Van Devanter	Wyoming	Taft	1911	1937	1859	1941
Joseph R. Lamar	Georgia	Taft	1911	1916	1857	1916
Mahlon Pitney	New Jersey	Taft	1912	1922	1858	1924
James C. McReynolds	Tennessee	Wilson	1914	1941	1862	1946
Louis D. Brandeis	Mass.	Wilson	1916	1939	1856	1941
John H. Clarke	Ohio	Wilson	1916	1922	1857	1945
WILLIAM H. TAFT	Conn.	Harding	1921	1930	1857	1930
George Sutherland	Utah	Harding	1922	1938	1862	1942
Pierce Butler	Minnesota	Harding	1922	1939	1866	1939
Edward T. Sanford	Tennessee	Harding	1923	1930	1865	1930
Harlan F. Stone	New York	Coolidge	1925	1941	1872	1946
CHARLES E. HUGHES	New York	Hoover	1930	1941	1862	1948
Owen J. Roberts	Penna.	Hoover	1930	1945	1875	1955
Benjamin N. Cardozo	New York	Hoover	1932	1938	1870	1938
Hugo L. Black	Alabama	Roosevelt	1937		1886	
Stanley F. Reed	Kentucky	Roosevelt	1938	1957	1884	
Felix Frankfurter	Mass.	Roosevelt	1939		1882	
William O. Douglas	Conn.	Roosevelt	1939		1898	
Frank Murphy	Michigan	Roosevelt	1940	1949	1890	1949
James F. Byrnes	S. Carolina	Roosevelt	1941	1942	1879	
HARLAN F. STONE	New York	Roosevelt	1941	1946	1872	1946
Robert H. Jackson	New York	Roosevelt	1941	1954	1892	1954
Wiley B. Rutledge	Iowa	Roosevelt	1943	1949	1894	1949
Harold H. Burton	Ohio	Truman	1945		1888	
FRED M. VINSON	Kentucky	Truman	1946	1953	1890	1953
Tom C. Clark	Texas	Truman	1949		1899	
Sherman Minton	Indiana	Truman	1949	1956	1890	
EARL WARREN	California	Eisenhower	1953		1891	
John M. Harlan	New York	Eisenhower	1955		1899	
William J. Brennan, Jr.	New Jersey	Eisenhower	1956		1906	
Charles E. Whittaker	Missouri	Eisenhower	1957		1901	

1 Resigned without ever sitting.
2 Unconfirmed recess appointment.

SELECTED BIBLIOGRAPHY

General

ASSOCIATION OF AMERICAN LAW SCHOOLS, Selected Essays on Constitutional Law (4 vols. 1938).

CORWIN, The Constitution and What It Means Today (11th ed. 1954).

FREUND, On Understanding the Supreme Court (1949).

HAMILTON, JAY, and MADISON, The Federalist.

HARVARD LAW REVIEW, Annual Review of the most recent Supreme Court Term.

HUGHES, The Supreme Court of the United States (1928).

JACKSON, The Supreme Court in the American System of Government (1955).

McLAUGHLIN, The Foundations of American Constitutionalism (1932).

NEW YORK UNIVERSITY SCHOOL OF LAW, Annual Survey of American Law (published annually since 1942).

SCHWARTZ, American Constitutional Law (1955).

SCHWARTZ, The Supreme Court (1957).

STORY, Commentaries on the Constitution (5th ed. 1891).

SWISHER, The Supreme Court in Modern Role (1958).

UNITED STATES, Annotated Constitution of the United States of America (Corwin, ed. 1953).

UNITED STATES, Documents Illustrative of the Formation of the Union (1927).

VANDERBILT, The Doctrine of the Separation of Powers and Its Present-Day Significance (1953).

WARREN, The Supreme Court in United States History (2 vols., rev. ed. 1926).

Judicial Review: The Balance Wheel of the Federal System

BOUDIN, Government by Judiciary (2 vols. 1932).

CAHN (ed.), Supreme Court and Supreme Law (1954).

CORWIN, Court over Constitution (1938).

CORWIN. The "Higher Law" Background of American Constitutional Law (Great Seal Books ed. 1955).

JACKSON, The Struggle for Judicial Supremacy (1941).

ROBERTSON AND KIRKHAM, Jurisdiction of the Supreme Court of the United States (Kurland and Wolfson ed. 1951).

Congress and the Legislative Power

BURNS, Congress on Trial; the Legislative Process and the Administrative State (1949).

FRANKFURTER, The Commerce Clause Under Marshall, Taney and Waite (1937).

RIBBLE, State and National Power over Commerce (1937).

WILSON, Congressional Government: A Study in American Politics (1894).

The President and the Executive Power

CORWIN, The President: Office and Powers (4th ed. 1957).

CORWIN AND KOENIG, The Presidency Today (1956).

ROSSITER, The Supreme Court and the Commander-in-Chief (1951).

Constitutional Limitations on the Power of Government

Bill of Rights:

AMERICAN CIVIL LIBERTIES UNION, Annual Reports.

ASSOCIATION OF THE BAR OF THE CITY OF NEW YORK, The Federal Loyalty-Security System (1956).

BARTH, The Loyalty of Free Men (1951).

CHAFEE, Free Speech in the United States (1941).

CHAFEE, How Human Rights Got Into the Constitution (1952).

CUSHMAN, Civil Liberties in the United States (1956).

DOUGLAS, An Almanac of Liberty (1954).

DOUGLAS, The Right of the People (1958).

GELLHORN, Individual Freedom and Governmental Restraint (1956).

GRISWOLD, The Fifth Amendment Today (1955).

HOOK, Heresy. Yes; Conspiracy, No (1953).

KONVITZ, Civil Rights in Immigration (1953).

NEWMAN, The Freedom Reader (1955).

PFEFFER, The Liberties of an American (1956).

POUND, The Development of Constitutional Guarantees of Liberty (1957).

STOKES, Church and State in the United States (1950).

Desegregation:

BLAUSTEIN AND FERGUSON, Desegregation and the Law (1957).

SHOEMAKER (ed.), With All Deliberate Speed (1957).

SOUTHERN EDUCATION REPORTING SERVICE, Southern School News (monthly since 1955).

VANDERBILT UNIVERSITY SCHOOL OF LAW, Race Relations Law Reporter (bi-monthly since 1956).

INDEX

THE DOCKET SERIES

PAPERBOUND .... **$1.00 each**
CLOTHBOUND .... **$3.50 each**

Volume 1—THE HOLMES READER
Opinions, speeches, biographical study and evaluative summaries of the great American jurist. By Julius J. Marke.

Volume 2—THE FREEDOM READER
Historic decisions on momentous questions in the development of our constitutional and administrative law. By Edwin S. Newman.

Volume 3—THE MARSHALL READER
The decisions, writings, speeches and other pertinent works by and about the Father of American constitutional law. By Erwin C. Surrency.

Volume 4—THE WILSON READER
Writings by and about his contributions to international law and political science. By Frances Farmer.

Volume 5—THE WEBSTER READER
A fascinating character in American history comes to life in this provocative collection of source and secondary material. By Bertha Rothe.

Volume 6—THE MEDICO-LEGAL READER
Readings in the areas of joint concern to doctors and lawyers. By Samuel Polsky.

Volume 7—THE BRANDEIS READER
Contains decisions, speeches and writings and appropriate evaluative comment on his work. By Ervin Pollack.

Volume 8—THE AMERICAN JURISPRUDENCE READER
All schools of American jurisprudential thought are represented in this collection of important source and evaluative material. By Thomas A. Cowan.

Volume 9—THE ALEXANDER HAMILTON READER
Writings by and about this great Federalist, in commemoration of bicentennial year of his birth. By Margaret E. Hall.

Volume 10—THE FREDERIC WILLIAM MAITLAND READER
A unique selection of readings by and about this most illustrious legal historian. By Vincent T. H. Delany.

Volume 11—DEANS' LIST OF RECOMMENDED READING
A compilation of books recommended by the deans and professors of numerous American Law Schools. Compiled and annotated by Julius J. Marke.

Volume 12—AN AMERICAN CONSTITUTIONAL LAW READER
A collection of readings and commentary which projects a picture of the growth and history of the American federal system. Compiled and edited by Robert B. McKay.